HARMONY, DISORDER AND SMILES

A visit to Thailand is likely to be an infuriating, alienating and head-scratching experience that will also provide the most wonderful and welcoming of culture shocks.

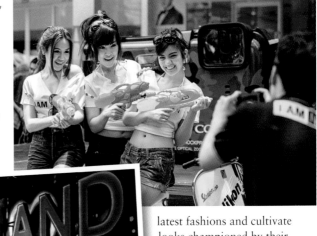

Thailand assaults the senses with an overload of activity—an explosion of colors, sounds, sights, smells and tastes. It possesses a seductive spirituality born not only from Buddhist values but from an ancient animist approach that has its origins in the country's folklores and forests.

This book is an attempt to understand one of the world's most visited countries—but goes beyond the usual tourist brochures and guidebooks. *A Geek in Thailand* is an exploration of why Thailand at once appears so foreign and chaotic yet familiar and ordered. Through a journey that includes understanding the complex cacophony of components that make up Thailand's food, noise levels, politics, traffic and contradictory character traits, we will begin to discover how seeking a balance, a harmony and a level of calm in all these integral elements is at the heart of the soul and culture of the country and essence of being Thai.

latest fashions and cultivate looks championed by their Japanese and Korean counterparts, Thais are inexplicably unique in their outlook. There is pride in the nation's individualistic Thai perspective that stems not only from it being the only Southeast Asian country to ever resist colonization by Western powers but also from the deep reverence and respect for the intrinsic national Thai values of Nation, Religion and Monarchy.

The longer you stay in Thailand, the more questions you are likely to ask. To understand Thailand, you must have a knowledge of its geographical position and the influence of

LOOKS CAN BE DECEPTIVE

Although young Thai men may wear T-shirts bearing the names of Western bands and cheer for English football teams on Saturday nights, and although Thai women may wear the

LIVING THE HOLIDAY DREAM

The story of how I came to live in Thailand is quite a common one for those who choose the 'Land of Smiles' as their adopted homeland. I came for a holiday, well no, actually, that's not entirely true.... I came seeking relaxation, to de-stress at the end of a joyless English-teaching contract in Korea. Rather than return to the gray and dreary streets of my hometown of Manchester in the UK, where I would be twiddling my thumbs until my Masters course in journalism began, I went to Thailand at the suggestion of my girlfriend at the time.

I headed straight for the holiday island of Phuket. I think it was on day three, while I was sitting on the sand at Kata beach looking out at the water and the cliffs and peaks and distant green hills, that the hustle and bustle and toil and trouble of my recent time in Korea began to feel like years, not mere days, away.

I stayed in Phuket for a month, writing the odd travel article for a local newsmagazine to help subsidize my English breakfasts, bowls of chicken fried rice and bottles of Singha beer. Being a sun-starved Mancunian, I then decided to do some more beach-hopping and ended up on the more remote and less-developed (at the time) island of Samui. I stayed in the Fishmerman's Village, a lovely little beachside town with cheap accommodation and a lively selection of bars and foreign and Thai restaurants. I spent my days jogging on the beach and learning shorthand and writing. In the evenings I worked my way through a seemingly never-ending menu of delicious spicy, sour and sweet Thai dishes to the sounds of live music.

Tourists on a jungle trek in Maetang get a good soaking.

understand Thailand is to understand the political divisions of its people, which at times seem to manifest itself as little more than a preference for a particular color of clothing.

Writing this book has involved adventures down alleyways, gallons of coffee in cafes, thousands of emails and phone calls and fascinating days spent with professors, experts, artists, musicians, writers, street vendors, waitresses, taxi drivers, businessmen and everyday Thais who make up the eclectic mix of contemporary Thai society.

This project has also, perhaps most importantly, been inspired and motivated by each and every stranger's smile, a reminder to this English geek of why he wanted to write a book about their country and culture in the first place.

its neighbors. To understand Thai people, you must at least know of the one-time existence of more than 50 ethnic groups that were 'unified' and rebranded 'Thai' by one of the country's most controversial and influential 20th-century prime ministers. To understand the Thai national character, you must have an awareness of its people's propensity to smile, to save face and to respect the 'tribe' above all else. To

Opposite top The Thai New Year, Songkran, is perhaps the world's biggest water fight. Opposite center Being happy in Thailand is important, and there are even military-led campaigns to encourage it. Opposite bottom I've met many interesting people in my time in Thailand. Performance artist and *Thailand's Got Talent* contestant Romadon is definitely in my top three. Above center The infamous Full Moon Party in Koh Phangan has become a rite of passage for young visitors. Above left Just dance: A cheerleading flash mob performing in Bangkok.

The time for me to return to the UK, and the responsibilities associated with it, was drawing ever closer. I decided that I should at least make an attempt at seeing another side of Thailand, something different from the idyllic paradise-like corners of the earth. I went to Bangkok, then to Chiang Mai and finally to Ayutthaya. In Bangkok I saw an urban Asian metropolis that straddled modernity and tradition and poverty and wealth like no other capital city I had ever visited. In Chiang Mai I saw a beautiful city surrounded by breathtaking countryside, with wonderful wildlife and awesome architecture, temples and ruins, and in Auutthaya I experienced a glimpse of the Thailand of the past.

I had spent three months in Thailand, a lengthy holiday by any stretch of the imagination. But the fact that as soon as I had completed my Masters degree, I looked at ways of returning to Thailand is testament to the attraction of the country, to the fact that everything just seems so dull, so gray, so cold, so non-spicy and so un-Thai in comparison.

Like many expats who choose Thailand as their adopted home, I came for a holiday and stayed for the laid-back lifestyle. I came because I loved something about Thailand, something that I couldn't quite put my finger on. When I left seven years earlier, I wasn't quite sure what it was, but I was determined to find out. So I returned and began to work for the same newsmagazine I had written for during my initial visit. For my first Christmas in Thailand, I bought a Christmas tree, but when January came around I threw the little plastic thing out as I doubted I'd be there when the bells started jingling again. After three more tree-less Christmas festive periods, I admitted to myself that I should probably buy one again. I now live and work in Bangkok.

As with most other expats in Thailand, there have been times when I've wanted to tear my hair out with the 'Thai' way of doing things, but the anger and incredulity always pass and I remain, with a smile on my face and a Christmas tree and water pistol for Songkran in my cupboard.

CHAPTER 1

THAI HISTORY AND CULTURE

How did ancient Siam come to be the colorful country of contemporary Thailand? Here, we will discover some of the most famous, influential and controversial Thais, both past and present. Religion, Nation, Monarchy are at the heart of Thai culture and are where, as geeks in Thailand, we will begin.

A BRIEF HISTORY OF THAILAND

The ancient kingdom of Siam—from the Sanskrit word Syama, meaning 'dark' or 'brown'—was renamed Thailand in 1948.

This was, in fact, the second time the country's name had changed. Siam was first renamed Thailand in 1939, at the onset of World War II, by then Prime Minister Field Marshal Luang 'Plaek' Phibunsongkhram who believed the name change would whip up much-needed ultra-nationalist spirit to unify or at least inform the approximately 50 ethnic groups resident in the country that it was a land for 'Tais', the dominant ethnic group at the time.

Although Thailand's hosting of Japanese forces and perceived alignment with the Japanese in World War II was retrospectively deemed to have been 'under duress' as opposed to being 'allied' (Thailand was 'occupied' by 150,000 Japanese troops), it was decided to revert to the pre-war name Siam at the end of the war, in 1945.

Field Marshal Plaek was subsequently forced out of office and put on trial for war crimes, but was acquitted owing to strong Thai public support. In 1947, he led a coup and once again became prime minister. The following year Siam, for the second and final time, became Thailand.

THAILAND'S FOUR KINGDOMS

Thailand has gone through a myriad of changes and been exposed to numerous influences throughout its history. The existence of a number of separate, distinct and often co-existing Thai kingdoms has been largely responsible for the formation of the multifaceted Thailand we know today.

Sukhothai The Sukhothai kingdom of Thailand (1238–1448) is considered to be the 'Golden Age of Thailand'. As the first independent Thai state follow-

SUKHOTHAI

ing the decline of the Khmer empire in the early 13th century, it is also believed to signal the beginning of modern Thai history.

The Sukhothai kingdom was a prosperous and plentiful place for the country and its people, one where 'rivers were full of fish and fields of rice'. It was also a time of relative peace, with good relationships with neighboring countries. During the Sukhothai period, it was believed that kings would keep bells outside of their palaces. If any subject had a grievance, he would ring the bell and the king would come to the gate and dispense justice accordingly. This leadership style was later to become known as 'father governs children' and is still relevant today, not only in the palace but also in the hierarchy of Thai companies and organizations.

Although its authenticity has subsequently been questioned, the Thai alphabet was created by King Ramkhamhaeng during this period, evidenced by the discovery of an inscribed tablet, the Ramkhamhaeng Stele. In the script, the king speaks of his benevolent leadership style. King Ramkhamhaeng's 'paternal rule' and the culture and traditions of Sukhothai were later to take on further significance during the 1932 pro-democracy revolution, when scholars

WHAT'S IN A NAME?

The word Thai in the Thai language means 'independence', leading many to believe the choice of name refers to Thailand's ability to resist attempts at Western colonization, the only Southeast Asian country to successfully do so. Others believe the name refers to those who were to become the country's most populous and dominant group of people—the Tais. The Tais were initially an ethnic group hailing from southern China, who migrated into the Chao Phraya River valley in central Thailand around AD 1000, an area already inhabited by two main Austro-Asiatic groups speaking Mon and Khmer. Present-day Thais are the product of the assimilation and fusion of these three groups.

In recent years, some Thai scholars, including historian Charnvit Kasetsiri, have called on the country to revert to its original name, Siam. Although the widespread practice of Theravada Buddhism has promoted racial harmony, Charnvit points out that it was only when the country became known as Thailand—'a land for Tais'—that its 50 other ethnic groups currently residing alongside the Tais, including Yuan, Lao, Malayu, Karen, Hmong, Chinese and, most recently, *farang* (people of European descent), were discriminated against and dissuaded from expressing their customs, dress and language in favor of a unified Thai existence or Thai-ness. Charnvit believes that a return to the name Siam would be the first step in signaling that not only the country's past but also its present is made up of many different ethnicities and ideologies, and is the only way to bring about reconciliation of its mosaic of peoples and cultures.

AYUTTHAYA

LANNA

THONBURI AND RATTANAKOSIN

argued that it was the 'Golden Age of Thailand' that, in fact, had given birth to what was to become a peculiarly Thai style of democracy.

Ayutthaya The Ayutthaya kingdom (1350–1767) is perhaps the best-known ancient Thai kingdom as its capital is still resplendent with historical buildings and artifacts. This period of Thai history witnessed huge economic growth as well as the establishment of relations with foreign traders, especially the Portuguese. With great power came great change and during the Ayutthaya period Thai society became distinctly hierarchical, with the large majority of Thais working as slaves or serfs for landowners, nobles and officials. Unlike the paternalistic rule of the Sukhothai period, the kings of Ayutthaya had absolute power and were perceived as incarnations of gods.

The Ayutthaya period was integral in developing the Thai arts where all members of society, from court officials to artisans and scholars of Buddhist learning joined together to make and decorate the area's temples and palaces.

But this period in Thai history was also fraught with wars and battles with Burma, which led to the ultimate sacking of the city in 1767 and subsequent destruction of a large number of records, palaces and temples. Despite this, for a long period during the Ayutthaya reign the kingdom was largely considered to be the strongest power in mainland Southeast Asia.

Lanna Much like the Sukhothai kingdom, the Lanna kingdom, which ruled from the 13th to 15th century in northern Thailand, had an incredible influence on Thai society and culture and is still nostalgically regarded.

The Lanna kingdom co-existed during the Sukhothai and Ayutthaya kingdoms, and at its height its power and influence were said to have rivaled Ayutthaya's with whom it had repeated battles and skirmishes. It was during this period that Lanna's culture and traditions of what is widely considered as the cultural capital of Thailand, Chiang Mai, were developed and firmly entrenched in Thai culture. Lanna architecture, woodcraft and masonry are easily identifiable and revered today. The kingdom eventually fell to the Burmese in 1558 but returned as a vassal state of Siam in the latter part of the 18th century.

Thonburi and Rattanakosin King Taksin the Great of Thonburi managed to reunite the country the following year, which gave birth to Thailand's shortest reigning kingdom, the brief age of the Thonburi kingdom (1768–82). The capital of Siam was moved to Thonburi and located on the opposite side of the Chao Phraya River where Bangkok now stands. As a result of numerous internal political problems, King Taksin was reported to have succumbed to stress and was subsequently ordained as a monk, disappearing from sight.

Because of its more advantageous position, Bangkok was then chosen as the new capital city, and in 1782 King Buddha Yodfa Chulaloke (Rama I) took over and became the first Chakri (royal ruling house) king in the Rattanakosin kingdom—the dynasty that presently encompasses Thailand.

SIAMESE TWINS

Chang and Eng Bunker (1811–74), who were joined at the sternum, were perhaps the first two Siamese men known to the larger world. Commonly known as the 'Siamese Twins', they toured the world as an exhibit of interest before settling and marrying two sisters in North Carolina, USA. Owing to their Chinese ancestry, they were known as the 'Chinese Twins' in Siam.

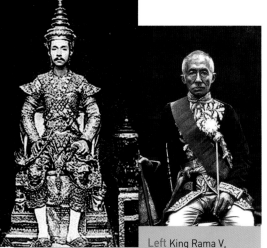

Left King Rama V, widely considered one of the greatest kings of Siam.
Above right King Rama IV, who provided the inspiration for the play and movie, *The King and I*.

ROYALTY IN THAILAND

The monarchy in Thailand is highly revered and staunchly protected by the lèse-majesté law. The current King of Thailand, Bhumibol Adulyadej (Rama IX), is the world's longest serving monarch and is dearly loved by the people of Thailand.

A testament to the Thai people's love for the king and the royal family, past and present, is the sheer number of royal portraits in premises throughout the Thai social structure, including homes, factories, offices and roadside garages.

Whether Thai or not, you are expected to show the utmost respect for the Thai royal family, and on occasions that demand it, such as before movie screenings and football matches, stand for the Thai national anthem, which is also played at 8 am and 6 pm every day. In public places, such as busy train platforms or market places, where the anthem is often broadcast through loudspeakers, it is remarkable to see everybody come to a halt.

Color of Love According to both Thai and Khmer astrology, each day of the week is associated with a particular color. As King Bhumibol was born on a Monday, which is associated with yellow, the most loyal of royalists can be identified by their choice of yellow clothing on Mondays. Blue garb is also a popular color to wear on Fridays out of respect for Queen Sirikit's birthday.

The King's Predecessors

Another much-respected member of the monarchy from the Chakri dynasty was King Rama IV or King Mongkut. Reigning from 1851 to 1868, he was known as the 'Father of Science and Technology' for embracing Western technologies and innovations, effectively beginning Thailand's modernization process. He also hired English and American missionaries to teach the princes English, and Western mercenaries to train Siamese troops.

King Mongkut's son, Chulalongkorn the Great, otherwise known as King Rama V (1868–1910), was also a hugely popular king. He is credited with abolishing the slave trade in Thailand, (depicted on the back of the B100 note), building railways, introducing electricity and through various reforms in the Thai feudal system and his influence in 'modernizing Siam', continuing to save the country from Western colonization.

The Man Who Brought Democracy

One Thai who has had immeasurable influence on modern Thailand is former prime minister Pridi Banomyong. He was one of the leaders of the 1932 Pro-Democracy Coup that saw the end of absolute monarchy and the adoption of the current and more popular constitutional monarchy. Pridi helped draft a new constitution and was, and still is, seen as a controversial figure in Thai history. He spent his remaining years in exile in France. After a generation overseas, his grandson, Ariya Banomyong, has returned to Thailand and is the current manager of Google in Thailand.

Making Siam 'Civilized'

Another influential but controversial figure among Thais is Field Marshal Luang 'Plaek' (Strange) Phibunsongkhram, who is also a former prime minister of Thailand. Phibunsongkhram was charged with inculcating a sense of nationalism among Thai people during his time in the National Assembly and Thai military. Through various mandates, he ordered the Thais to learn the national anthem, salute the flag in public and communicate in public only in the Thai language.

Phibunsongkhram was also responsible for promoting the use of forks and spoons instead of hands for eating and adopting more Western attire. Indeed, up until a 1940 Thai Cultural Mandate, the common traditional costume for women, especially in rural areas, was a wrapped sarong and little else. Despite being the son of a Chinese immigrant, he was also responsible for the launch of numerous anti-Chinese policies and the closing down of Chinese schools all over Thailand. Many older Thai people remember him for his simple and easy to remember mandate of 'Wear a hat and become civilized.'

Like his political nemesis Pridi, Phibunsongkhram died in exile, his final years being spent in Japan.

Field Marshal Luang 'Plaek' (Strange) Phibunsongkhram

Left A protestor waves a flag at the popular pro-democracy site, the Victory Monument, in Bangkok. Above Thousands gathered every day in the capital, listening to speeches, attending rallies and mainly blowing whistles.

THE COLOR OF POLITICS

Thaksin Shinawatra is a former prime minister of Thailand (2001–6) who remains both revered and disliked. After courting previously neglected rural Thai voters, he won two landslide election victories and arguably changed the face of Thai politics forever. Many of his policies, including providing universal affordable health coverage and low-interest agricultural loans, were hugely effective and consolidated his support base among the poorer classes.

Thaksin's emerging power and popularity unsettled the élite, the middle classes and Thailand's traditional establishment who had, almost exclusively, been in the political driving seat for decades.

Thaksin is also controversial for leading Thailand's 'War on Drugs', which saw around 2,275 drug traffickers and addicts killed over a three-month period in 2003. The government claimed that only 50 deaths were the result of police actions, the rest being assassinations and revenge attacks by drug dealers and gangs. In 2006, the telecommunications billionaire was stripped of his family fortune of $1.4 billion by the Supreme Court after being found guilty of corruption. Since then, half has been returned. He lives in self-imposed exile in Dubai following protests led by the conservative royalist People's Alliance for Democracy (its supporters known as Yellow Shirts), which overthrew his government in December 2006 while he was abroad—one of 19 military coups and attempted coups since the founding of the constitutional monarchy in 1932.

After Abhisit Vejjajiva from the People's Alliance for Democracy replaced Thaksin as prime minister, supporters of Thaksin, made up of mostly poor and rural Thais, known colloquially as Red Shirts, have clashed many times with the Yellow Shirts. During the tenure of what the Red Shirts consider the illegal, undemocratic and unlawful appointment of Abhisit, there have been numerous Red Shirt protests. The most notable occurred in 2010, when hundreds of thousands of Red Shirt protesters took to the streets. Violent clashes between the protesters and the military left 92 dead and more than 2,000 injured.

In 2011, Thaksin's sister Yingluck Shinawatra, leader of the Pheu Thai party, was elected prime minister. One of the populist policies on the Pheu Thai party's agenda for 2013 was to pass a blanket amnesty bill which would have retroactively exonerated political criminals from crimes they had committed. This would have allowed her exiled brother Thaksin Shinawatra to return to Thailand without fear of charges. Needless to say, the Thai people opposed and supported the plan in equal numbers.

Many of the protesters in 2013–14 were unified in their anti-Shinawatra sentiments.

Support for Sale

The Red Shirts and Yellow Shirts are not officially aligned with any political party. Rather, they are independent supporter groups. Many believe that the two high-profile supporter groups could one day officially launch their own political parties.

WHAT TO DO BUT LAUNCH A COUP

When Yingluck Shinawatra, the leader of the Pheu Thai Party, won a landslide victory in the 2011 elections, many Thais were prepared to give her a chance despite the fact that she was the sister of the deposed Thaksin Shinawatra. For others, old wounds heal slowly and allegations came swiftly that she was merely a puppet for a political party that Thaksin would still be controlling.

The final straw for the non-believers came in November 2013 when Yingluck attempted to pass a broad amnesty bill that would, in effect, allow Thaksin to return to Thailand where he would not face any charges nor serve the two years in prison that he was sentenced to in absentia, and, most controversially, have all his seized assets returned. Anti-government protests quickly formed up and down the country, especially in Democrat stronghold areas like Bangkok and Phuket, with pockets of protesters traveling to Bangkok to join the street marches. Their aim, as seen on various items of merchandise made quickly available, was to Shut Down Bangkok in order to Restart Bangkok.

SUTHEP STEPS UP

Former Democrat Party Secretary-General Suthep Thaugsuban quickly became a figurehead and spokesperson for the anti-government protesters, and later formed the People's Democratic Reform Committee (PDRC). Fearing that the present government was so corrupt that any elections or attempted reforms would be rejected or dealt with unfairly, he called for Yingluck to be ousted in favor of installing an unelected people's council. His aims were dismissed, mainly by outside foreign and international observers, as fanciful and unrealistic. Despite this, Suthep and the protesters, clad in merchandise emblazoned with the Thai flag, continued marching every day, whistles blowing. Donations were collected, often by Suthep himself, which went to cover the cost of providing food and water for the faithful. Protesters set up camp on the streets and even in Lumphini Park and there were regular concerts and speeches to boost morale.

In December 2013, Yingluck dissolved the House of Representatives and scheduled a general election for February 2014. She ignored plans to step down in the interim, maintaining that it was her duty to continue to lead the country as a caretaker prime minister.

DON'T VOTE FOR DEMOCRACY

In the run up to election day, February 2, anti-government protesters called on the Thai people not to vote and on the day itself blocked many polling stations, preventing people from voting. They feared that despite all their whistle blowing, the vast majority of Thais (in the rural north of Thailand at least) would go ahead and vote in a party that was sympathetic to the Red Shirt (Thaksin Shinawatra) cause and all the marching and blowing of whistles would have been for nothing. It was a minor victory for the PDRC but not for democracy, as the elections were nullified in March. This enraged pro-government supporters and there were numerous Red Shirt protests held in retaliation, mainly in the north. As the weeks progressed, there were also mounting rumors that the protesters might be heading to Bangkok. In the meantime, skirmishes between protesters and riot police in the capital had turned violent, leading to 28 deaths, including those of two child protesters. Each group blamed the another and accused the police of siding with the opposing faction.

IT'S NOT A COUP (REALLY...)

Something had to be done. In May 2014, following six months of protests, Yingluck and nine other ministers were removed from office by the Constitutional Court. A few weeks later, martial law was imposed under a law promulgated by King Rama VI almost a hundred years earlier to the day.

Like many generals before him, General Prayut Chan-o-cha, Commander of the Royal Thai Army, launched a coup d'état against the caretaker government. The junta was known as the National Council for Peace and Order (NCPO).

From the outset, General Prayut was quick to point out that what was taking place was not a military coup in the traditional sense of the word and there would be no violence. In fact, he stated that the coup was launched to prevent the kind of violence that was being seen at that time in Ukraine. Many Thais and

HAPPINESS FESTIVALS

Throughout the month of June 2014, the Royal Thai Army staged a number of 'Happiness Festivals' in the capital, including at the highly symbolic site of the Victory Monument, popular with protesters past and present, with the aim of restoring happiness to the people. Activities included music concerts, free movie screenings, a petting zoo, free haircuts, free meals and even a sexy coyote performance.

Apart from a few tourists intent on obtaining a soldier selfie, there were many more who were wary of the political situation in Thailand and visitor numbers plummeted.

The Tourism Authority of Thailand hit upon the idea of promoting Martial Law Tourism, stating that, in fact, the country was now safer than ever, what with soldiers, machine guns at the ready, guarding the streets.

Following the murder of two British backpackers in late 2014, the Thai Tourism Minister stated that she had another idea to ensure the safety of the country's visitors: every single one of them would be asked to wear a wristband containing a serial number that corresponded with their ID, which would work much like a sort of rudimentary tracking device. It was met with a mixture of incredulity and ridicule and the idea was soon dropped. A curfew for tourists was another idea that was quickly dismissed.

From July 2014 onwards, the sight of soldiers in the streets became less and less common and life returned to as normal as it has ever been for the Thai people.

visiting foreigners seemed to agree, with some posing for pictures with bemused soldiers holding machine guns.

Despite the 'it's not a coup' claims, a curfew was swiftly imposed from 10 am to 5 pm, which quickly had the desired effect of removing the protest camps that were sporadically placed throughout the capital and elsewhere in the country, regardless of color.

BACK TO 'NORMAL'

Once the coup was imposed and the country was, for the twelfth time, under military rule, Thailand began to return to a sense of military normalcy that almost every generation since 1932 had experienced at one time or another. Suthep shaved his head, joined the monkhood and disappeared from public view for the next few months, while Yingluck went abroad to catch up with her brother. Towards the end of the year, however, she began to be spotted at glitzy events in the capital. The good times weren't to last, however. In January 2015, Yingluck, despite no longer being in office, was impeached and banned from participating in politics for five years.

The NCPO had cleared the streets and seemed to have been successful in reminding the two warring factions about what really mattered. All that remained was to try to convince the general public that they were doing the right thing. And so began the Happiness campaign in June 2014.

HARDLINE POLITICS

Although the NCPO initially said that it was their ultimate intention to hold elections in the latter part of 2015, when Prime Minister Prayut would step down, the former general also hinted on a number of occasions, especially on his weekly Friday night TV address, *Kuen Kwam Suk* (Returning Happiness), that this would only be the case if he thought that the government and Thai society were in a stable enough position for him to do so.

Although martial law was finally lifted in April 2015, it was quickly replaced with the invocation of Article 44 from the interim constitution. Commonly referred to as 'dictator law', it gave Prayut absolute power to override any branch of government as long as such actions were done in the name of national security.

Above Prayut, Suthep and Thaksin were front page news for much of 2014 and 2015.
Below Protestors changed tack, from anti-Shinawatra to anti-coup, in 2014.

THE LAND OF PLENTY

Once touted as a land of plenty because of its rich, varied and abundant agricultural products, Thailand is still able to make such claims, albeit in a slightly more corporate and less romanticized rural way. It continues to have one of the lowest levels of unemployment in the world.

The story of the Thai economy really began to change pace, along with its main characters, when King Rama V, in an attempt to sidestep the sort of bloodshed seen during the American Civil War, abolished slavery and serfdom in 1905. From then onwards, opportunities were available not only to wealthy landowners and noblemen but also to a new wave of entrepreneurs and merchants. Soon after, the export of agricultural products, including most significantly rice, became paramount in the steady growth of the economy and Thailand's inclusion in the global market.

A cultural and economical hangover from Siam's reliance on serfdom is, arguably, still present in Thai society. As such, living like a king or a queen, or at the very least a master, is relatively achievable, at least for the middle and upper classes. Taking taxis everywhere, eating out every day, having regular massages and employing gardeners, maids and cleaners is not seen as particularly indulgent for a large percentage of the kingdom's residents. Of course, this is only made possible by Thailand's huge socio-economic disparity, its ingrained, clearly defined hierarchical structures and its slew of servile jobs. In Thailand, there are whistle-blowing car park attendants, guards who appear to be guarding little more than their plastic seats, well-dressed doormen employed solely to salute customers at shopping malls, and countless other subservient jobs that have disappeared from many a developed country's workplace.

Gender inequality is another remnant of traditional Thai culture that hasn't dramatically changed over the years. Although women can be found on construction sites, collecting trash and

Although rice fields can still be found in the countryside, many rural Thais have migrated to the cities to find work.

generally doing any job that men do, they also tend to earn, on average, 81 percent of what men earn for doing the same job. Thai women have to compete with very traditional, stereotypical and downright sexist views, both inside and outside the office. At home, they are expected to take care of the children and perform all domestic duties, all of which are done with virtually no governmental assistance.

Most Thais work long, hard days, the average being from 8 am to 6 pm, five days a week, often with a half or full day on Saturday.

WHEN **DISASTER** STRIKES

As long as Thai workers have not been fired or have left their position without due cause, they are eligible for up to 15,000 baht (US$450) unemployment benefit per month, depending on the amount of social security contributions they have made. Although this may not seem like a huge amount, the minimum wage in Thailand is just 300 baht a day ($9), so 15,000 baht a month is actually a well above average monthly amount.

Any Thai who earns less than 150,000 baht (US$4,500) per year is exempt from paying tax, meaning, in effect, that a huge percentage of the Thai population and workforce do not pay taxes or make any social security contributions whatsoever. This includes Thailand's street vendors, fruit sellers, DVD merchants, tourist touts, illegal taxi drivers, and all those employed in cash-in-hand industries. A downside of this seemingly kind concession is that should disaster strike and they find themselves unable to sell pineapples, or without customers, then they will invariably find themselves on their own, unable to receive any help from the state. In Thailand, one must be part of and pay into the system to benefit from it.

Foreigners in Thailand who find themselves in a similar situation are also rarely entitled to any financial support despite the significant tax and social security payments they may have made. This is because a foreigner's residence and status as a non-tourist in Thailand is usual dependent on having a work permit. Once that is taken away, so too are the majority of a foreigner's rights to aid.

It is fortunate, therefore, that at least statistically Thailand enjoys one of the lowest unemployment rates in the world, standing at around 0.8 percent.

THE NEW THAILAND

A walk around any Thai supermarket or shopping mall, where an unbelievable number of smartphone-using staff are sitting down and chatting, is testimony to the unnecessarily high level of employment in Thailand. From the spare tire store worker whose only duty appears to be glancing slightly over the shoulder of an unattended customer to the staff who monitor and wield flashlights while commuters walk through metal detectors at train stations, many of Thailand's shops, stores and industries seem to employ around a third more workers than a foreigner is normally used to. Indeed, it often appears that Thailand creates a job and employs somebody to complete a task that only needs doing because it wasn't done by the relevant person in the first place.

Do not make the misguided assumption, however, that this increase in numbers of staff correlates with an increase in productivity or efficiency. Asking the whereabouts of an item in a Thai store merely results in an extended game of Chinese whispers. Salaries being so low, combined with staff numbers being so high, often results in either an unwillingness or an unrequited ability to think or perform a duty outside the very narrow remit of a job.

The flip side of the 100 baht note depicts King Rama V freeing slaves.

CAN I HELP YOU?

Appearances are doubly deceptive, with many economists suggesting that Thai employment figures probably aren't as rosy as they first appear. A significant percentage, they suggest, are merely not officially unemployed or are working fewer than 20 hours per week. There are also many Thai workers, especially in the tourist industry, who suffer from off-season unemployment.

As millions of Thais are not required to pay tax, the knock-on effect contributes to the woefully inadequate welfare system, which often means little or no help when Thais get down on their luck and really need it.

Like many welfare programs in Thailand, child care, and even a knowledge of it, is mainly only available to those within the system and those who have made social security contributions. For those who have, a pilot child welfare program was launched in 2015 that

equates to, on average, around 400 baht (US$12) a month for children up to one year old. After that, parents are on their own. In contrast, the Thai government is more accommodating towards senior citizens, regardless of whether they have paid social security during their lifetime. They qualify for a state pension of 600 baht per month in their sixties, 700 baht in their seventies and so on.

Some 40 percent of Thailand's workforce is engaged in the agricultural sector, 40 percent in service industries and 20 percent in manufacturing. The combined success of the manufacturing and service industries, alongside Thailand's strong, steady industry of agricultural exports, has resulted in a reduction in the number of people living below the poverty line from 65 percent in 1988 to 13 percent in 2011. According to the World Bank, Thailand is one of the great development success stories of the 20th century.

Left Long commutes to work are often part of the daily slog.

Below Four hands are not necessarily better than two.

THE THAI LANGUAGE

With seemingly lax one-size-fits-all rules regarding tenses, relatively simple sentence structures and mainly monosyllabic words, the Thai language appears to be one of the easier constructed languages.

Once you dig deeper, however, you will learn that the tonal language of Thai, with its subtle nuances, is incredibly difficult to master. There are also different dialects depending on region, and particular words, sentence structures and phrases that are only used in certain circumstances. There are even different registers, including Religious Thai and Royal Thai. There are also masculine and feminine versions of some Thai words. *Krab* for men and *ka* for women, as polite particles to end sentences, are the most commonly used.

The spoken language of Thai is purported to have originated from the border of Vietnam and China and has similarities with the languages of Laos, Myanmar and northern Vietnam. In fact, around 70 percent of the words from the Thai dialect of Isan (bordering Laos) and the Lao language are the same, as is the sentence structure. Despite these similarities, however, there are still enough differences to mean that someone who speaks only Thai, Thai Isan or Lao will not necessarily be able to understand other languages.

'THAI ONLY'

The majority of residents of the rural Thai area of Isan are ethnic Lao and as such are bilingual. Although Thai is now taught and used in schools, as decreed by Field Marshal Plaek through his process of 'Thaification', a mixture of Thai and Lao is used in the social environment. 'Thaification' was also imposed on the Chinese community in Thailand, resulting in the teaching of Chinese being banned in favor of the Thai language.

HARDER THAN IT LOOKS

On paper, it gets harder, with written Thai at first, second and third glance resembling little more than a series of squiggles. It is believed to have been introduced during the reign of the third Sukhothai sovereign, King Ramkhamhaeng, in 1283. Written Thai was based on the pre-existing Pali, Sanskrit and Indian writing systems and has remained largely unchanged since its inception.

One of the most difficult aspects of the language is that unlike English and other European 'alphabet languages', Thai is a tonal (phonemic) language. This means it contains a much greater degree of variation in the pronunciation of its syllables. There are five lexical tones in Thai (low, mid, high, falling, rising), which makes for a very melodic but consequently hard to decipher language. For example, the word *mai* means 'new' if said with a low tone, 'no' if said with a falling tone, 'silk' if said with a rising tone but creates a question if used at the end of a sentence.

Thai people have a great love of puns and double entendres as heard in the sometimes risqué *molam* (country music) lyrics, which adds to the complexity.

HEARING THE DIFFERENCE

The Thai written language uses a phonemic alphabet of 44 consonants and 32 vowels. Perhaps because of the diversity and range of sounds, most Thais carry all their lives a school-learned mnemonic picture association

Above Easy as A, B, C. Most start off by learning the Thai alphabet.

Left Although many signs are also in English, there is no guarantee you won't get lost.

Above Believed by some, but not all, to be the first example of Thai writing.

THANON NAKHON SAWAN

GRUNT LIKE A LOCAL

All manner of grunts, exclamations and interjections pepper Thai conversation. Here are some of the most common you're likely to hear:

Aow! Used to show either surprise or disappointment.

Hoh! Used to show admiration or astonishment.

Ore! Used to show sudden realization, understanding.

Eh! Used to show confusion.

Oie! Used to show anger or frustration.

Uh! Used to show acknowledgement that the person you're speaking to has finally understood.

---

with every consonant, for example, *gaw gai* (chicken), *taw tao* (turtle), *law ling* (monkey). In fact, tones are so important that quite often a Thai speaker will add extra sounds when speaking a foreign language. This is most noticeably done when an extra vowel is added between two consecutive consonants. 'Steak' becomes 'st-ay-ke' and 'stamp' becomes 'sa-ta-m'. Sometimes the Thai speaker may just decide to omit sounding one of the consonants altogether.

The characters are written left to right, and spaces are only used to indicate the end of a sentence, not to separate words. The Thai language also has its own set of Thai numerals based on the Hindu Arabic numeral system, but nowadays the standard Western system is more common. Thai numerals can, however, still sometimes be seen, especially at places employing a dual pricing system.

Scholars fear that more letters, sounds and, of course, cute accompanying pictures will be lost to future generations as younger Thais seek new, quick and easy ways to communicate in text-speak.

In Thailand, a popular way of showing the 'efficiency' of the large smartphone screen is by showing a young Thai texting quickly on the 'large-enough-screen' that can accommodate all of the Thai letters, consonants and vowels.

Learning TINGLISH

Anybody who stays in Thailand for an extended period, even if they make little or no effort to learn Thai, will find they will begin to possess a rudimentary level of 'Tinglish'—a hybrid of Thai and English based on existing Thai rules of grammar and cultural practices.

Tinglish tends to omit pronouns and the verb 'to be' as these are not necessarily used in the Thai language. For example, instead of saying "We don't have...," a cashier might say, in Tinglish, "No have," as this is the most accurate translation from the Thai for *Mai mee*.

Walk past any taxi driver in the kingdom and the likelihood of him enquiring in Tinglish "Where you go?" is not necessarily rude and intrusive but merely a direct translation of the common Thai greeting/enquiry *Bai nai*? ("Go where?")

Also quite common in Tinglish is the addition of a Thai particle, for example, *ka/krab/na*, at the end of a perfectly well-constructed English sentence to indicate polite conduct, as these particles are always used to end a sentence if the speaker wishes to speak formally. I hope you understand *krab*.

Other common mistakes made in Tinglish include:

I am boring = I am bored

Although it may initially seem like a refreshingly honest statement, it is likely that the Thai speaker merely wishes to convey their lack of interest in a particular activity. This misuse of the present continuous is simply a result of not understanding or remembering the difference in use and meaning. The Thai equivalent of bored (*beau*) and boring (*naa beau*) is created in a totally different way.

I play Internet = I go on/use the Internet

This is simply a case of first language interference, as in Thai the verb *len* (play) is used in conjunction with all games, including football and computers. In Thai, to work is associated with making money, while to play is any activity that doesn't involve making money.

Same, same = Similar/the same

The doubling up of 'same' is, again, a result of direct translation. In Thai, one way of saying 'similar' can be *deeokwan deeokwan* or *khlai khlai gap*.

After a few months of living in Thailand, do not be surprised if some bad grammatical habits start to form. As there are no articles ('a', 'an', 'the') in Thai, and pronouns are largely omitted, new arrivals may suddenly find themselves speaking a rather neanderthal version of English, with utterances like "Want beer".

There is also no Thai equivalent of 'some' or 'any', and when forming a question in Thai, the subject normally begins the sentence. This means that once the feckless foreigner masters the modern art of Tinglish, he will probably begin constructing sentences like "Beer have?" It's not all bad though, as he is likely to also add *krab* on the end of every sentence.

Wat Arun is a particularly beautiful Bangkok temple, especially when viewed at sunset. Although more like a theme park than a tranquil place of contemplation, the Grand Palace attracts thousands of visitors every day.

THAILAND'S MOST IMPORTANT RELIGIOUS SITES

Many of the most stunning and historically significant Thai *wat* (temples) are located in the cities of Ayutthaya, Chiang Mai, Chiang Rai and, of course, Bangkok. Thai temples are often used for multiple purposes and are therefore central to Thai life.

Some Thai temples act as rehabilitation centers, while others serve as festival venues. Some host huge annual temple fairs, complete with funfair rides, games, contests, live music and an obligatory Thai market. Entry to temples in Thailand is free for Thais but there may be a small entry fee for foreign visitors.

Wat Arun (Temple of Dawn) is located on the west bank of the Chao Phraya River in Bangkok. This iconic riverside structure is breathtaking and when viewed from the water the temple's reflection makes for a truly memorable experience, especially at sunset or sunrise. This beautiful structure is further characterized by its two central *prang* (spires), decorated with multicolored ceramic, that seem to stretch right up into the sky.

Another popular temple site is **Wat Phra Mahatat** in Ayutthaya. The temple ruins are in a similar state to

Wat Pho

As its name suggests, Wat Pho (Temple of the Reclining Buddha) contains a 151 ft (46 m) long gold leaf-covered reclining Buddha statue. It is the biggest temple complex in Bangkok and is home to the Thai Traditional Medical and Massage School, where weary travelers can revive their aching feet, shoulders and body with a traditional Thai massage for a very reasonable price. Aspiring masseurs can even take a Thai massage course.

WAT PHRA KAEW

WAT PHRA MAHATHAT

WAT SAKET

WAT SUTHAT

other sites in Ayutthaya. However, it is the spectacular Buddha image embedded in a tree trunk that prompts many to visit. Theories vary as to its existence. Most Thais believe that Burmese ransackers had tried to steal the head,

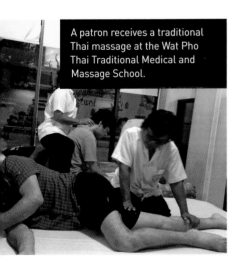

A patron receives a traditional Thai massage at the Wat Pho Thai Traditional Medical and Massage School.

failed because of its weight, dropped it and that trees had subsequently grown around it.

Wat Phra Kaew (Temple of the Emerald Buddha) is perhaps the most important temple in the whole of Thailand. Situated within the grounds of the Grand Palace, the exquisite structure contains a Buddha image dating from the 15th century, raised high upon a platform.

Wat Saket (Temple of the Golden Mount) in Bangkok dates back to the Ayutthaya kingdom. The Golden Mount refers to the manmade mound upon which the temple sits. To reach the top of the mount, worshippers and visitors have to climb 300 steps. The crowning glory of Wat Saket is the wonderful golden *chedi* (stupa).

Wat Suthat is not only one of the

largest temples in Bangkok (it covers around 10 acres/4 ha) but also one of the oldest. A huge red teak arch at the entrance is all that remains of a giant swing that once welcomed visitors to the complex. Inside the complex are wonderful murals, numerous pagodas and a 25 ft (7.6 m) tall bronze Buddha image.

WAT TRAIMIT

Housed in **Wat Traimit** in Chinatown, Bangkok, is the world's largest golden-seated Buddha. Carved in solid gold, the 5 ft (1.5 m) high statue, which weighs around 5 tons, is believed to date back to the Sukhothai period. It is well worth a visit if only to learn more about the interesting story of the structure.

Wat Ratchabophit is a temple designed in rather a unique manner and is well worth a visit. Although its layout includes a traditional Thai circular courtyard, complete with golden *chedi*, the interior design of the temple was heavily influenced by the gilded Italian architecture of the time. There is also a royal cemetery in the temple grounds.

The otherworldly design of the interior of **Wat Paknam** is strikingly beautiful. Unlike other traditional Thai temples, the ornate décor is colored with unconventional light blues and reds, and unusual shapes and hues. The temple is also well known for its meditation lessons, and monks here instruct in Buddhism and meditation in both English and Thai and therefore attract many visitors each day.

Another Thai temple worthy of mention is **Wat Rong Khun** (White Temple) in Chiang Rai. As its name suggests, it is a completely white structure (representing purity) that would not look out of place in a *Lord of the*

Wat Benchamabophit

Wat Benchamabophit is widely regarded as one of the most beautiful temples in Thailand. Designed by Prince Naris, a brother of the king at the time, it stands out from the majority of temples in Bangkok as it uses the finest Italian marble. This major tourist attraction draws huge numbers of visitors who come to marvel at the majesty and beauty of the temple and its 52 Buddha statues that decorate the exterior.

Wat Rakhang

Wat Rakhang (Bell Temple) is a popular temple for visitors who wish to ring in good fortune to their lives. The ringing of the temple bell is a common practice for those wishing to bring positive influence in their life. Wat Rakhang is also well known for its artistic exterior design.

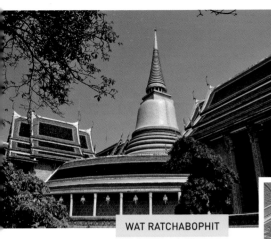

WAT RATCHABOPHIT

WAT RONG KHUN

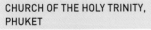

WAT PAKNAM

Rings movie. The unconventional temple was designed in 1997 by Chalermchai Kositpipat, who once said that it would never be finished in his lifetime. He plans to build—or have someone build—another nine dream-like structures and aims to have them all finished by 2070.

OTHER PLACES OF WORSHIP

Thailand is also home to some beautiful Christian churches. Increasingly of late, more and more Russian Orthodox churches have sprung up around the kingdom. One incredible structure, built in a classic cross-shaped plan and topped with a gold onion-shaped dome, is the Church of the Holy Trinity Church in Phuket.

Because of the relatively large Muslim population in Thailand, there is understandably more than a fair share of spectacular mosques in the kingdom. A stand-out mosque is the Pattani Grand Mosque, situated in the troubled south of the country. Easily the largest mosque in Thailand, the Pattani Grand Mosque, opened in 1963, is also widely regarded as one of the hundred most beautiful mosques in the world, with the large dome in the center and four smaller surrounding ones often drawing comparisons with India's Taj Mahal.

PATTANI GRAND MOSQUE

CHURCH OF THE HOLY TRINITY, PHUKET

The best-known Sikh temple (Gurdwara) in Thailand is located in Bangkok. The structure that stands today, the Siri Guru Singh Sabha, was originally built in 1933. Located in the Phra Nakhon district, known to the locals as Little India, this six-story temple, trimmed in gold and topped by a gold dome, is steeped in Sikh culture and heritage.

Owing to the sizable Nepalese community in Thailand, there are also a number of Nepalese temples in the country, including Phuket. A temple stands at the top of Patong hill and is immediately recognizable and distinguishable from Thai Buddhist temples owing to the use of more vibrant and mixed colors and, of course, the representation of the multitude of Hindu gods.

THE IMPORTANCE OF THAI BUDDHISM

If you're an early riser in Thailand and regardless of whether you're in the metropolis of Bangkok or the smallest village in Surat Thani, it is likely you will see orange-robed monks walking through the neighborhood giving blessings and receiving alms.

Around 95 percent of Thais are Buddhists, the highest percentage of Buddhist nationals in the world. The Thai version of Buddhism is chiefly derived from the Theravada or southern school of Buddhism, which originated in Sri Lanka, but over time has incorporated elements of Thai myths and folk stories and, owing to the large Thai Chinese population, various Chinese gods. Thai Buddhism has also been heavily influenced by Hinduism.

In 2013, following the death of Kanchanaburi born Supreme Patriarch Somdet Phra Nyanasamvara, who was also Sangha Leader of the Buddhist World as bestowed by the World Fellowship of Buddhists, King Bhumibol ordered a 30-day national mourning period.

The importance of Buddhism in Thailand cannot be understated. Around 50 percent of Thai boys and young men typically enter the monkhood or become ordained at least once in their lifetime. King Mongkut himself was a monk for 27 years. In days gone by, the king of Thailand was seen as a protector of the religion. Kings, queens, princes and princesses therefore take part in religious ceremonies, attend services and make merit each year.

MAKING MERIT

Thai people 'make merit' (do good things as prescribed through religious doctrine), whether giving alms to monks or visiting temples on birthdays, significant dates and religious holidays. They make merit to bring inner happiness, become successful, gain guidance and cease earthly desires.

It is quite common for a Thai home to have some sort of Buddhist shrine, complete with Buddha image, to which family members pray, meditate or make merit. Outside homes and places of business, daily food offerings are made to the spirits and ancestors in a bid to appease them.

MULTIPURPOSE MONASTERIES

Many Buddhist temples in Thailand double up as retreats or places of rehabilitation. Each year, thousands of young Thai offenders are dispatched to their local temple for guidance, instruction or therapy. Treatment often involves taking an alcohol or drug vow against the use of either for a certain period of time. Attendees also purge themselves regularly and drink herbal concoctions that make them vomit into large trough-like areas in the temple.

A much-revered monk, who ran the country's largest drug rehabilitation program at Wat Thamkrabok in Saraburi province, was former police officer Phra Chamroon Panchan. His treatment of those suffering from narcotic addiction was internationally recognized. In the 1970s, at the end of the Vietnam War, the temple also became a shelter for up to 30,000 hill tribe (Hmong) refugees from Laos. Controversy has,

Left Novice monks accept morning alms at Amphawa Floating Market.

Below Monks set out to get their daily food donations.

The disgraced, disrobed
Luang Pu Nen Kham.

MONKEY BUSINESS

Although Buddhism in Thailand is arguably as strong as it ever was, there is a gradual sense that many, especially among the younger generation, are becoming somewhat disillusioned. The year 2013, especially, was not a good one for Thai Buddhist monks, with many being caught on camera carrying Louis Vuitton bags, shopping for iPhones and even endorsing air humidifiers. Such 'vulgar' displays of consumerism and earthly objects are strictly against the principles of Dharma (law of nature) and, as such, were met with much condemnation in Thailand. According to the National Office of Buddhism, there are around 61,000 monks in Thailand.

however, surrounded the temple since it was first used as a rehabilitation center in 1959, and in 2003 the Thai military sent hundreds of troops to the temple to investigate accusations that the temple was being used as a base for drug and arms trafficking. As a result, the Hmong were fenced into the temple grounds for more than a year. The fencing has since been removed.

Phra Chamroon Panchan died in 1999, aged 73, but the temple still offers help to Thai and foreign addicts who wish to experience a Buddhist approach to drug rehabilitation. There have been a number of famous Westerners who have completed treatment at Wat Thamkrabok.

ISLAM IN THAILAND

Islam is Thailand's largest minority religion and is practiced by around 7.5 million people, or about 12 percent of the population. The majority of Thai Muslims are ethnically Malay, and speak Malay as well as Thai, but there are also many of Middle Eastern, Bangladeshi, Pakistani and Cambodian origin.

Although Thai Muslims and mosques are scattered throughout the kingdom, the highest concentration of Thai Muslims is in Bangkok while 18 percent live in the southernmost provinces of Narathiwat, Pattani, Yala, and Satun bordering Malaysia. The former Islamic sultanates of Yala, Pattani and Narathiwat were handed to Thailand by British Malaya as part of the Anglo-Siamese Treaty of 1909 that defined the modern border between the two nations.

In many areas of Thailand, Muslim communities live peacefully side by side with Buddhist communities. However, there is serious and very real unrest in southern Thailand, with an increasing level of fighting between Muslim military insurgents and the Thai army in the three main Muslim provinces. The conflict has seen almost 6,000 people—Muslims and soldiers— killed since 2004. A large percentage of residents in the majority Muslim areas in the south feel they are under-represented at a political level and would like to have independence from Thailand, and insurgents are therefore fighting for autonomy.

Above Thai Muslim girls enjoy a cold drink.
Below Bang Tao Mosque.

OTHER RELIGIONS IN THAILAND

Despite a relatively small number of followers, Hinduism has had a huge impact on Thailand's culture and its interpretation of Buddhism. The clearest example of the religion's influence is the adoption and adaptation of the Hindu epic *Ramayana* into the Thai version, the *Ramakien*, which came to be used as inspiration for Thai theater productions, dances, songs, art, and even modern-day Thai soap opera plots.

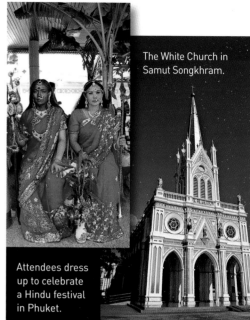

The White Church in Samut Songkhram.

There is also a small community of Sikhs, mostly engaged in the business sector in Thailand, with high numbers in the larger cities of Bangkok, Chiang Mai and Phuket.

Christianity was introduced to Thailand by European missionaries as early as the 1550s and the missions played an important role as agents for the transmission of Western ideas, such as medicine and education. Soon after, King Narai ordered the building of St Joseph's Church in Ayutthaya for the use of missionaries and foreign religious workers and local converts, mostly Chinese. There are currently around 500,000 Christians in Thailand.

Attendees dress up to celebrate a Hindu festival in Phuket.

GHOSTS IN **THE VILLAGE**

Tales of ghosts, spirits and unearthly beings are not just reserved for Halloween in Thailand. It is quite common to see shrines, better known as spirit houses, erected in a prominent spot outside homes, offices, hotels and other buildings in order to provide an appealing shelter to wandering spirits. Offerings must be presented regularly at these spirit houses.

Many ghost stories have their origin in traditional Thai folklore and animism but have also become intertwined and adapted by traditional Buddhist mythology. The omnipresence and continued popularity of the Thai spirit world can also be seen in the recurring theme of both good and evil ghosts in Thai movies and Thai soap operas. In 2013, Thai ghost movie *Pee Mak* became the highest selling Thai movie of all time.

Villagers in the northeast and rural communities of Thailand still believe in black magic and ghosts. They will sometimes wear bracelets made by monks to protect themselves from harmful ghosts. One of the most common ghosts terrorizing rural communities is Pee Mae Mai, a lonely widow, who is believed to prey on the men of a village. If a large number of men die or disappear from a particular community, Pee Mae Mai is believed to be responsible and is thought to be lurking about. Villagers will rush to make basic puppets of men, often fashioned from sticks with coconuts on top, to hang outside, along with a sign that reads 'No men inside' in a bid to throw Pee Mae Mai off the scent.

Another feared ghost is a female witch called Pop, who uses black magic to destroy or haunt people, make them fall in love or get sick. By day she could be the rice seller at a popular restaurant, but at night she becomes a ghost and exists to haunt villagers. It is believed that a tell-tale sign of a Pop is somebody who eats raw, live meat or perhaps a whole chicken. Even today, it is quite popular for villagers to organize witch-hunts to seek out and kill a village Pop.

Right Spirit houses are highly visible outside public buildings and private residences.

Below right A teenager reads a Thai ghost comic.

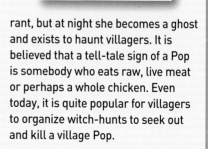

THAI FOLKLORE

The importance of myths and folklore and how they interweave and are relevant to Thai cultural thinking is not to be taken lightly. Stories of spirits and of mythical creatures are to Thailand what fairy tales and superheroes are to the West, and are similarly used as cautionary tales and to entertain successive generations.

A 'lucky' 20 baht fish.

The fact that so many Thais still carry charms, wear amulets, make merit and choose particular phone numbers is a clear indication that myths and folklore are still an influential part of everyday Thai life, if not perhaps as widespread and staunchly believed today.

Some Thais choose auspicious dates to buy cars to avoid accidents. Some don't point at rainbows to avoid losing their finger and many don't have their hair cut on a Wednesday to steer clear of bad luck. All have their origins in Thai mythology and folklore.

Even today, Thai TV shows featuring fortune-tellers and clairvoyants or people recounting their experiences with ghosts and spirits is a common staple. Each year there are tales of hauntings, possessions and things that go bump in the night, which are, in a cyclical manner, given credence and reaffirmation with the regular coverage. As Thai belief decrees that a premature death often results in ghosts haunting the area in which someone died until they are given an official and religious send-off, news of ghostly sightings following the 2004 Thai tsunami became commonplace in newspapers and on TV shows, with one story in particular quickly cementing its placement as a modern Thai myth.

STORIES BECOME MYTHS

Apparently, a few weeks after the tsunami, a Phuket taxi driver was flagged down by four tourists who asked to be taken to the airport.

On the journey there, they all chatted freely until they arrived at their destination. Upon turning around to inform his passengers that they had arrived, the driver found that his cab was empty. As a result of such tales, and in order to encourage ghost-fearing visitors back to the island post-tsunami, hundreds of monks took to the beaches to perform cleansing ceremonies and allow the restless spirits to be able to depart this world.

In 2013, upon apparently seeing the ghost of an old lady in the sleepy beach-side town of Khao Lak, near Phuket, 21 schoolgirls and one schoolboy were taken to hospital, checked and treated for fear of mass possession.

In the past, but to a lesser extent today, *mor duu* (fortune-tellers) occupied the same cultural space that psychiatrists, careers advisers and doctors do in the West. Some Thais also go to *mor phi* (witch doctors) for help with invisible spirits, to avoid difficulties, to remove bad luck or even to place a curse on an enemy.

CAN I HAVE YOUR NUMBER?

Many Thais believe the number nine is an incredibly auspicious and lucky number and go to great lengths to get number plates and phone numbers bearing as many nines as possible. King Bhumibol is also Rama IX in the Chakri dynasty, which earns him an extra special place in people's hearts.

At the other end of the scale is the number 25, or, more specifically being 25. Thais consider this a particularly precarious stage of life, where one is more likely to get involved in accidents or be a victim of misfortune. In order to counter bad karma, many 25 year olds make merit and visit temples in the hope of banishing bad luck.

Considering Thais' preoccupation with the meaning behind numbers, it is not surprising that the only legal form of gambling in Thailand is the lottery. Interestingly, the 'underground lottery' (based on the last two or three digits of the government lottery) is much more popular. Except for a few government sanctioned arenas, gambling at every other event is illegal.

A Thai cultural theme show, like *Siam Niramit*, is a great place to go for a crash course in Thai myths.

THE SPIRIT OF BUDDHISM

Before the introduction of Buddhism, Thais believed in animism, along with other forms of what is commonly referred to as folk religions. They worshipped spirits, practiced magic and used talismans. Over time, the main tenet of animism—that natural entities, including plants, animals and even inanimate objects like shrines and statues, contain spiritual souls— became intermingled with Buddhist and Hindu philosophy and tales. Contemporary Thai Buddhist spirituality, therefore, is quite an eclectic mixture of superstitions and beliefs. Ghosts and mythical characters remain popular in Thailand, especially the ones that take on animal forms or have a grounding with their natural surroundings.

The ghost of Pee Nang Takian, for example, haunts Takian trees (*Hopea odorata*), and it is believed that if such trees are ever felled she will haunt the area and bring great misfortune to the person(s) responsible.

Although over time Thais' reliance on the land and its animals, and by extension their relationship with nature, waned, the beliefs evolved to become superstitions, and it is still therefore common to see various animal-inspired talismans adorning the walls of Thai businesses, for example, a spider, which helps trap passing custom in the traders' proverbial webs.

Even the Thai national emblem is a half man/half eagle character called Garuda hailing from the Himaphan Forest that features in Hindu mythology. It has been used as a symbol of Thai royalty since King Vajiravudh (Rama VI) in 1911. As ancient kings and their subjects believed in divine kingship, Garuda, in his role as vehicle for the god Vishnu, became synonymous with royalty and its image thus came to be used as a royal seal. The powerful Garuda is omnipresent and can be seen everywhere, perched high above government gates and on banknotes, passports or any official document.

Another hugely influential mythical creature in Thai culture is that of the legend of Kinnaree, a half female/half bird character that lives among other mythical creatures in the mysterious Himaphan Forest. Kinnaree is believed to belong to a group of perfectly beautiful sisters who have wings and tails and can fly between the human and mystical worlds. Throughout Thai history, in its literature, poetry and art, Kinnaree has always reflected the ideal of Thai beauty and quality and is often used as the symbol for femininity.

The most popular of myths featuring Kinnaree is called Manora and is about a Kinnaree who was kidnapped from the Himaphan Forest to marry a prince. This story is also retold in various famous Thai traditional dances.

What could be a more fitting symbol and character for Thailand's Tourism Awards (Kinnaree Awards) than the Kinnaree? Beautiful, mythical and gentle, she is the essence of Thai grace.

A typical half human/half bird Kinnaree commonly seen at Thai temples.

STARTED WITH A MYTH

The majority of Thai festivals can be traced back to a particular myth, for example, that of Paya Nark (Great Naga). This giant snake appears in many Thai and Buddhist tales, and images of it can be seen in temple architecture, boat designs and Buddhist sculptures. Some Thais still believe in the Great Naga, with cracks and damage to roads often blamed on the giant serpent tunneling underneath. Every year, thousands even await its appearance in the Mekong River around the end of October. Its visit is usually accompanied by a *bang fai paya nark* (naga fireball), a collection of sparkling circles that come from the river or from fireworks, depending on perspective, and float in the air.

An often dangerous, even deadly, festival is Boon Bang Fai (Rocket Festival), held in Isan every March. During the three-day festival, people make merit and pay respect to the spirits that they believe provide rain. They do this by launching huge bottle rockets filled with gunpowder into the sky.

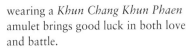

wearing a *Khun Chang Khun Phaen* amulet brings good luck in both love and battle.

REFLECTIONS OF SOCIETY

Thai myths present unwavering examples of ideals of masculinity and femininity, where women appear as symbols of delicate beauty while men are presented as strong, charming and talented in some way, usually with magic. The symbolism in Thai mythology reflects Thailand's ever-present social, gender and class hierarchical structures, and also the very patriarchal, polygamous and often hypocritical Thai society of yesteryear.

Phra Apai Manee and the male characters from *Khun Chang Khun Phaen* are talented men who, as was the case with Thai men of status in the past, have several wives along their journey.

Meanwhile, Wanthong, the female protagonist in *Khun Chang Khun Paen*, is executed at the end of the story, partly for being unable to choose between her two suitors. The legend of Wangthong continues to this day, with the commonly used Thai idiom "Nang Wanthong song jai", which translates as "Wanthong who has two lovers at the same time", being a shorthand slur for a woman with loose moral values.

THAI ARTIST AND MYTHS

Chakrabhand Posayakrit, a Thai National Artist in Visual Arts (Painting), is a celebrated portraitist and painter whose themes are mainly taken from Thai dance theater and literature, including mythological characters such as Kinnaree.

Chakrabhand has also participated in mural restoration work at Wat Phra Kaew (Temple of the Emerald Buddha) and created new, yet traditional themed murals at Wat Trithosathep in Bangkok and Wat Khao Sukim in Chantaburi.

Men, masks and merriment at the Phi Ta Khon festival.

Above left and right Locals turn out in droves for the Boon Bang Fai (Rocket Festival).

At the annual Phi Ta Khon ghost festival held in the mountains of Loei province in Isan, male residents dress up in colorful garb and masks (*khon*) and wield wooden phalluses (*palad khik*) in homage to a party that was once held to welcome the return of Buddha, a party that was so raucous it woke the dead.

Characters with links to the mystical world or who are well versed in magic are often the protagonists in Thai literature, both past and present, with *Phra Apai Manee*, a 30,000-line epic written by Sunthorn Phu, perhaps the best known. A popular, handsome and charming prince, Phra Apai Manee was skilled in both magic and battle. The story follows the young prince's adventures after being sent from the palace to learn about the world, armed with just his magic flute and winning smile. Adapted from folklore, the story is taught in schools and has been sold in book form for generations and made into countless movie adaptions.

Most Thais are also familiar with the characters from the epic poem *Khun Chang Khun Phaen*, a story about a charming, talented soldier who is also proficient in magic. This story is also told in schools, and it is believed that

Above The wonderfully decorated Royal Barge Procession.

Right The Grand Palace.

THAILAND'S ROYAL PALACE

The Grand Palace has been the official royal residence for the Thai monarchy since it was built for King Buddha Yodfa Chulaloke (Rama I) in 1782. The building of the Grand Palace, as the official residence of the new king, signified the metaphorical and literal transfer of power from the city of Thonburi, the capital during King Taksin's reign, to the new capital of Bangkok.

Encompassing an area of 60 acres (24 ha), the Grand Palace comprises numerous buildings, temples, structures and courtyards and was, until 1925, the home of every ruling king of Thailand in the Rattanakosin era.

During Thailand's period of absolute monarchy, the Grand Palace was also the seat of the government, where the government's decisions were made and at one time housed thousands of guardsmen, ministers, servants and concubines. As the Grand Palace was seen very much as a city within its own right, special laws were also drafted to govern the inhabitants.

After the current king, King Bhumibol Adulyadej (Rama IX), took up residence at Chitralada Palace, which is also located in Bangkok, the Grand Palace was used more as a location for official events and worship.

Although it is also a hugely popular tourist attraction because of its many beautiful temples, buildings and architectural splendor, certain sections of the Grand Palace are out of bounds as it is still technically a 'working palace' with many senior royal officers having their offices there.

As the complex stands today, the Grand Palace is divided into four areas separated by walls and gates, namely, the Outer Court, the Middle Court, the Inner Court and the Temple of the Emerald Buddha.

THE OUTER COURT

During the absolute monarchy period of Thai history, the Outer Court was the seat of royal government and was occupied largely by government agencies and officials. Even today, the area has a distinct business and administrative feel, with many buildings inside used for official meetings. Visitors may also be interested in a small museum called the Pavilion of Regalia, Royal Decorations and Coins.

THE MIDDLE COURT

The Middle Court is arguably the most important and oft-visited section of the Grand Palace. It houses all the Grand Palace's residential buildings, many of which have been designed with an eye-watering level of beauty and detail. Here you will find the various former residences of the most influential people of the kingdom. Although it is no longer used as an official residence for the Thai monarchy, it still has its fair share of armed Royal Guards, who stand sentinel throughout the day.

THE PHRA MAHA MONTHIAN GROUP

The Phra Maha Monthian group refers to a number of interconnecting buildings situated within the Middle Court. This walled structure was where the actual abode of the king was located. All Royal Coronations now take place here. This was also where all foreign missionaries and ambassadors were received and granted audiences with the king.

THE INNER COURT

The Inner Court, situated adjacent to the Middle Court, is closed off to the public. Whenever a king of Thailand was resident in the Grand Palace, this area would house the royal consorts and female attendants. The section was completely forbidden to outsiders and to all men.

The Royal Family

Bhumibol Adulyadej was born in Cambridge, Massachusetts, USA, in 1927 and was installed as the King of Thailand in 1950, making him the longest reigning monarch in the world. If assets managed by the Crown Bureau are included, he is also believed to be the world's richest man, with an estimated net worth of $30 billion. Queen Sirikit has been King Bhumibol Adulyadej's wife and royal consort since April 1950 and they have four children.

The name Bhumibol loosely translates as 'Strength of the Land'. King Bhumibol is also widely known as the 'Development King' owing to his numerous charities, rural development programs and attempts at making villages sustainable and self-sufficient. In fact, many members of the Thai

ROYAL PUBLIC HOLIDAYS

Numerous royal holidays are observed and celebrated with much gusto throughout the year. For example, Commemoration Day, a nationwide public holiday, is held on May 5 to celebrate the coronation of the King in 1950.

Queen Sirikit's birthday, which has subsequently come to be known as Mother's Day, is celebrated on August 12. On this day, Thai people celebrate the Queen's birthday as well as their own mother's.

Likewise, King Bhumibol Adulyadej's birthday is celebrated on December 5 and is known in the kingdom as Father's Day, where Thai people not only celebrate the King's birthday but also their own father's.

October 23 is another public holiday with royal significance. This holiday is known as Chulalongkorn Day and commemorates the birthday of the much-loved King Chulalongkorn (Rama V).

Above left The coronation of King Bhumibol Adulyadej in 1950.

Above right King Bhumibol is loved and revered like a god in Thailand.

The royal family of Thailand on the occasion of King Bhumibol's 85th birthday in 2012.

royal family, both past and present, are well known for their philanthropy and are associated with specific charities and causes.

Besides attending numerous annual religious and royal ceremonies, such as the Royal Barge Procession and the Changing of the Robes of the Emerald Buddha, members of the Thai royal family have many other official duties to perform, including the awarding of degree certificates during the majority of graduation ceremonies.

Most years, generally on auspicious dates, including the King's birthday and most recently Princess Maha Chakri Sirindhorn's birthday, there are also Royal Pardons, which are entirely up to the discretion of King Bhumibol. In 2015, to coincide with the Princess's 60th birthday, for example, 38,000 prisoners were released early and 140,000 prisoners had their sentences commuted.

Every evening at 7 pm, most Thai TV channels run a nightly program featuring the latest happenings and royal news. Footage may show a member of the royal family visiting a school or perhaps inspecting the new facilities at a museum.

With the much-loved King Bhumibol now in his late eighties, and considering the hugely pivotal role that he has played in stabilizing the country and in Thailand's political affairs, the prospect of succession to heir-apparent Prince Vajiralongkorn, who in 2014 divorced his third wife, remains a delicate and contentious subject. Although very unlikely, there are some who believe that the King's daughter, Princess Maha Chakri Sirindhorn, who is unmarried and without child, may even become the ruling monarch. Discussion on such matters, however, is restricted in the kingdom amid fears of contravening the lesè majesté law.

The debate is fueled further and given extra significance by a well-known old prophecy that the Chakri dynasty would last only nine generations.

What will become of Thailand once the reign of King Bhumibol comes to an end remains a sensitive issue.

CHAPTER 2

THAI DESIGN AND CRAFTSMANSHIP

Thai style is subtle, simple, yet stunning. The secret of Thai style lies in the pursuit of an aesthetic that is in harmony with the surroundings, nature and culture. It is expressed not only in the country's arts, crafts, silk wear and tribal textiles but also in the architecture, including the beautiful five-star resorts that dot the country, the serene temples that are the focus of towns and the traditional homes that form the center of Thai life.

STYLE STARTS AT HOME

It is not only in the intricate craftsmanship that Thai style is expressed but in the desire for calm amidst chaos. It's visible in the harmonious lifestyle of slum-dwellers who live in noisy, close quarters; in the hustle and bustle of the markets; in the traffic on the street. Thai style, and the desire for balance and functional oneness with the surroundings, is everywhere, especially in the Thai home.

The teak wood 'stilt' house is the typical traditional home in Thailand, especially in the rural areas of the north, center and south. Although the size of these structures often differs, depending on the social status of the owners, and the materials used also varies, the principles behind the design of the house have remained consistent over the centuries.

The stilt house has a multipurpose practicality. Because of the regular monsoon seasons, most of the living areas of a Thai house are built on raised platforms to avoid being flooded. It is for this reason also that many tradition-al Thai houses have sharply angled roofs, which allow rainwater to run off. The elevated position of a stilt house also allows for cool breezes to pass below the platform and keep the structure from becoming overly warm in the hottest months. This one-floor structure was typically made using teak wood (now a restricted material in Thailand) because of its strength and insect-repellant properties. The use of hardwoods, bamboo and dried leaves also helped keep the house cool.

Top left The elephant shrine in the lobby of the Anantara Golden Triangle Elephant Camp.

Top right A raised door frame, seen in temples and houses to keep spirits out and babies in.

Above Beautifully crafted wooden furniture is a dominant feature of traditional Thai-style houses.

Left A traditional Thai stilt house.

INSIDE THE THAI HOUSE

As with Thai temples, visitors to Thai homes take off their footwear before venturing inside. There is no danger of footwear being stolen. Even in the poorest, most ramshackle and dodgiest apartment blocks you will see dozens of pairs of shoes that will remain untouched outside doors.

One of the most interesting archi-tectural features commonly found in traditional Thai homes and temples is visible before one even steps foot in the building. Many Thai homes and temples have raised door frames at the threshold that require visitors to step over and into a room. These are designed not only to strengthen the structure but, it is also believed, to prevent demons from getting in and, in the case of homes, babies from crawling out.

As a result of the gradual Western-ization of Thai society, the interior of contemporary Thai homes resembles other nation's homes, except for the ample floor space. Whereas in Western homes space would typically be filled with sofas, chairs, cabinets, coffee

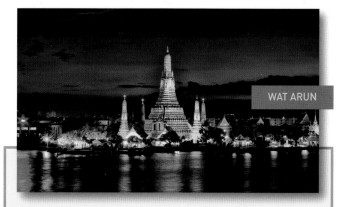
WAT ARUN

GET IN TOUCH WITH NATURE— ADD A PLANT

Considering the Thai cultural relationship between plants and animals, it is not surprising that a vital part of Thai architecture, past and present, is how it interacts and blends seamlessly with nature. This is why, regardless of whether in the middle of the city or in the rural countryside, most Thai rooms, buildings, apartments or houses will have a plant or two.

As to be expected in Thailand, if you are in the market for a plant, then there is a market for a plant, along with a plethora of seeds and flower bulbs. Also to be expected in the land of street life is a visit from the local plant man at some time over the weekend. Pick-up trucks or carts laden with pots in a variety of sizes and shapes and all manner of flowers and plants will make the slow crawl from remote pockets of the countryside to the inner cities and suburbs of Thailand to sell their wares.

The Father of Thai Design

Many of today's young Thai designers graduate from the world-renowned Faculty of Decorative Arts at Silpakorn University and are proponents of what is known as Thai modern design. An early mentor, Prince Narisaranuvativongse, considered the 'Father of Thai Design', combined Western design methodology with Thai tradition. The late prince's traditional wooden residence and studio, Ban Plainern, in Bangkok, contains samples of his art works and is an important center for performing arts. Every Sunday, students and others with an interest in traditional Thai arts attend Thai classical dance and music lessons.

The Golden Era of Thai Architecture

Assistant Professor of Architecture at Silpakorn University Faculty of Architecture, Dr Pattrapon Vetayasuporn, believes that to understand Thai architecture is to understand Thailand's geographical position in relation to the two great civilizations of India and China as well as nearer neighbors. Shapes, lines and motifs from these places are integral features of the Thai architectural landscape.

"You see both Indian and Chinese influence in the design of different temples. One of Thailand's most famous temples, Wat Arun, for example, is a real melting pot. Images of ancient Chinese soldiers and animals are around the base of the Khmer-style central tower while other sculptures are inspired by Indian Hindu gods and goddesses like Shiva. If you want to understand Thai architecture, you have to trace its historical origins," says Dr Pattrapon.

Thai architecture also differs according to the location, and what Dr Pattrapon calls 'resource of space'. The further north you travel, he says, the more likely you are to see houses made from teak, whereas in the south, because of the absence of native teak wood, houses tend to be made from a variety of other materials. It is for this reason that Dr Pattrapon believes that in addition to the three broad Thai architectural categories of temple and shrine architecture, palace architecture and traditional Thai house architecture, there are other differences that stem from variations in location and the ethnicities, background, beliefs and lifestyles of the inhabitants.

Dr Pattrapon considers the Sukhothai period of Thai history to be the 'golden era' of Thai architecture, arts and craftsmanship. It was because of the kingdom's prosperity and stability that both time and money were spent on building, developing and creating culture and towns, as opposed to fighting. "Even the Buddha was smiling," he remarks.

The future of Thai style, of Thai design, however, is uncertain he feels. "Thais don't appreciate Thai architecture and culture anymore. It's a real shame. It's a situation where foreigners appreciate and see the value in it more than locals do."

tables, TV stands and ornaments, care is taken in Thai living rooms and bedrooms, in particular, to have space for makeshift dining or sleeping areas.

At mealtimes, a low table is brought out and reed matting or cushions are placed around it. Thai people still prefer to eat seated on the floor. This, again, has its origins in functionality. In most social situations, Thais are preoccupied with social status and hierarchy and the potential for embarrassing scenarios caused by chairs of different heights. If, however, everyone sits on the floor, then everyone is equal and potential problems are avoided. The host just has to be careful with the allocation of the floor cushions.

Most Thai houses also have a shrine area, complete with Buddha images, photos of deceased relatives and photos of the King and Queen of Thailand.

In many Thai houses, the cooking area or kitchen is situated outside, usually at the rear of the house and often at ground level to keep cooking smells away from the living areas. The fridge, however, is often placed in the living room for ease of access.

Traditional Thai houses are also commonly known as Thai knock-down houses, referring to the ease with which they can be dismantled and reassembled in another location, a common practice in the past because of the migratory nature of rural Thais. This adds a completely new meaning to the term 'moving house'.

In recent years, many Thai architects have revisited the architecture of the traditional Thai home, in particular the rural home, which they have come to regard as sustainable, multipurpose and stylish, and reflecting the essence of Thai style and design. The time when all Thais lived in such homes rather than in apartment buildings or Western-style concrete homes is nostalgically perceived as reflecting a richer culture and a simpler, more peaceful existence, when fish were in the sea, rice was in the fields and Thai society was less fraught with political and other struggles.

Today, the subtle blending of nature and functionality with elegant design is at the heart of much of Thai architecture. This is seen in Thailand's most iconic contemporary buildings and structures, which often blend traditional Thai style with modern Western conveniences.

The Influence of Foreigners

The contribution of foreign artists and architects and their works deserves special mention in the development of Thai art and Thai style. Several influential foreign artists, some working alongside local artists, had a profound impact on the development of Thai art and sculpture. One such person was Italian-born Corrado Feroci, who was invited to Thailand in 1923 by King Rama VI to teach Western sculpture in the Fine Arts Department of the Ministry of Palace Affairs. He later served as the court artist of Siam. In 1944, he changed his name to Silpa Bhirasri and became a Thai national in order to avoid arrest by the invading Japanese army.

Along with Prince Narisaranuvativongse, with whom he worked, Bhirasri is widely credited as being one of the fathers of modern art in Thailand. He designed and sculpted many of Bangkok's monuments, including the Democracy Monument and Victory Monument and the statue of King Rama I at Memorial Bridge. He was also instrumental in the founding of Silpakorn University, the University of Fine Arts, in 1944. His birthday, September 15, is observed every year as a public holiday.

The tradition for European or foreign-influenced art has continued in Thailand. In 2013, a *European Heritage Map* listing 65 sites of historical importance in Bangkok and Ayutthaya was published by the European Embassies and Delegation of the European Union. A year later, an app was released. It includes some of the best as well as lesser known pieces of European architecture, including the Hua Lamphong Railway Station in Bangkok.

Left The interior throughout contains a mixture of Western and Eastern influences.

Below Marble, as opposed to wood, is used to keep feet cool.

Bottom The exterior of the Jim Thompson House after the tourists have all left.

The Jim Thompson House

The late Jim Thompson, famous for revital-izing the Thai silk industry, and later for his mysterious disappearance in the jungles of Malaysia, is also well known for his former residence, the Jim Thompson House, located alongside a canal in Bang-kok. The house comprises six separate buildings built from disassembled century-old teak homes, and has been turned into an official museum. Its hundreds of pieces of art and items of interest make it a must-visit place for those who wish to learn about one of Thailand's most interesting foreigners and entrepreneurs while enjoy-ing a tour around an immaculately kept and beautiful traditional Thai home.

THAI ANTIQUES AND CRAFTS

Most tourists leave Thailand with a souvenir or two, but while visitors may find it easier to take home a miniature elephant statue or wooden frog instrument, Thailand has a wonderful assortment of handicrafts, pottery and other unique and worthy items to compete for that valuable luggage space.

BENCHARONG

PEACE AND PATRONAGE

Thai craftsmanship started to flourish during the Ayutthaya period (1350–1767) of Thai history. It was then that artists, artisans, musicians and craftsman tended to create under the patronage of the kings, and as such were encouraged to produce the finest and most noteworthy pieces.

CERAMICS, COLORS AND CRAFTSMANSHIP

Thai ceramics, one of the earliest recorded examples of Thai craftsmanship, have been found dating back to 3000 BC. The earliest ceramics were earthenware, made of clay, and were basic in design. The most famous and celebrated of Thai ceramic-making came during the Sukhothai period (1238–1448) and these exquisite bowls, boxes and jars were often used in foreign trade.

From the 18th century onwards, a unique type of polychrome enameled porcelain with Thai motifs, called *bencharong* ('five colors'), was made in southern China exclusively for Siamese royalty. There is now some modern reproduction in Thailand.

ORIGINAL 3D SCREENS

Although the commercial use of teak wood in Thailand has been restricted since 1989 in an attempt to replenish Thai forests, there are still a number of skilled craftsmen and carpenters in the large cities, with Chiang Mai perhaps the best place to find all manner of furniture expertly crafted from teak and other types of wood.

Thai spas, fine dining restaurants and even temples adorn their walls with intricately hand-carved wooden panels. Chiseled from wood, sometimes teak, in a variety of sizes, the level of detail of these 3D works of art is often quite breathtaking. They often depict images of Buddha or Thai mythological creatures, and are finished with varnish, oil or sometimes paint.

KNACK OF LACQUERWARE

Lacquerware, made by applying successive coats of translucent colored lacquer layers to a wood or bamboo base, then embellishing it with designs, most often gold and black lacquer figures or traditional motifs, was originally made almost exclusively for temples and palaces. Many household objects, from simple bowls to large cabinets, are still made by this ancient process, though modern lacquerware makes use of a wide range of base materials, including ceramics and metal.

LACQUERWARE

Like many of the craft traditions practiced in Thailand, the origins of lacquerware can be traced to Chiang Mai, where the finest pieces are still created.

CARVING OUT A NICHE IN HISTORY

Although it is unclear as to whether vegetable carving originated in Japan or Thailand, the delicate, intricate and flawlessly beautiful art, which has since been extended to fruit and soap carving, can be seen in Thai hotel lobbies and at cultural fairs, markets and restaurants around the country.

Vegetable carving is believed to date back more than 700 years to the Sukhothai era, when, in much the same way that other Thai arts developed, a servant to the king who was charged with making a *krathong* (a boat-shaped offering made from banana leaves), decided to carve a pattern of a flower as decoration.

CARVED WOOD

SOAP CARVING

NIELLOWARE

VEGETABLE CARVING

UNIQUE AND GREEN

Thai celadon pottery, a type of high-fired stoneware, is lauded as among the finest of its type in the world. Celadon refers to the pale blue-green color, which is not painted or lacquered on but is produced by a wood and ash glaze during the firing process, which also produces fine crackling. Patterns are incised or carved into the pottery items before glazing and mostly comprise simple linear and floral motifs.

Celadon is one of Chiang Mai's most popular crafts. Here, artisans produce fine replicas of old designs, both Thai and Chinese, for home decoration and everyday use as well as smaller items like jewelry.

THAI METALWORK

Thailand is one of the few remaining countries still producing nielloware, an ancient art in which an amalgam of metals is applied to carved portions of a silver object to create silver or gold patterns against black backgrounds or vice versa. Since ancient times, nielloware, decorated and produced with meticulous attention to detail, signified status and was usually presented to the king or others in high positions, including foreign dignitaries. In the early 20th century, the King and Queen of Thailand initiated efforts to stimulate the modern-day production of nielloware.

Over the years, the popularity of this ancient art has gone through ups and downs but it is still taught from the age of 11 in most Thai schools.

The techniques of vegetable carving differ, as do the base produce and tools that are used, but the most popular patterns for smaller vegetables like carrots and radishes are roses and carnations. With larger fruits like watermelons, the artist has the opportunity to create more intricate designs and details. I have seen human faces and teddy bears etched into the skins of watermelons. After 700 years, however, the most popular patterns on carved vegetables, fruits and soaps continue to be flowers.

There are numerous academies and courses where visitors can learn how to carve fruit and vegetables and also national and international competitions in which the world's finest carvers compete for prizes and the honor of being crowned the best.

CELADON

GOLD NIELLOWARE

Chiang Mai's Craft Villages

Partly because of traditional skills passed down from generation to generation and partly because of its relative isolation from the changing fashions of metropolitan Bangkok, Chiang Mai has preserved its strong crafts tradition.

Baan Tawai, about 9 miles (14.5 km) from Chiang Mai, is a great place to pick up handmade wooden items ranging from sculptures and knick-knacks to expertly designed pieces of furniture. There are many stores and factories in the village where you can purchase carved wooden goods at great prices and see the craftsmen at work.

The residents of San Kamphaeng, around 8 miles (13 km) from Chiang Mai, are known for their long history of excellence in making teak furniture, celadon and lacquerware. Also located in the San Kampaeng district is the traditional Lanna-style village of Bo Sang, where the finest handmade umbrellas and parasols are crafted. Bo Sang's unique mulberry paper umbrellas are admired the world over for their vibrant colors and handmade motifs. Every January a festival is held to celebrate the exceptional craftsmanship of these two towns.

Thai silk fabric is generally one, two or three ply, which refers to the number of threads used for the weft when weaving the silk fabric. More ply means more strength and thickness but at the expense of sleek smoothness. Heavier silk shawls, designed for colder temperatures, typically contain more ply.

The colors and patterns of Thai silk vary from simple two-tone designs to intricate tie-dye patterns created by tying and dyeing the warp and weft threads in different color combinations. Popular patterns and designs include flowers, elephants and religious motifs.

QUALITY THAI SILK

Recognizing the harm that cheap imitations could have on the reputation of genuine Thai silk products, the Thai Agriculture Ministry introduced a unique ranking system to differentiate and authenticate different types of Thai silk products. This comprises four variations of peacock emblems, with a gold peacock being the highest rank, indicating 'premium Thai silk'. This verifies that the product has been made using traditional methods by hand and with native Thai silkworms.

There are many ways to ensure the product you are buying is indeed good quality, genuine handmade Thai silk. As Thai silk is woven by hand and is of a naturally soft but coarse texture, you should be able to feel, if not see, minor imperfections. With Thai silk, if it looks and feels too good to be true, it probably is. If 'handmade Thai silk' feels too smooth, it is likely to be machine woven using non-Thai silkworms.

REVIVAL OF THE THAI SILK INDUSTRY

Thai silk products are known the world over for their extremely high quality. Beautiful, vibrant and exotic in design, color and texture, authentic Thai silk products can last a lifetime. A name that has become synonymous with Thai silk is that of American-born Jim Thompson, who revived the industry after World War II.

Thompson was perhaps the most famous foreigner living in Thailand after the war (1945–67) and his influence on the Thai silk industry was considerable. He is widely credited with revitalizing the Thai silk industry in the face of competition from foreign textiles, especially Chinese and Japanese silk imports, after the war and with bringing the beautiful and luxury product to the international stage. He introduced superior looms and modern colors and oversaw better and more efficient production practices in the industry. His pioneer company remains one of the biggest and best silk producers in Thailand, and visitors to the kingdom are likely to see one of his many stores in the best shopping districts.

The booming industry of today depends to a large extent on silk from the northeast of Thailand, on the Khorat Plateau, a rural area known as Isan, that has been home to generations of female Thai silk weavers since Chinese merchants introduced the process thousands of years ago. One of the factors contributing to the superiority of Thai silk is the handcrafted manufacturing process. Each level of production is carried out by skilled weavers, many of whom have their own machinery, looms and silk weaving implements in their homes. The Khorat Plateau also exports the vast majority of the fabrics used to create luxurious pieces, both within and outside Thailand.

Above Jim Thompson relaxing at his home in Bangkok.

Top A traditional Thai shawl and skirt made from the finest Thai silk.

Authentic Thai silk products contain the printed pattern on only one side of the fabric, the colors of which should change when held up against the light. The other side should not change color.

As it is hand-dyed, there should be different levels of hues visible in the material, creating a unique look to each piece that cannot be replicated, as opposed to the uniform appearance of commercially processed silk.

Although not recommended trying in a store, unless you ask and it is agreed upon, the burning of a thread should smell like hair and produce very fine ash. Fake silk drips when burnt and emits black smoke.

The Silk Making Process

Thai silk is produced mainly on the Khorat Plateau in northeast Thailand from the cocoons of Thai silkworms, or caterpillars, that come from the eggs of a silk moth (*Bombyx mori*). The caterpillars are raised on a diet of locally grown mulberry leaves, and when mature each builds a cocoon from its spittle on a mulberry twig frame. The cocoons are them boiled to separate the silk thread from the caterpillars inside.

The color of natural Thai silk thread varies from light gold to light green, with each thread measuring 1,640 feet (100 m) long! The threads, however, are much too thin to be used by themselves and have to be combined with others during the hand-reeling process, done on a spindle, to create a stronger, more durable and uniform fiber for weaving.

The raw silk threads are then soaked in hot water, bleached, dyed in vats of the desired color and dried before they are woven into lengths of fabric using hand-operated looms for making a range of wonderful Thai silk products, including clothing items and home furnishings.

Clockwise from top left Silk attire is often worn during Thai festivals and events. Weavers work on looms at Ban Tha Sawang Silk Weaving Village to make all types of silk cloth. The tools of the silk weaving trade. Hanks of dyed raw silk waiting to be woven into cloth. Lengths of handwoven silk fabric ready for sewing.

Colorful fabrics handwoven by the Karen community.

THE ARTISTRY OF TRIBAL TEXTILES

The hill tribes of Thailand are the descendants of tribal people from China, Tibet and Laos who migrated to the remote Thai borders. There are six recognized hill tribes in Chiang Mai and the surrounding areas, each with their own language, belief system and culture.

In the past, much of the income of the hill tribes came from either opium production or subsistence farming employing now illegal agriculturally unsound slash-and-burn farming techniques. As they are no longer allowed to participate in these activities, Thailand's hill tribes have become among the world's most marginalized, impoverished and at-risk communities. The fact that a large percentage of them are denied Thai citizenship and are thus technically viewed as criminals because they mostly occupy national forests has worsened their situation.

Some communities were forcibly resettled to the lowlands in the 1980s but many have remained in the hills and the dense jungles of Thailand, living at around 3,200 ft (975 m) above sea level. For many, life is tough and dealing with outlaw soldiers, opium traders and illegal smugglers is a daily struggle.

Although there are plenty of opportunities for tourists to visit Thailand's hill tribes, it should be noted that over the last generation or so many so-called 'cultural preservation centers' have turned into little more than human zoos in the name of 'ethnic' tourism. This is especially true of those tours advertising authentic 'Karen Padung' trips where visitors can view Padung women, a subgroup of the Karen, who have 'stretched' their necks to epic proportions since early childhood (purportedly merely an illusion) through the use of a succession of brass rings.

AFTER OPIUM

More ethically sound sources of income include the growing of coffee beans, Duang Dee Hill Tribe Coffee, for example, being a highly successful project. There is also the very distinctive, colorful and immediately identifiable hill tribe handicrafts and textile industry.

Hill tribe women's exquisite weaving and sewing skills have been passed down from generation to generation and are used nowadays to make all types of handmade clothing, bags, scarves, musical instruments, utensils, weapons and handicrafts. As well as being available from the hill tribe communities themselves, craftswomen often make the long trip from the lowlands or mountainous regions to the tourist areas of Chiang Mai, Bangkok, or even as far afield as Phuket, to sell their wares to tourists.

CULTURAL HOMESTAYS

Many hill tribe communities offer homestay programs, including those tailored specially for gap-year students. The idea is that the culturally curious traveler gets to observe and interact with locals and their culture and way of life. A homestay program could include going fishing, helping out on a farm, visiting a local market, eating traditional food or learning the age-old traditions of weaving cotton on a primitive loom or making a piece of silver jewelry. It is best to do some online research before visiting any particular group or tribe, partly to see what activities are available and partly to check out the companies offering such programs and the testimonials of previous participants.

There are various registered education and charitable programs and initiatives designed to help the hill tribes of Thailand.

Top left A hill tribe woman from northern Thailand weaves on her front porch.
Left A visitor examines textiles being sold by a long-necked Padung Karen woman in Chiang Rai.

HMONG HILL TRIBE

Thailand's Traditional Hill Tribes

The Karen form the largest minority hill tribe group, with an estimated nine million people scattered throughout Thailand, Burma and Laos. The Karen people are well known for their fine handcrafted silver jewelry. Good quality silver has always been prized over other minerals, including gold. They make intricate silver bracelets, earrings, necklaces and pendants. Quite often the designs reflect those used on their woven textiles or have a braided or woven look. Both men and women craft silver and each follows the same process of melting the 99 percent pure silver, cooling, hammering, shaping, chiseling and finally engraving it. The Karen are also skilled at making handicrafts from bamboo, wood and other materials.

HILL TRIBE SILVERWARE

The Akha hill tribe, particularly the women, are immediately recognizable by their elaborate traditional costumes and pointed head-dresses adorned with silver and beads. Their traditional dress is typically handwoven and utilizes local vegetable dyes to produce either blue or black fabrics. Akha men are also distinctively recognizable from their garb: a long black jacket with intricate and geometric designs, typically in red, embroidered within.

Although the Hmong hill tribe people have maintained many of their customs and traditional skills, including embroidery, agriculture and jewelry making, they are also the most integrated into Thai culture and society and as such are the most prosperous. A sizable number of Hmong have emigrated to Western countries, including America, Canada and France since the early 1980s, while others have been, more controversially, forcibly repatriated to Laos by a United Nations scheme to aid Thailand in closing refugee camps.

KAREN HILL TRIBE

AKHA HILL TRIBE

FOUR SEASONS, KOH SAMUI

CONRAD, KOH SAMUI

LITTLE PIECES OF PARADISE

Thai hospitality—gentle, caring and thoroughly indulgent—is famous the world over for its exceptionally high quality. Hand in hand with such hospitality are wonderful villas, stunning resorts and other luxurious accommodations.

From beachfront huts on the coast of Krabi and stunning luxury resorts in the heart of Bangkok to secluded private lodges nestled in the lush hills around Chiang Mai, Thailand has it all and a lot more.

Here are some of the most remarkable places to stay in the kingdom.

CITY RESORTS

One of the oldest and most instantly recognizable hotels in Thailand is *The Mandarin Oriental Hotel* in Bangkok, located along the Chao Phraya River. Its convenient location, international standard facilities and understated Thai elegance have made it the holiday accommodation of choice for numerous famous guests over the years, from author Joseph Conrad to football and fashion icon David Beckham. The hotel is as stunning and luxurious today as it was when first opened in 1876.

The Peninsula, which is also located beside the Chao Phraya River, is the 78th tallest building in the world and as such allows some wonderful views of Bangkok. There are also both Rolls Royce and BMW limousines available to hire on an hourly basis.

The world-famous *Shangri-La Hotel* in Bangkok offers a great combination of peaceful retreat and immediate access

to some of the most popular tourist destinations and shopping districts. The Thai-inspired décor and airy, natural design is calm, soothing and luxurious in a way that is only possible in Bangkok.

Unique design and décor, combined with a top level of service and hospitality make the *Sukhothai Bangkok* hotel stand out amidst the busy city of Bangkok. The atmosphere is elegant and understated, and although located in the center of the city it is quiet, soothing and incredibly peaceful.

BY THE BEACH

Situated away from the busier tourist areas of Phuket, the *Mai Khao Dream Villa Resort and Spa* is a true oasis on one of the quietest and most unspoilt stretches of Phuket beachfront. Each of the private pool villas comes with butler service and easy access to the award-winning spa.

The *Amanpuri* resort in Phuket is a little slice of jungle heaven. Designed in a traditional Thai style, blending harmoniously with acres of tropical foliage and surrounding jungle, it is a resort that inspires calm and relaxation from the moment one arrives.

The private pool villas of the *Conrad, Koh Samui* are built on a stunning and unspoilt stretch of the Koh Samui beach,

allowing uninterrupted views of the beautiful sea and nearby islands.

Nestled within its own private bay, the *Four Seasons, Koh Samui*, with its charming southern Thai-style hillside pool villas and residences, offers a secluded escape overlooking the islands and Gulf of Siam.

The *Phulay Bay*, a Ritz Carlton Reserve, is situated in Krabi along one of the quieter shores of the Andaman Sea. The resort is designed around, rather than on, fantastic natural scenery, including limestone cliffs, reefs, caves and corals. As such, there are all sorts of wonders and activities right on the doorstep of this stunning resort.

IN THE JUNGLE

A stay at the *Four Seasons, Chiang Mai* is sure to add a new meaning and significance to the words 'peaceful' and 'secluded'. Set among the unspoiled mountains of Chiang Mai, the hotel immediately becomes your private oasis.

The majestic, palace-like surroundings and decor of the *The Dhara Dhevi* in Chiang Mai is sure to leave a long-lasting impression. Designed in the Lanna architectural style of the region, the resort is set among rice fields and lush foliage, which creates a seamless bridge between nature and resort.

AMANPURI, PHUKET

SUKHOTHAI, BANGKOK

THE DHARA DHEVI, CHIANG MAI

THE MANDARIN ORIENTAL, BANGKOK

FOUR SEASONS, CHIANG MAI

PHULAY BAY, KRABI

Elephant Treks to the Border

The architecture and grounds of the Anantara Golden Triangle Elephant Camp and Resort in Chiang Rai make it a stunning place from which to explore the ancient Lanna culture of northern Thailand. Situated on the Thai border of the Golden Triangle, the resort offers guests the chance to go on elephant treks in the dense jungles, visit nearby hill tribes and enjoy breathtaking views of neighboring Cambodia and Laos.

A SHOPAHOLIC'S PARADISE

If there is one thing that Thai people love to do even more than eating, it is shopping. Touted as 'serial shoppers', the Thais have two main choices: gritty markets for street-level survival and glitzy malls for conspicuous consumption.

THAILAND'S STREET MARKETS

Regular outdoor markets are held several times a week throughout the kingdom. These are typically located on the busiest stretches of road and are open in the cool of the evening, from around 5 pm to 10 pm. They are full of local color and bargains—haggling is permissible; start by offering 40–50 percent of the asking price—and everything under the sun is available. Sometimes a 'stall' may consist of little more than a blanket thrown on the ground on which the wares are displayed. Others are more traditional stall spots manned by a regular vendor. Sellers range from artists seeking exposure, high school students flogging their handmade cutesy objects to hardcore souvenir hawkers.

The markets also act as meeting places for Thai people and a place to come and visit, hang out, eat some delicious food and browse, haggle and pick up some wonderful and weird products. It is a great opportunity for visitors, especially in the lesser-known tourist markets, to experience a slice of real Thai life.

There are also the larger, more established weekend markets or bazaars where you will find all of the weekday market offerings as well as pirated DVDs, counterfeit handbags and designer label products, tourist tat, perfume, pets and, quite literally, anything else that you can think of. These are more tourist-friendly places with sellers often able to speak some 'Tinglish' to draw the foreign buyer in.

Top Shoppers explore the Siam Square Night Market. Above Siam Paragon, just one of Bangkok's many malls.

THAILAND'S MEGA MALLS

Thailand is also home to some huge, ultra modern shopping malls, many in Bangkok, among them Siam Paragon, Central Plaza Rama 9, MBK and Siam Square. On Saturday afternoons, Siam Square turns into an endless stream of impromptu fashion parades as teenagers and young fashion-conscious Thais turn up to show off the latest artistic expressions and styles and to mingle with the fellow fabulous.

These behemoths of consumerism have everything you would expect to find in a Western-style shopping mall—brand-name stores, book shops, clothes stores, foreign restaurants, food courts and even cinemas—all in air-conditioned comfort.

There are also shopping malls of note in Pattaya (Central Festival Pattaya Beach), Chiang Mai (Kadsuankaew), Udon Thani (Central Plaza Udon Thani) and Phuket (Jungceylon). Many more are currently under construction. Whether these will eventually eclipse the smaller stores and markets, whose popularity continues unabated, remains to be seen.

Above Dedicated followers of Thai fashion at Siam Square. Right Make sure you're hydrated before tackling MBK Shopping Mall.

THAILAND'S INCREDIBLE WEEKEND MARKETS

Two of the largest markets in Thailand are the marvelous yet crazy Chatuchak Weekend Market in Bangkok (see overleaf), which has around 15,000 stalls, and the wonderful institution that is Chiang Mai Sunday Walking Street Market.

Every Sunday in Chiang Mai, a half-mile stretch along Ratchadamnoen Road as well as some of the minor side roads are closed to vehicles. Along with many handmade products, clothes and souvenirs, there are also plenty of entertainers, musicians, artists and eccentrics to brighten up the whole shopping experience.

CHATUCHAK WEEKEND MARKET

CHIANG MAI SUNDAY WALKING STREET MARKET

Communicating Via Calculator

Although many traders in the larger bazaars and markets will speak a smattering of English, generally enough to get by in the trade exchange, quite often a calculator will act as a conduit for the bargaining ritual.

Many of the market stalls sell identical items and stalls with similar objects tend to be grouped in the same sections. If you don't like the price, ask for a better one and if the vendor is unable to meet it, walk away. There will be other little wooden elephants.

It's also a good idea to be able to speak some basic Thai. This is to at least give the impression that you know what you are talking about and are familiar with how much things should be.

Useful phrases include *Tao rai krab?* (How much please?)

Peng! Lod raka dai mai krab? (Expensive! Can you lower the price, please?)

If all else fails, revert to the trusty calculator. As a last resort, turn on your heel and walk away. If the seller calls after you, that means he's willing to barter some more. If he doesn't, just continue walking.

A BORDER TOWN MARKET

For the dedicated bargain hunter in Thailand, the best places to go to find incredibly low prices are the border town markets. A good example is the sprawling Rong Kleu Market in Sa Kaeo, on the border with Cambodia, which is famous for clothes. Historically, Cambodians came to the border to sell clothes that were 'donated' by international aid. Although such donations no longer happen with such regularity, the trade in second-hand clothes has continued. Sometimes real brand name garments are mixed in with counterfeit goods, so keep a keen eye open for genuine bargains and, of course, haggle and bargain—it's all part of the fun at a Thai market.

Nowadays, the market sells secondhand goods exported from places like Japan, Korea and Hong Kong. When the goods arrive at the market, they are repaired and cleaned by merchants who then sell them on. Around 90 percent of the traders in the market are non-Thai.

A MARKET FOR EVERY PURPOSE

If there's a market for it in Thailand, there's usually an actual market for it. Thai people love to socialize and the marketplace is the perfect place for the harmonious combination of both.

CHINATOWN MARKET

Music, eating, talking and having *sanuk* (fun)—there's a reason why Internet shopping has not yet taken off in Thailand to the same extent as other parts of the world. Thai people love market shopping because they love the human contact and interaction that it entails. Although there are all-purpose markets like Chatuchak Market in Bangkok, or the weekend markets up and down the country, there are also specialized marketplaces for a more specific and tailored shopping experience.

PLANT MARKET

Food Markets If you want a true taste of Thailand, then visit a *talad sod*. These daily food markets are where you go to get the freshest produce. They are typically open very early in the morning (5 am) until late at night (11 pm–1 am). The permanent food markets are arranged fairly logically, with separate sections for meats, seafood, vegetables, fruits and cooked food. Some also have a small section of plastic tables and chairs where diners can eat.

Clothes Markets If you want a glimpse into the current Thai fashion trends, then forget the shopping malls with their international clothes lines and visit the weekly clothes markets. Here, budding designers and young entrepreneurs with access to a T-shirt press or sewing machine turn up with handmade trinkets or a clothes range from the capital. Prices are cheap and open to negotiation. Quality is adequate and the experience is fun.

Fruit Markets One of the best things about Thailand is that you can buy a fresh pineapple, or any number of wonderful tropical fruits, from the side of the road throughout the day. Although not technically markets, there are lots of fresh fruit stands, trucks or even carts set up alongside roadsides, where vendors are happy to expertly chop and bag your fruit for an exceptionally low price.

Plant Markets Much like the fruit markets, if you're looking for that one particular plant, then you will likely not need to travel too far, as there's a veritable jungle of plants and foliage in roadside plant stores, where workers can advise or give suggestions on what is best for you.

OTOP Markets The OTOP (One Tambon (area) One Product) markets were set up with the express purpose of promoting locally made produce, whether it be pottery, clothes or snacks. The level of adherence to that ethos has come into question over the years, with many market holders

Chatuchak Weekend Market

Although it may seem like a never-ending, twisting and turning monster of a market, exploring the largest outdoor shopping area in Bangkok, Chatuchak Market or Jatujak (JJ Market for short), is a great morning, afternoon, evening or even whole day out.

The western section of Chatuchak Market, known as Jatujak Plaza, is open daily, but it is only at the weekend when the 35 acre (14 ha) maze of a market, containing 30 sections and 9,000 stalls,

opens that Chatuchak truly comes alive. It is estimated that around 200,000 people visit at the weekends.

At first glance and perhaps even second and third walk around the market, it may seem an impossible task to make rhyme or reason of the layout, but after maybe the fourth circuit it will all start to make sense. There is one main walkway off which there are 62 numbered side alleyways called Soi 1, etc. As long as you can make it back to the main walkway at any one time, then you can simply do the loop and you will get back to where you started. This is in theory, of course, but even if you do get lost, it's half of the fun.

A serious piece of advice, however, is to keep hydrated and carry a bottle of water around with you. Thankfully, there are plenty of food and beverage stalls dotted around, where shoppers can take five minutes out and indulge in a spot of people-watching.

Getting to Chatuchak Market is quite easy. You can take the BTS Skytrain to the Mo Chit station and follow the throngs of happy shoppers or take the MRT subway to Chatuchak Park station, exit no 1.

If you'd like a break away from the crowds, you can visit the nearby Chatuchak Park before heading back into the madness for another souvenir or trinket or two.

Chatuchak Market is open on Friday from 6 pm to midnight and from 9 am to 6 pm on Saturdays and Sundays.

resorting to selling counter-feit goods, including DVDs, CDs and clothes. Contrary to how it may seem, the buying and exporting of such products is, in fact, illegal in Thailand. It is also, strictly speaking, illegal to take images and statues of Buddha out of the country. A grand and very public show of raiding, seizing and subsequently destroying 'pirated goods' happens regularly, where everything from Louis Vuitton bags to Billabong tops and DVDs are burned.

FOOD AND NIGHT MARKET

Night Markets These are a lot of fun and the perusing of souvenirs, perhaps stopping off to have a drink or roadside foot massage, is a great way of spending the evening. Most tourist areas have one, with Silom Road in Bangkok a great example of how the Thai sidewalks come alive in the evening, with food, fake brand-name goods and people. Another great night-time market worth visiting is the Night Bazaar in Chiang Mai.

Made For Walking As well as attempting to reclaim the Thai beaches, the NCPO also announced that it would clear the capital's sidewalks of illegal operators, at least during the day, in a bid to enable pedestrians to actually walk on the sidewalks. Street vendors were promptly advised to shut up shop.

As with many Thai attempts at resolution, however, where the proclamation of intended action often trumps actual enactment, compromises, allowances, and pure failure to enforce eventually won out, and apart from a few areas of the city many vendors gradually crept back into action.

A law that is upheld by all but the most rebellious of street vendors, though, is the banning of all carts and stalls (typically food-based) on Mondays, as this is the day that Bangkok's streets are giving a thorough and much-needed cleaning.

Traversing the Silom sidewalks in the evening is indeed an unforgettable experience, with stalls and beggars, touts and masseurs competing for space and attention. Not to mention the odd motorcycle using the path as a short cut.

FLOATING MARKET

Floating Markets Although Thai floating markets, consisting of hundreds of vendors congregating by boat, usually in the early morning, have all but disappeared and there are very few, if any, authentic ones left, a visit to Damnoen Saduak Floating Market in Ratchaburi, 60 miles (96 km) southwest of Bangkok, is a great experience, if only to get an idea of how traders used to operate in small rowing boats along the canals dug to connect provinces. Prices of produce are quite high and the vast majority of people who actually use the markets are tourists.

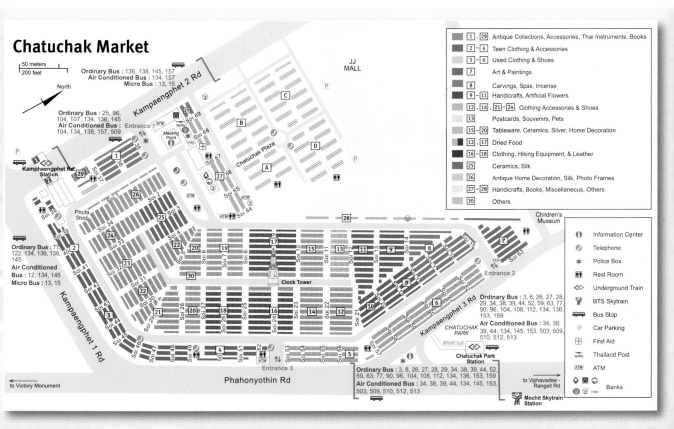

CHAPTER 3

THE UNIQUE THAI CHARACTER

Take a peek behind the Thai smile to learn about the paramount importance of religion, the 'tribe' and fun in the lives of the Thais. Explore the diverse ethnic origins of the people and the historical and contemporary influence of the Chinese. Take a look also at the intriguing world of Thai Pretties, Thailand's third gender, and profiles of other everyday Thai people. And learn about what it is like working with Thais, the uneasy position that foreigners occupy, and what to do and avoid if you wish to work in the country.

MAI PHEN RAI: BEHIND THE THAI SMILE

Thailand is known as the Land of Smiles, a reference to the commonly held belief that Thai people are happy, amiable people who like to smile regardless of whether—by Western standards—the situation is appropriate or not.

To enjoy your time in Thailand, either as a tourist or expatriate resident, it is important to know what underpins the Thai national character and the subtleties involved in communicating with the Thais. This will allow you to remain calm in any situation and to simply go with the flow of Thai life.

If there is one phrase that will stand you in good stead during your time in Thailand it is *mai phen rai*, which loosely translates as 'never mind', 'no problem' or even 'there's nothing that can be done'. Theorists suggest that this philosophy stems from Thailand's Buddhist roots that promote forgiveness, gentleness and non-aggressiveness.

Standing in line at a bank waiting for the teller to complete a transaction but she forgets to do it? *Mai phen rai*—she'll do it now. Overcharged at a restaurant? *Mai phen rai*—the bill can be amended. A neighbor's poor tethering results in a piano falling from the top floor of an apartment building almost killing you? *Mai phen rai*—you are still alive.

Although the *mai phen rai* attitude, combined with the ever-present smiles, may seem rather irritating and unnerving to a Western visitor, remember that it is central to the Thai philosophy of interactions and relations.

KEEP CALM

Rectifying potentially problematic situations will be achieved much more quickly and with far less hassle if you adopt this attitude. Shouting, getting angry and even presenting logical reasons will not. *Mai phen rai*—you are in Thailand. All that your actions will likely do is make the Thai you are confronting 'lose face', which will have repercussions.

Thai people are very proud, with a heightened sense of self-esteem and dignity. Any situation that threatens, criticizes or insults a Thai or is deemed an affront to their ego is likely to result in a strong emotional reaction, if not at the time then almost certainly later on.

Saving face, recognizing one's place in the hierarchical structure and maintaining ego are extremely important to Thais and thus must be remembered in all interactions. Regardless of the hierarchical structure between those involved, all parties must, in fact, be respectful of the others' ego. What initially may seem like a rather timid and useless character trait, is, in fact, a carefully cultivated technique for dealing with potentially fractious situations.

BE CONSIDERATE

Another common Thai trait is the ability to possess *kreng jai*. The direct translation is 'awe of the heart' or 'deferential heart'. This is often at the heart of many difficulties that foreigners experience in Thailand. Being considerate of others' feelings, even if the other person is in the wrong, is essential, even if it is also unfathomable. For example, if a colleague promises to do work at the weekend but doesn't do it and, in fact, had no intention of doing it, one must try to exhibit *kreng jai* and attempt to understand why the person didn't do it in spite of saying they would. In accepting the work, they were being considerate of your feelings by not offending you through refusal.

KEEP CALM AND BE CONSIDERATE

Criticism avoidance techniques are incredibly important in Thai social interactions. One has to be flexible and understanding, even if a situation is highly irritating. *Kreng jai* and *mai phen rai* therefore work hand in hand in many situations in Thailand.

Many believe that *kreng jai* is the essence of Thai-ness—the attempt to not disrupt the harmony or status quo of interactions and to value other people's

The Thai smile is the default expression in Thailand, so unless you want to stand out from the crowd, smile.

WHY WAI? **THE GRACEFUL GREETING THAT CHARACTERIZES THAILAND**

In Thailand, the importance of the *wai* is paramount. The gentle bowing and pressing of the palms together in a prayer-like pose, similar to the Indian Namaste salutation, is an ancient and traditional Thai greeting.

Despite the rapid modernization and Westernization of Thailand, the *wai* remains as popular and integral as ever. It is quite common, therefore, to see Thai toddlers *wai* before they are able to speak.

Thai people will *wai* one another instead of shaking hands and, generally speaking, it is the younger (deemed inferior) who should *wai* the elder (deemed superior), who will then return a *wai*.

It is, however, not always essential or deemed appropriate to reciprocate.

If, for example, you are checking into a hotel and the staff *wai*, you don't need to *wai* back because you are a guest and therefore superior. Likewise if you receive a *wai* at a convenience store or supermarket.

There are varying degrees of *wai* in Thailand. To perform a standard *wai*, the palms are pressed together at chest level while smiling and looking at the person being greeted. For a more formal *wai*, perhaps for a parent or teacher, people bow their heads and raise their hands until they touch the tip of their noses. The most formal *wai*, reserved for a monk or some such revered figure, involves a slight bowing of the head and the raising of the hands until the tips of the fingers touch the forehead.

happiness, sometimes at the expense of your own. Difficulties arise in Thai–foreigner relationships when a foreigner accepts a Thai person's *kreng jai* without reciprocating, perhaps because it is thought unnecessary or a sign of weakness. Interestingly, many Thais do not mind bending the truth slightly or even lying straight out to avoid arguments or to spare the feelings of the person they are lying to. Confusing, indeed, but in order to enjoy living in the Land of Smiles one needs to be able to navigate the Thai character's complex web of sensitivities by recognizing the above traits and using the same techniques so as not to offend their sensibilities.

BELIEF IN THE 'OTHER'

The majority of Thais are not Buddhist scholars, nor do they pretend to be. This, coupled with the fact that over time Thai Buddhism and the Thai belief system came to be intertwined with animism, folklore and belief in the spirit world, means that for most people the contemporary Thai belief system boils down to a superstitious belief in gods, spirits, magic and ghosts. It is quite common

for Thai people to visit *mor duu* (fortune tellers) or *mor phi* (witch doctors) and take part in black magic rituals if they want to change their lives. Such visits are used to bring about both positive and negative adjustments, such as to entice an ex-boyfriend back or to harm someone.

It is also quite common for Thai people to wear Buddhist amulets or have religious tattoos on their bodies in the belief that they carry protective powers. Unfortunately, it is not out of the ordinary to see a dead Thai on the side of the road who has decided to forgo the wearing of a 300 baht motorcycle helmet in favor of a 300 baht amulet he had bought from the local temple.

The influence of these superstitions and fears permeates all aspects of Thai society, including the educated, who will often choose to open a business, buy a car or get married on a perceived auspicious date or time of day because of its intrinsic superstitious value.

KEEP CALM, BE CONSIDERATE AND SMILE

In the Land of Smiles, orders are usually masked as a request with the help of a smile and the suffix *ka* or *krab*. Smiles are sometimes used at totally inappropriate times in Thailand, for example when the 'smiler' feels awkward, embarrassed or ashamed. A mechanic once beamed at me when it was discovered he had forgotten to replace the oil in my motorbike, costing me thousands of baht in repairs.

Do not underestimate the power of the smile and its ability to diffuse potentially embarrassing situations, endear yourself to strangers or just help life pass by smoothly and happily. A nice genuine smile goes a long way and is at least as important, if not more, than a please or thank you.

THE ROLE OF RELIGION

Thailand is predominantly a Buddhist country, where many of its citizens, regardless of their path in life, are quite pious, at least on a relatively superficial level. Each act performed by a Thai is done with the knowledge that it brings either merit or demerit. This concept of acting in a positive manner in order to bring good karma has a huge impact on Thai behavior.

Another commonly held Thai belief rooted in Buddhism is that everybody is born with different levels of *bun wassana* (good karma), which often leads to blind acceptance of one's achievements, failures or status. Born poor? One has low *bun wassana—mai phen rai*. Better luck in the next life.

It is also generally believed that Thai men can gain enlightenment as well as repay their parents by undergoing training as a monk, usually before they marry and start a family of their own and often for three months during the rainy season. Most Thai men, therefore, enter the monkhood at 20 in an elaborate ordination ceremony at a temple.

This option, of course, is not open to Thai women and thus many Thai women must continue making merit and performing selfless acts their whole lives. It is for this reason, some argue, that prostitution in Thailand is relatively accepted. The women who enter the industry are predominantly from extremely poor backgrounds and typically become prostitutes to help their families. They send money back home to their parents or, in some cases, their children. As such, prostitution is seen as an act of making merit and probably also the result of having no *bun wassana*.

LIFE IS TO BE ENJOYED

While in Thailand, one should also never underestimate the Thai idea of *sanuk* (fun). Enjoying oneself and taking pleasure from life is incredibly important. Life is to be enjoyed, not endured. This is why it is quite common for young Thais to try out several jobs or even partners and minor partners (*gik*) until they find the right one, or one that is sufficiently enjoyable.

The Thai work environment is generally much less formal than in the West. People natter, giggle, eat and smile at what to Westerners appear to be ridiculously unacceptable levels. *Kreng jai, mai phen rai.*

Most activities in Thailand are done en masse as it's just more fun: dancing, eating, hazing, supporting, protesting, the list goes on....

MY NAME IS....

Up until 1913, Thais were not formally required to have and use a surname or last name. Traditionally, Thai people preferred—and still do—to be known by just one name, which, unhelpfully, may be neither their first or last name. Nowadays, many Thais prefer to be identified by their *cheu len* (play name/nickname).

Like in English, Thai has titles that you can add in front of names, which are designed to establish who is 'superior' and 'inferior', especially among family and friends but also for very formal occasions and in written communications. In most cases, Thais use their first name with the honorific Khun (Mr/Mr/Miss). The same goes for foreigners, meaning I am referred to as either Khun Jody or Mr Jody.

Thai nicknames serve another purpose, especially for Westerners, but also for some Thais who often find it difficult to pronounce some excruciatingly long Thai names. Although Thai nicknames may sometimes be common English names like Jane or Joe, often they are something quite strange like Ant, Nail or even Beer. Those searching for deeper meanings behind these names may be disappointed, with common explanations, delivered with straight faces, being perhaps that their father or mother simply liked ants or nails or beer.

Animal names are also frequently used as adjectives to describe people and their particular characteristics, a throwback to Thailand's animist belief system. *Kwai* (buffalo) is used in a derogatory sense for somebody of low intelligence; *hia* (monitor lizard) has become a byword for somebody slimy, smelly and generally pretty low; *moo* (pig) is pretty self-explanatory, while *rat* (rhinoceros), is used to describe a sassy, sexually aggressive woman.

Other Thai nicknames are equally confusing, for example, *Jiab* (chirp), and for someone with a darker complexion *Dam* (black). Indeed, no Thai person

escapes having a potentially embarrassing play name. Even fascist dictator Field Marshal Pibunsongkhram was known as Field Marshal *Plaek* ('strange') owing to his strange appearance when he was younger.

Thai people's nicknames are often included alongside their full names on business cards and may be the only time their full names are ever mentioned. Indeed, Thai people's historically grounded propensity to use only one name makes it difficult to apprehend criminals or indict employees who have done wrong, when the only record of their identity is an inkling that perhaps their father liked a particular farmyard animal.

The odd nicknames of Thais cannot be explained as simply lost in translation.

What's Good for the Tribe

Thai people have what is often described as a 'tribal mentality', meaning they have a clear understanding of social place and social structure. Historically, Thais believe in an ingrained and widespread network of patronage as opposed to any particular type of democratic political ideology. Respect for the 'tribe'—whether corporate or family, urban or rural—thus wins over respect for the nation. Reverence and deference and respect and loyalty are expected to be accorded brothers and family members, social superiors, the faction, the department, the boss and local government official at all costs, even if that involves covering up corruption or other social misdeeds. There is an expectation to toe the line, to do your bit—quite often with a smile—and woe betide anyone who chooses not to.

One must protect the tribe by protecting the superior. In order to do so, it is important to know one's place. This is why, no matter the age of the individual, they are either *nong* (younger sibling) or *pee*

(older sibling) according to who they are with. This is not only limited to family members but also colleagues, friends and even strangers.

Thais are always mindful of status. A clear example of this is when someone of a perceived lower status will physically crouch in order to be below the eye line of a superior who is passing by. This is the case even when the superior is sitting, which results sometimes in some amazing impromptu contortions.

Traveling around Thailand's cities, rural areas, seaside destinations and border towns will remind visitors that the country has never been racially homogenous.

ETHNIC AND REGIONAL DIFFERENCES

If you were to view Thailand only through its soap operas and advertisements, you would think its people were, by and large, white-skinned and tall, with European features. While there are Thai people who do look like this (Thai Chinese and mixed race, *luk kreung*), Thais do not have a single distinct look.

The simple explanation is that Thailand has never been a racially homogenous country. It is a mosaic of people and cultures from about 50 different ethnic groups that have inhabited the country and surrounding areas throughout the country's history.

The dominant ethnic group in Thailand after who, it has been suggested, the country was named are part of the larger Tai group of people who can be found not only in Thailand but in neighboring Southeast Asian countries and China. Ethnographers suggest that the Tai originated from the southern Chinese regions of Guangzi, Guangdong and Yunnan. This subgroup goes by different names depending on where they originated or continue to live. In China they are known as Dai, in Burma as Shan, in Vietnam as Tay and in Thailand as Tai or Thai. Ever since Siam was renamed Thailand in 1935, Thai has been used as a collective term for descendants of these various groups born in Thailand.

THE 'ORIGINAL' THAI

Among the wide variety of diverse ethnicities making up the people of Thailand is a small community (around 300) of forest dwellers and hunters and gatherers of African and Andamanese origin scattered around southern Thailand and Malaysia. They are known among

Left A Thai man 'blacks up' to collect donations to help put on the play *Sangthong*.

Right Most Chinese festivals are celebrated throughout Thailand, not only in its Chinatowns.

Thai people as *ngor*, which is the Thai word for 'rambutan', a reference to their Afro hair that resembles the hairs on the skin of the fruit. Another Thai name for the nomadic group is Sakai, which translates loosely as 'barbarian' or 'strong wild person'. Understandably, these people prefer to call themselves Mani, meaning 'human' or 'our group' in a Mon-Khmer dialect, the language they originally spoke before a southern dialect of Thai was widely adopted.

The Mani have featured in many stories throughout Thai history, with the most famous perhaps being *Sangthong*, written by King Rama II, about a banished prince who finds a costume that turns him into a Mani villager and blesses him with superior jungle-like powers. A page boy of King Chulalongkorn (Rama V), who was a Mani named Kanang, was the inspiration for the king's poetic verse *Ngor Pa*, which is about Kanang's life in the jungle, a piece that is highly regarded as a classic of 19th-century Thai literature.

THE CHINESE IN THAILAND

The largest distinct ethnic minority in Thailand are the Chinese, who initially arrived as traders, settling first in coastal areas in the south before moving to other areas. Thailand is, in fact, home to the largest overseas Chinese com-

POISONING THE WATER

In 2014, the movie *By The River* (*Sai Nam Tid Chua*) was released to critical acclaim. It was based on the real-life story of how, in the 1990s, a local lead mine poisoned a river used by the Karen hill tribe community for fishing and bathing deep in the forest of Kanchanaburi. More than 30 villagers were subsequently diagnosed with lead-toxic illnesses, with some losing their sight as a result of swimming in the river and eating the fish caught there.

Although the lead mine closed, no aid or alternative food and water supply were provided to the villagers. It took almost two decades, after numerous tests, campaigns and help from activists, to get the Administrative Court to rule, in 2013, that the Pollution Control Department (PCD) should pay 177,000 baht (US$5,250) to each of 22 recognized victims as a form of compensation.

Many Thai Muslims are of Malaysian heritage.

Muslims in Thailand

Another large community in Thailand are the Muslims, who comprise predominantly Malay immigrants, but there are also significant numbers of Cambodian, Indonesian and Bangladeshi Muslims in Thailand.

In the three southern provinces of Pattani, Yala and Narathiwat, the vast majority of the population are Malay in origin and to this day speak a Malay dialect as well as Thai.

There are also those who are considered indigenous Thai Muslims who have intermarried and live in mixed communities or in separate small Muslim communities throughout central and southern Thailand.

munity in the world, many arriving in the 18th to early 20th centuries. Numbering around nine million (14 percent of Thailand's population), large and distinct Chinese communities exist in many of the big cities and townships.

Despite the struggle and persecution the Chinese have faced through-

out Thailand's history, and despite now sporting Thai surnames as decreed during King Rama VI's reign, many Chinese are proud of their heritage and what their community has achieved. Indeed, they have good reason to be proud. In the last century or two, they have made a substantial contribution to the GNP

THE THAI SEA GYPSIES

A lesser-known minority and marginalized group in Thailand are the Chao Le (Sea Gypsies). Visitors to the Andaman coastal region of Thailand, especially Phuket and Krabi, will hear of these communities, yet few know of the plight that affects them. Chao Le have been in Thailand for hundreds of years and are of Moken descent, an Austronesian ethnic group with their own language, culture and distinct way of life. They are seafaring people who, to the present, survive by fishing

and spend great periods of time living off and on the sea.

Permanent sea gypsy villages exist in a few locations around the region, including the popular tourist destination of Rawai, Phuket. They are typically poor, and like many of Thailand's hill tribes are denied citizenship, meaning their children often resort to begging for money and remain unschooled until they are old enough to become fishermen like their fathers.

Increasingly, the livelihood of Phuket's sea gypsies and even their homes are under threat, with various

landowners in the region claiming that in the absence of papers proving land ownership—a practice and concept technically only introduced in Thailand in the 20th century (prior to that, the king owned all land)—the sea gypsies' 'prime tourist real estate', which they have lived on for generations, belongs to them. As the majority of the older generations of sea gypsies speak a different dialect and, in many cases, cannot read or write, few have the relevant paperwork to prove that they own the land and have lived there for generations.

Right Davika Hoorne.
Far right Thai-Norwegian model and actress Urassaya 'Ya Ya'.
Below right Mario Maurer.
Below Tata Young, singer and actress.

Mai Davika Hoorne
X
CPS CHAPS 35ᵗʰ ANNIVERSARY

VGI GLOBAL MEDIA

of Thailand and are well represented at all levels of Thai society, especially in business and politics. Thanks to extensive assimilation, it is often difficult to distinguish them as a separate ethnic group. Many of the wealthiest Thai people today share some part Chinese heritage, with former prime minister Yingluck Shinawatra, for example, being part Chinese. The family's original Chinese name of Sae Khu was replaced with Shinawatra, meaning 'routinely appropriate action', in 1938. It is estimated that around 40 percent of the total population of Thailand has some Chinese blood.

A possible explanation for the Thai Chinese community's success is that although many of them arrived penniless in the 18th and 19th centuries, they came as free immigrants and not indentured workers. Whereas the majority of Thai commoners were serfs and thus tied to feudal lords and kings, the Chinese could move anywhere and work in any profession.

THE NEW THAIS

The increase in relationships between Thais and Caucasians has led to a greater number of mixed race children (*luk khrueng*). Many of these children have benefited from the financial stability that a foreigner is often able to bring to the family and generally enjoy a privileged position in Thai society.

Mixed race children who have typical Western features, pale complexions and height often find opportunities in the Thai entertainment industry because of their exotic looks. In fact, a lifestyle in entertainment is almost expected of them. Singers, actors, models, TV presenters, there is no area of the Thai entertainment industry where they do not have a powerful presence.

One example is Thai-Norwegian model and actress Urassaya 'Ya Ya' Sperbund. Like many *lakhorn* (soap opera) actresses, she was discovered in a Thai TV advertisement at 14. She gained national recognition in the Channel 3 soap opera *Peun See Long Hon*. Ya Ya has also won many awards in modeling competitions, including Seventeen Choice Hottie Female.

Doing for the female-watching Thai public what Ya Ya has done for the

male is Thai-Chinese-German actor and model Mario Maurer. He gained national recognition for his role in the soap opera *Tai Fah Tawan Diow* and went on to act in the highest grossing Thai film of all time, *Pee Mak*. Mario is relatively proficient in Mandarin and starred in his first Chinese language movie, *Love on That Day*, in 2012, which was well received by his huge Chinese following. He has since had a starring role in *The Love of Siam*.

Interestingly and rather symbolically, both leading actors of the remake of the Thai classic *Plae Kao*, a romance drama set in rural Thailand, were played by *luk khreung*. As the original version featured typical Thais with brown skin and broad noses, light-skinned Chaiyapol Julien Poupart and Davika Hoorne both had to be 'browned up' with make-up in order to play the roles of country-dwelling field workers.

THAI 'PRETTIES': THE THAI IDEAL OF BEAUTY

Thailand is a beautiful place, from its nature and scenery to the delicate subtlety of design and architecture and even the careful arrangement of food on a plate. Appearances matter in Thailand and the Thai pursuit of beauty is a multibillion dollar business.

To be pretty in Thailand is incredibly important, in fact, it can even be an occupation. For many young Thai women who meet certain criteria—tall and slim, with big eyes and a small mouth and, most importantly, fair skin—a job as a Thai 'Pretty' is a surefire way of earning a sizeable income.

A Thai Pretty is hired as a promotional tool. She is transported to various exhibitions to stand around looking, well, 'pretty' and, at least on a subconscious level make the product look all the more desirable. Products may range from mobile phones, cars, hardware, clothes and condominiums to, naturally, beauty products.

Sometimes the Pretties are asked to welcome crowds and make announcements over a microphone, but in general they just stand at stalls, smiling and welcoming crowds of both men and women to the product they are representing.

ATTAINING THE IDEAL

Achieving the 'Pretty' look is, for many young Thai women, almost a full-time job. It may require eyelid surgery, nose reconstruction, breast enlargement and

the use of industrial amounts of skin whitening creams.

In Thailand, having light skin is not only a symbol of beauty but also a symbol of social class. To be dark-skinned is associated with the poorer rural classes who work outside, perhaps in the rice fields. It is for this reason that many Thai women shun the sun, keeping in the shade or moving from one air-conditioned room or building to the next. Even on a trip to a beach, if given the choice, Thai women will sit under a parasol or in the shade and only venture into the sea if fully clothed.

Regardless of how scientifically attainable it is for these naturally light brown people to become as white skinned as those appearing on TV and in maga-

You can probably hear Thai Pretties before you see them—beautiful young women rolled out in public places and armed with microphones to help sell anything from the latest European car to household cleaning products.

zine adverts, a huge percentage of Thai women invest heavily in skin whitening products.

Many of the cosmetics sold in Thailand contain chemicals that are banned in other countries. For those who cannot afford the expensive brand-name products or appointments in clinics, there is a wide array of illegal and highly dangerous skin bleaching products on the black market. There are apparently no places that could not benefit from whitening, with the recent trend of vagina whitening growing alarmingly.

At present, the Thai ideal of beauty lies somewhere between a Korean soap star and a Japanese cartoon character.

The Dangers of Getting White

The multibillion dollar business of skin whitening came under scrutiny in 2013. In that year, a Japanese cosmetics company received 15,000 complaints from customers reporting outbreaks of blotches on their skin after using the company's skin whitening cream. It was also the year that a Thai cosmetics company got into hot water over the moral and societal implications associated with their campaign to find the Thai university girl with the brightest, whitest skin. The advertisement was criticized for racial discrimination for its depiction of darker-skinned students as dim and gloomy and white-skinned girls as happy and intelligent.

This is not the first time that Thai companies have been accused of being offensive and even racist in their advertising campaigns. A Thai girl turning 'blackface' after eating a chocolate donut sparked outrage in 2013, as did an advertisement for a miracle working skin whitening product that showed a white-skinned receptionist being outed as having African parents.

Even men, though to a lesser extent, buy into the phenomena of light skin equals good and handsome, and dark skin equals bad and ugly. However, for the Thai male, such techniques are not all that aggressively marketed and therefore not as big business. But the poster boy image of the young, tall, handsome, often *luk kreung*, white-skinned, English-named singer or movie star remains popular in Thai media. They are, however, invariably soft spoken and cute, meaning they are much more like their Korean counterparts than their Western ones.

THAI LEADING WOMAN

Former prime minister Yingluck Shinawatra very much fits the Thai female ideal—tall, slim, pretty and white skinned. Although public opinion has changed dramatically since, when Yingluck first came to power it was seen as a huge step for women in Thailand. Here was a woman who was going to use her brain, and of course her good looks, to bring about positive change for the people of Thailand. Here was the future of Thailand and, as such, women voted for her in droves. There were, however, many Thai feminists who were not so easily taken in and argued, as they have since, that the main reason she was elected was because of her brother, former prime minister Thaksin Shinawatra.

Indeed, after a short time, Yingluck did nothing to allay fears that she was merely a very pretty puppet. She was once quoted as saying she would use her femininity to work for Thailand. Opponents argued that a true feminist would never say this or have to resort to

such actions and said that although she had the anatomy of a woman she very much thought 'like a man'. In reality, Yingluck's Pheu Thai Party did very little for women's rights in the kingdom, and even less to address issues of violence against women and discrimination in the workplace. The perception remains that from the Go Go bars to the highest echelons of Thai government, Thai women sell their beauty as a commodity. Sometimes it's the only commodity they have.

PAINFUL LENGTHS FOR PERFECTION

Khunying Tobnom, or Madam breast-slapper as she is known in English, is the go-to woman if you want to have your breasts slapped in Bangkok. She performs the practice not for fun or even for punishment but to allegedly boost her clients' bust sizes by at least a cup without the need for surgery.

A session with Madam Yingtobnom doesn't come cheap. She charges around 18,000 baht (US$600) for two sessions—one breast per session. She also offers a face-slapping service, which apparently induces slimness. Why the face-slapping technique doesn't result in the client getting a more voluptuous face is another matter, but what is important is how it reveals the painful lengths that Thai women will go to for the perceived perfection of beauty.

ANYTHING YOU CAN DO

It is not only Thai women who go to excruciating lengths in the attainment of

Tall, slim and fair but ultimately unable to step out from her brother's shadow.

beauty. Documented since the 14th century, many Thai men, especially in northern Thailand, have had *fang mook* (pearl beads) inserted into the shaft of their penis. The main reason it was done, and still is, was to enhance pleasure for the recipient. It carries obvious health risks.

Adding a Touch of Color

Beauty pageants are still incredibly popular in Thailand, and winners of the larger national and international ones are usually showered with gifts, acclaim and lucrative advertising contracts. Thailand's entrant for Miss World, Nonthawan 'Maeya' Thongleng, caused quite a stir when she won Miss Thailand World in 2014, a title that is usually won by paler-skinned Eurasian-looking Thai woman, because of her honey-hued, naturally light brown skin.

After the crowning, the Surat Thani native from the south of Thailand, spared no time in announcing that she had entered the beauty contest for all the darker-skinned women around the kingdom. Since the competition, Maeya has become a role model for Thai girls and women and regularly receives messages from young girls stating that they no longer wish to change their skin color by using the drugs, creams and ointments available on the market.

The media were quick to nickname her Pocahontas and the 'colored beauty queen'. Maeya is also a singer and often appears on a variety of TV shows to showcase her vocal skills and for people to marvel at her beauty and compare skin tones.

Whether Maeya's natural look signifies a long-lasting shift in the perception of beauty for Thai woman remains to be seen.

LADYBOYS: THAILAND'S THIRD GENDER

Thailand's third gender is an endless source of fascination for visitors, who are invariably astonished at the seemingly high numbers of *kathoey* (ladyboys) in Thailand and the comparatively privileged place they occupy in society. The only time most tourists see *kathoey* is at overtly sexualized cabaret shows or in the 'entertainment' zones of Bangkok, Phuket and Pattaya, where they will dance, have their picture taken and provide comfort, all for a price. It is for this reason that Thai ladyboys are often equated with the seedier side of Thailand. They are often viewed, at least by the tourist, as a highly sexualized caricature, albeit attractive, and are thus objectified.

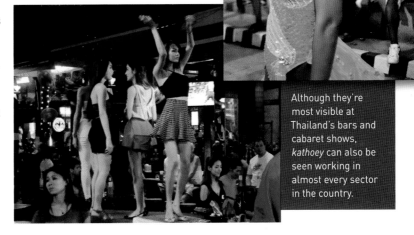

Although they're most visible at Thailand's bars and cabaret shows, *kathoey* can also be seen working in almost every sector in the country.

This is both unfortunate and unfair as the *kathoey*, away from the neon-lit bars and huge cabaret shows, have become integrated into most areas of Thai society. It is quite common to see a ladyboy bagging groceries in a supermarket, serving food in a restaurant or working in a beauty salon, for example. They can also be found in many less traditional female occupations, a famous example being Nong Toom, a Muay Thai fighter whose trademark was to kiss her vanquished male opponent on the head. A movie of her life was released in 2003, entitled *Beautiful Boxer*. Some saw the introduction, in 2011, of an all-*kathoey* air hostess staff aboard PC Air airline as a positive high-heeled step up for the community, while others viewed it as mere exploitation. The airline ceased operations in 2012.

Ladyboys in Thailand seem to be much more visible, respected and accepted than in other Asian and Western countries. It is probably for this reason that tourists turn out in droves to gawp, point and have their pictures taken among these beautiful and remarkably feminine people. Others have suggested that it is perhaps something darker, something more akin to the fascination people had for the Bearded Lady of yesteryear.

BEAUTY IS IN THE EYE OF THE BEHOLDER

The dramatically different way in which ladyboys are perceived in Thailand may go some way towards explaining why it appears that there are, proportionally, so many more of them in Thailand than elsewhere. Maybe it is simply a matter of Thailand creating a safer haven for transgender and transsexual people to come out. Being transgender in many other places is still seen as something shameful, to be hidden away and even to be repressed. But in Thailand this is not the case. There is pride in being a *kathoey*. There are celebrated *kathoey* models, singers and actresses. There are also annual beauty pageants, with Miss Tiffany the best known, the winners of which garner almost as much interest from the public and press as do women contestants in traditional competitions.

Theorists speculate that the high percentage of Thai nationals who are ladyboys could be indicative of something more ominous. Rumors abound that in impoverished rural areas of Thailand very poor families will start to give their young children hormone tablets so that they will be able to provide for them as *kathoey* entertainment workers when they grow up. It is certainly the case that there are a large and disproportionate number of Thai *kathoey* working in the sex trade.

There are also many *kathoey* who profess to have been the victim of extreme discrimination in Thailand. Many large companies are unwilling to employ *kathoey*, so many resort to criminal activities and consequently fall foul of the law. Interestingly, however, there have been reports that when in prison *kathoey* enjoy a level of freedom not experienced on the 'outside'. In jail, many ladyboys become 'prized prisoners' and are treated exceptionally well. Post-op ladyboys are segregated from male prisoners and are thus highly valued. It is only when cut off from Thai society at large that they realize, perhaps for the first time, how unfair and discriminatory life as a *kathoey* can be in Thailand.

The Tom-Dee Couple

Another widely accepted alternative lifestyle frequently seen in Thailand is that of lesbian couples. In Thailand, this often takes place between a *tom*—a young woman who dresses in traditionally male clothes, has short hair and speaks using male speech patterns—and a *dee*—a stereotypically feminine girl with long hair and an outwardly female appearance.

Such relationships tend to occur during the teenage years, with many *dee*, especially, choosing to adopt a more standardized romantic and heterosexual life when they get older. However, as displays of affection between girls are quite common anyway, *tom-dee* relationships largely go unnoticed in Thailand. Much like gay and ladyboy relationships in Thailand, to be a *tom* or even a *dee* is perceived to be retribution for a transgression in a past life.

GETTING BETTER
Life for the Thai ladyboy is unquestionably better today than it was in the past. There was a brief period, from 1993 to 1997, when homosexuals (which *kathoey* were categorized as) were prohibited from attending teacher training courses. It was only in 2002, under pressure from the gay community, that the Thai Department of Mental Health removed homosexuality from its list of mental disorders. The Thai military followed suit in 2005, discontinuing its practice of dismissing transsexual and gay recruits from the army on the grounds of severe mental disorder. In 2007, the legal definition of rape was changed to include same-sex criminal attacks. Before this, if a man raped a man or ladyboy, it would only be classified as sexual molestation.

MOVING FORWARD
The Thai *kathoey* community, however, still argue that things could be more equal in Thai society. Any time a *kathoey* appears in a Thai soap opera or on TV, she is cast as a horrible caricature. Loud and brassy, *kathoey* usually play the role of fools.

Kathoey continue to campaign for equal rights regarding civil partnerships and for the legal right to change their gender on identity cards and passports. They also bemoan a lack of employment protection rights. In Thailand, a paradox exists where, on a superficial level, *kathoey* enjoy immense freedom unparalleled in Western societies, a freedom, however, that is not reflected within the Thai legal system.

Although the tenets of Buddhism purport tolerance in all aspects of life, many Thais perceive the lives of *kathoey* as deeply unhappy, and, as such, explain their existence as karmic retribution of a past life. They believe that *kathoey* were playboys in previous lives and are thus destined to live a life, in a cruel twist of fate, as a woman trapped in a man's body, resigned to a life without true love. In Buddhism, there are four genders. In addition to male and female, there is also *bhatobyanjuanaka*, which was originally translated as hermaphrodite but has now widely come to mean transgender or transsexual, and *pandaka*, which probably referred to eunuchs.

Runners-up flank Sophida 'Baimon' Siriwattanakul, the winner of Thai transgender beauty contest Miss Tiffany 2015.

LIVING IN THE CITY

Away from farms, fields and traditional teak wood houses, the majority of Thais don't refer to their homes as apartments but as rooms, and this is a much more accurate description of the 215–322 sq ft (20–30 sq m) units that many live in. Despite the small living quarters, the cities offer Thais a myriad of opportunities and lifestyles that are not available in rural areas and smaller towns.

BE TRUE TO YOUR SCHOOL

As noted earlier, many Thai people have what is often described as a 'tribal mentality'. While this can sometimes result in a healthy pride in the community, the village and the company, it can also provoke unacceptable behavior and have dangerous repercussions.

Combine this tribal pride with the teenage desire to belong and the restlessness and misplaced, unfocused energy of youth and you have the all too common occurrence of inter-college rivalry that results in a shocking number of gang fights and fatalities every year.

In Thai universities, it is quite common for freshmen to have to complete a number of initiation ceremonies set by older students to show their allegiance. In recent years, many argue, such rituals, including being forced to drink spirits, shout loudly in public or be tied up, border on abuse and a form of hazing. Such activities are often encouraged and therefore legitimized by the universities themselves. This deference to seniority and submission to orders is referred to by the acronym SOTUS, which stands for Seniority. Order. Tradition. Unity. Spirit.

While initiation/bullying may be commonplace in Thai universities, in the technical colleges such energy is often directed in more dangerous ways. In Bangkok, especially, the incidents of rival school gang violence show no sign of slowing and it is quite common for students to carry weapons.

Younger students are expected to show respect and reverence to the college as well as to their elders by often fighting or fiercely defending the honor and reputation of their college. In 2012, there were more than 1,200 incidents of student violence reported in the Bangkok area, 20 of which resulted in death. The year 2012 was a particularly bad one for student brawls and

deaths, but rarely a month passes without an incident of inter-college violence. Social networking sites contribute to the increase in more organized mass brawls.

Both the military and Buddhist associations of Thailand have, for a while, been involved in seeking solutions to this violence. A common scheme is for 'problem' students to attend boot camps where they live, work and even meditate side by side with rival students. Quite often they will be asked to build a house together or other group-based activities.

In the latter part of 2014, Prime Minister Prayut weighed in, announcing a zero-tolerance policy and banned 21 vocational colleges from accepting enrolments from students with histories of violence or tattoos. He also threatened to close down colleges that couldn't control

Thais are taught from a young age to respect their teachers. They prostrate in front of them during the annual Wan Khru (Teacher's Day) and display fierce pride in their faculty. It's natural, therefore, that inter-college and university rivalry often becomes unfriendly.

I'LL TAKE YOU THERE

Unlike their *tuk-tuk* driving counterparts who charge extortionate amounts to tourists, the life of a *motorsai* (motorcycle) taxi driver is a hard and comparatively honest one. They eat at roadside restaurants or from street vendors and work all day, or night, depending on their shift. This is a job that is typically done by Thai men until they are quite elderly.

A large section of the Thai population use the *motorsai* method of transport for getting from A to B. It is cheap, quick and convenient. These men possess an incredible level of street knowledge and know all the short cuts, some illegal, to get you to your destination.

Taking a *motorsai* taxi is a tourist attraction in itself, but not for the fainthearted or for those without travel insurance. Drivers zip in and out of lanes, somehow managing not to clip wing mirrors, they drive on pavements, run red lights and, by and large, manage to get you to your destination in one piece. Quite often they will not have a helmet available for their passengers despite being required by law to do so, so keep an eye out for a driver who does.

If legal, they work from taxi stands, and as such have to be registered with the local transport department and are, in return, issued with a vest that clearly shows which area they have to operate from.

Motorsai drivers can be found in small groups, underneath shade in makeshift waiting areas. Quite often you will not see them but will be alerted to their presence by the proffering of services. Owing to the comparatively cheaper fares compared with taxi and *tuk-tuk* drivers, they often have to work long hours to earn enough.

The bikes they use are often on their last legs, so caution must be taken when choosing your driver. A short journey is usually just 20 baht (US 60 cents), but for foreign users it is probably best to agree on a price before setting off.

Chiang Mai to save and send money back home to their parents, or even their husband, to provide for their children. Bar girls tend to live together, with four or five sharing one small room.

Many bar girls are from Isan, the poorest rural area in the north of Thailand. They are paid to entice men into the establishment. Some dance in Go Go bars, some fix drinks and some make conversation with punters. Some do all three.

Bar girls often work on commission, so if a customer buys a 'lady drink' then she will later receive a percentage of the bill. Many, but not all, bar girls also offer sexual services in exchange for money. A customer first needs to pay the 'bar fine', an amount of money paid to the bar owner to cover the potential loss of money resulting from the bar girl's absence. It is then up to the bar girl and punter to decide upon an agreeable figure to complete the business transaction.

Many bar girls move to the tourist destinations with the hope of meeting and marrying a wealthy foreigner who can then take care of them and their family back home.

LIFE IN THE CITY

The life of a Bangkok-dwelling city slicker is so far removed and so different from that of a rural farmer, or somebody in the service industry, that they might as well be from a completely different country. A Bangkok city clicker is much like one from any other Asian metropolis. They have money and they like to spend it on brand-name goods, fashion and socializing.

Impeccably dressed, they are never seen out in scruffy clothes or without

Different costumes, different signs, but the back story of the Thai bar girl is often very similar.

their students and, true to his word, did just that, with two schools remaining closed for more than a month.

A student will attend a Thai technical college between 16 and 21 and typically study vocational subjects such as how to be a mechanic or an electrician as opposed to students who attend a university, from ages 18 to 22 for a four-year period.

FALLING IN LOVE AT THE BAR

Many of the girls and young women you see working the bars in the entertainment districts of cities will have a similar back story. They will invariably come from poor backgrounds and are working in the predominantly tourist destinations of Phuket, Pattaya, Bangkok and

make-up. They drive expensive foreign air-conditioned cars or travel in air-conditioned subways, shop in air-conditioned shopping malls and eat in air-conditioned restaurants.

For the Bangkok city slicker, life begins, ends and revolves around the capital. They work hard, shop hard and play hard. A higher level of income means that as well as sending money to their family back home—which most Thai children do—they also have more money to spend on clothes and recreation.

Thailand's wide social and economic disparities mean that many live exceedingly well, thanks to the servitude and low standard of living of even more Thais.

CAN SHE HELP YOU?

Prapaporn 'Izzy' Kaewkhub, a 22-year-old from the southern province of Songkhla, has been working as a guest service agent at a beachside hotel in Phuket for four months. The hours are long—10 hours a day, five days a week—and when she's not at work she splits her time between university and friends or colleagues. Izzy has always wanted to work in the hospitality sector, mainly because, she explains, all the jobs with the highest salaries in Thailand are in the tourism industry.

Do you live onsite? Yes, I share with one other girl, but she's not around most of the time so it's like having my own room basically. It has air-conditioning and a bathroom but no kitchen, but there is one in the common area, along with a television, refrigerator and sofas for other staff to use. Unfortunately, there is no Wi-Fi, but I heard they're going to set it up soon. Shared accommodation is convenient and I can save on costs.

What is the most challenging aspect of working at a hotel? Dealing with guests' complaints. I find it difficult to calm customers down when they get upset over something they want but are not entitled to. A couple came to me once and said that as they had been staying there for quite a long time they wanted a late check-out of 8 pm. I checked for availability, then tried to explain that it was impossible because their room was booked for

that night, so if they wanted to stay they needed to move to another room and pay an additional charge, but they didn't want to do that. Finally, they chose to leave the room on time. They were a little disappointed but understood the situation.

What are the best things about working at a hotel? The occasions I am able to negotiate and deal with guests' requests and get them something extra or something they aren't expecting.

Any interesting stories so far? Once a guest wanted a free upgrade. He spoke loudly from the time he arrived. I'm not sure if that was his personality or if he did it on purpose. Everybody felt uncomfortable about attending to him because he was also a little bit aggressive. I was the one who had to deal with him when he checked in. He asked the price of an

upgrade to a pool villa and I offered him the fixed additional price. He said it was too much and wanted it for free and said he would give us a good tip. I was shocked for five seconds and had to concentrate on what I had to say. I told him that I didn't have the authority to provide a free upgrade. Luckily, my general manager was around and he offered him a 50 percent discount and the guest took it. Personally speaking, doing that kind of thing is shameful. It was a weird day.

The world-famous *wai*—how many times, on average, do you do it per day? About 20.

How long do you plan to work in the industry? I'd like to gain around seven years' experience and then open my own business, such as a restaurant or coffee shop.

THRIVING COMPANIES IN THAILAND

It is little surprise that many of the richest families in Thailand have amassed their fortunes by focusing on sectors that appeal to contemporary Thai lifestyles. Industries concerned with Thai food, Thai drink, shopping and telecommunications thrive, partly due to a lack of international competition.

Channel 3 and Channel 7 are two of Thailand's most popular commercial television stations.

After spending just a day or two in Thailand, it's easy to see why these sectors are so popular. After all, which Thai doesn't like to eat, drink, shop, watch TV or use their smartphone?

Many of the country's richest conglomerates are not content to just dominate the domestic marketplace but are heading overseas to take on international rivals and some of the biggest brands in the world.

BANGKOK BROADCASTING

The main source of income in Krit Ratanarak's US$1.95 billion fortune is generated from ownership of Bangkok Broadcasting & TV, which runs the very popular and profitable Channel 7. Two other avenues of income derive from stakes in banks and cement companies.

THE CHAROEN POKPHAND GROUP

Estimated to be worth around US$11.5 billion, the second richest billionaire in Thailand is Dhanin Chearavanant, the head of the Charoen Pokphand Group. The group's humble beginnings started when Dhanin's father, who emigrated from China, opened a seed shop in Bangkok in 1921. The group wisely kept that Chinese connection strong and now generates half of its income from China. There isn't much that the Charoen Pokphand Group is not involved in. Its business interests range from animal feed production and chicken farms to shopping malls and telecommunications (TRUE). It also holds the hugely profitable sole license for 7-Eleven convenience stores in Thailand.

THAI BEV AND RED BULL

The third and fourth richest families in Thailand are both involved in the drinks market. Third spot goes to Charoen Sirivadhanabhakdi's Thai Bev company, Thailand's largest brewer and manufacturer of the hugely popular Chang Beer. Controversially, Charoen recently released a logo, in appearance very similar to that of Pepsi, for a drink called Est, with the aim of dominating the soft drink market as well as the alcohol market in Thailand. He also has commercial and residential properties around the world.

In fourth spot, the Yoovidhya family has also made its billions from the sale of Thai drinks brand Red Bull, which is now the most popular energy drink in the world. Founded in 1976 by Chaleo Yoovidhya, in 1984, under a partnership with an Austrian investor, Red Bull was marketed worldwide. Energy drinks are very popular with truck drivers and manual laborers in Thailand, with Red Bull being just one of many available on the market.

Controversy hit the family in 2012 when a grandson of the Thai founder, Vorayuth Yoovidhya, was involved in a hit-and-run incident involving his Ferrari and a Thai police officer on a motorbike. The police officer died. Vorayuth was released on bail and the case is ongoing.

TOURISM

A special mention must go to Vichai Srivaddhanaprabha who owns a string of retail stores and, more importantly, airport shops. The ever-rising number of tourists passing through Suvarnabhumi Airport in Bangkok has led to an exponential increase in sales and catapulted Vichai into the ranks of one of Thailand's richest businessmen.

COMMUNICATIONS

Despite living in Dubai in self-imposed exile to avoid prison for a corruption conviction, former prime minister of Thailand and one-time owner of Manchester City, Thaksin Shinawatra still regularly makes the top ten list of Thailand's richest people. Although his fortune was initially seized by the Assets Examination Committee following numerous allegations of corruption, Thai authorities returned a sizable chunk (US$1 billion) in 2012. His fortune was largely amassed by founding the largest mobile phone operator in Thailand, AIS.

Medical Tourism

Paralleling the rise of medical tourism in Thailand is Chalerm Harnphanich's rapidly burgeoning bank balance, which is estimated as over US$300 million. Chalerm has a 50 percent stake in the Bangkok Chain Hospital, which offers moderately priced healthcare services, as well as in international standard premium luxury hospitals.

THE CENTRAL GROUP

The richest family in Thailand is the Chirathivat family, owners of the gigantic retail and hospitality company Central Group. With a combined net worth of US$12.7 billion, the Central Group owns five department store chains in Thailand, China, Indonesia, Italy and Denmark. The most popular in Thailand is the Central Department store, which has outlets in Phuket, Bangkok, Pattaya and Udon Thani.

The Central Group is also the operator of the leading Thai luxury hotel chain Centara Hotels and Resorts, which has properties all over the country. An off-shoot sister brand of Centara is spa brand Spa Cenvaree, which operates in 29 locations in Thailand.

If you've shopped in Thailand, chances are you've probably done it in one of Tos Chirathivat and family's malls.

5 Thai products I now couldn't live without

Energy drink M-150 Yes, it makes my teeth sting and if I drink more than one a day I feel like there's a good chance my heart will burst out of my chest like a scene from *Alien*, but it's only 12 baht and a great pick-me-up.

Weird-flavored crisps Cheese & Onion, Salt & Vinegar? Boring.... When I'm in search of a quick snack, I head straight for Seaweed flavor. Yep. Don't knock it until you've tried one of those green bags of goodness.

Banana in a bag I'm out, I'm about, there isn't a food market or roadside restaurant nearby (unlikely, but still...), but there is, of course, a 7-Eleven. At just 10 baht a banana, it's cheap, healthy and saves me carrying around a bunch.

Dried stringy squid/seafood things The Thai equivalent of beef jerky, but for seafood lovers. At just 20 baht, what's not to love?

Thaibasco A clever name for a delicious but devilishly hot sauce. If I'm not adding sweet chilli sauce to my dishes, I'm reaching for this bottle to sprinkle a few drops of spicy peppery explosion on my food.

WORKING WITH THAIS

For foreigners working in Thailand, one of the biggest challenges is understanding office politics, which can be just as convoluted and confusing to an outsider as real Thai politics at Government House. It can also be as drama-laden as its soap operas, but generally with a slap or two less.

From prime ministers to office cleaners, disagreements need to be handled as delicately as possible.

Whenever living and working abroad, it is best not to automatically expect the foreign workplace and workforce to operate in exactly the same way as at home, or to possess the same values or to communicate in the same manner that you're accustomed to, even if, from your perspective, this is the wisest and most mature and professional way.

Many Thais have characteristics that may seem odd, unnecessary or even counterproductive, but much like the complex web of telephone wires that line Thailand's roads, the system works in its own way and has worked like that for a long time. If you are planning to join a Thai company, you are expected to join their system, to find your space and to hang in there!

According to Thai social structure and hierarchy, respect and reverence are always afforded the *phu yai*—Mr or Mrs Big—which, in the case of office politics, will be the boss or line manager, or even a person who has been at the company longer than the new arrival.

This ingrained expectation of deference means that, in general, Thai staff are much more compliant and unquestioning than Western workers. Even if a Thai worker fundamentally and whole-

WORKING 9–5, SORT OF

Differences in the Thai workplace begin before the actual work day itself. A Westerner may be startled to notice that many Thais approach the concept of punctuality as a challenge, with a rather laissez-faire attitude at best and an affront to liberty at worst. But again, perceptions between how things look and how things actually are can be quite different.

Although a Thai worker may arrive at the office more or less at the time expected, quite often she (usually a woman) will have a bag of rice or a breakfast snack with her. 'Start' time, therefore, invariably begins after eating breakfast. Taking phone calls, sending messages and tweets and maintaining her Facebook profile is likely to work up quite an appetite, so later on in the day a cookie or other type of snack will be brought out and, to be fair, generally shared with colleagues.

Thais generally have a much more relaxed style of working than Westerners. They crack jokes, walk around, even nap but—and this is crucial—they will invariably get the job done. Although Mr Smith may arrive on the dot of nine, it is pretty likely that he'll also be leaving pretty much as soon as the little hand on his watch hits five. Thais, on the other hand, will stay and work late if the job requires it. As Thai companies rarely pay overtime, this show of willingness to work late is again, albeit superficially, another way of showing that the worker values the team, the harmony of the workplace and, of course, the *phu yai*.

heartedly disagrees with what the manager is saying, or has an idea that he/she believes may improve things, they would probably be hesitant to make suggestions or disagree with the boss as a form of *kreng jai* to avoid either side potentially losing face.

This is why many Thai meetings will remain relatively quiet until jokes are cracked and that pesky matter of business is 'sort of'

completed. This 'Yes Men' culture may irritate the Western worker, especially if he sees something that needs addressing or fixing.

Having experience or good ideas is not necessarily the most important thing in the Thai workplace. To succeed in a Thai company, it is more important to establish harmony with the rest of the team. In this sense, professionalism and efficiency are not as highly prized as the ability or willingness to be affable with team members, to get along with them, especially the Thai boss.

THINKING OUTSIDE THE BOX

Showing initiative and thinking outside the Thai box is a risky business in Thailand. You will rarely be rewarded or encouraged for doing so. In some cases, you may even be admonished for it. I was once told by a Thai 'superior' to basically stop working so hard or asking so many questions. Such a request seems farcical, insane almost, if computed without a Thai sense of understanding of how the workplace operates.

Thais seem reluctant to step forward, to show themselves, for fear of highlighting how comparatively far behind other team members they are.

It is quite common to simply put problems in a multicultural workplace down to subtle cultural differences, or to blame the foreigner for not being sufficiently able to understand the elusive concept of Thai-ness.

MY BOSS IS BIGGER THAN YOURS

If there's a problem with another member of staff, the person who is aggrieved is more likely to approach their *phu yai* than the person they have the problem with. As opposed to the involved parties sitting down together to try to resolve the issue or find a solution, it is likely that the *phu yai* will then talk to the other party separately, or if the other person is in another department or perhaps a foreigner (essentially the same thing), then the *phu yai* of A will speak to the *phu yai* of B. It is then up to *phu yai* B to relay the message, order, complaint or issue and allow B to respond. Then *phu yai* B will go back to *phu yai* A to relay the message and comments. This approach to problem solving is, more often than not, left in the Western playground as it is incredibly time consuming and not a particularly efficient way of solving a problem. On the other hand, it serves to avoid confrontation, which is of utmost importance in Thai society and, by extension, the Thai workplace.

For the Thai worker, this is the correct protocol, but if B is a foreigner, then this approach, what is essentially talking be-

PROBLEMS IN PARADISE

It was the wise words of Tim Canterbury from British sitcom *The Office* who said of spending such a comparatively huge amount of time with colleagues as opposed to family: "All you've got in common is the fact that you walk round on the same bit of carpet for eight hours a day." While this is true for anybody working with anyone in any industry anywhere, when combined with more than a fair share of cultural differences, situations in the Thai workplace are bound to arise, so it is wise to take a deep breath and try to understand things from both sides.

hind backs, albeit sanctioned official backs, is likely to be interpreted as snide, cowardly, immature and, most of all, unprofessional. But again, this is from a Western perspective. In the Thai workplace, harmony and happiness are placed above all else and must be maintained at all costs. It is for this reason that it is highly unlikely that people will argue or raise their voices in a Thai office. Instead, a Thai will just ignore the person that he/she has a problem with. It's the ostrich head in the sand method of dealing with things, but it's a technique often employed, as actually dealing with the problem would require relevant parties to go above and beyond, or over heads, or do more than what is expected of them.

The hierarchical foundations that most Thai companies are built upon are dramatically weakened when part of the structure is changed or replaced or interpersonal 'renovation' is carried out. It's a delicately stacked house of cards, a flawed production, which is why most often very little will change until the director, the manager or the *phu yai* leaves a company. But again, much like their Government House-based brethren, it is not unheard of for employees to launch a sort of company coup, and in these cases, when sufficient numbers of staff have a unified voice nobody is safe, not even the *phu yai*, as long, of course, as somebody has access to or an email address of a bigger Mr Big.

In the Thai workplace, it's much easier and less stressful to just go with the flow.

PUTTING A FOREIGN FACE ON

The biggest challenge facing foreigners working in a Thai company is deciding whether they can be satisfied with doing only what is asked of them. Unless they have a financial investment in a company, bringing about any change to the Thai work culture or psychology will take a long time, if at all. Once the moral debate is carried out, the foreigner will likely find the absolution of responsibility and the requirement of significantly less work in a more relaxed workplace rather pleasant.

It is when a blinkered foreigner enters the workplace expecting it to be like the UK or Japan or the US and is unwilling to adapt that he will find the Thai workplace extremely stressful. The Thai workforce can be quite segregated, both literally and figuratively, with a number of invisible barriers separating Thais and foreigners in the workplace. The language barrier is an understandable obstacle, made almost insurmountable if both sides of the divide make little to no attempt to connect.

Ajarn Aum with some of her new recruits, ready to fly away.

FLY AWAY AS AN ANGEL

Monchaya 'Aum' Khuptawinthu makes dreams come true by changing Thai women into angels. After working for just under five years as a flight attendant, Ajarn (Professor) Aum decided to open Perfect Angels, a school that prepares Thai women, and a few Thai men, for a career in the sky. Also a trained pilot, the native Bangkokian talks about an industry that, in Thailand, is still regarded as incredibly glamorous.

Since the school opened in 2008, you've helped almost 3,000 students find a job. What's a typical day like for you? I get hundreds of emails a day. Tonight, like many nights, we'll be finishing [teaching English, practicing interview techniques and 'personality development'] at 3 am. This is normal because most students also work or are at university. We're like a One Stop Shop. People come here to improve their English, develop their personalities and learn how to create the right first impression. Competition in Thailand for the major high-end airlines is very fierce. There are 2,000–3,000 applicants for 20 or 30 positions so you have to make a good first impression.

So how do you make a good first impression? It depends. We need to identify what the selling point of each student is. Each one is different. Of course, smiling and eye contact are a must, but some applicants might be friendly, polite or confident, professional, flirty or funny. I have some students who aren't pretty but we train them to impress the interviewers and get a job. Sometimes girls come to me and say they can't become a flight attendant

because they're so clumsy, or some are overly confident or have other unsuitable character traits, but I always say to them, "Listen you have two choices, you can be the way you are or you can open your mind and let me change you." In most cases, I can change people because they're scared of me. I can change them into someone funny or entertaining. They don't have to be pretty or glamorous.

What about presentation? How should a Thai flight attendant look? When some students come to me, they look plasticky and I can spot immediately that they've had surgery. I don't want a Thai girl with a European nose. I want something natural. I tell the girls that most airlines don't want girls with V-shaped faces. We mainly send students to dermatologists because it's important to have spotless skin, with straightened white teeth. The age limit is generally 28. We weigh and measure them when they first come in. The minimum height requirement is around 62 inches (158 cm), so sometimes we suggest they do yoga or other types of posture improvement to increase their height.

Why do you think working as a flight attendant is such an attractive occupation in Thailand? The salary is very high, that's the first reason. If you're an office worker, you have to save for about 10 years to get a house, or without parents' help even longer, but flight attendants nowadays can get a nice car within six months, and a house within a year or two. It's always been a glamorous job in Thailand. We call them angels and think of them as smart, beautiful girls who get to travel all over the world. In the past, and still to an extent today, it was very hard for Thais to fly abroad because of visa restrictions and finances, so at that time there was really only one way to see the world and that was to work as a flight attendant.

Do you still keep in touch with your angels? Yes, every day I receive up to 1,000 messages on my phone from past students. In fact, every flight I take I see my angels. Sometimes I've trained up to half the cabin crew. Before the flight, they run to me and take photos, put them on Instagram and Facebook and tell me about their life and how much they've changed, but when the service starts they all disappear.

On Friday nights, many Thai open-air restaurants, bars and beer gardens fill up with an eclectic mix of expats, tourists and colleagues enjoying some after-work drinks.

MIXING BUSINESS AND PLEASURE

In the West, encounters outside of the workplace are quite infrequent and are usually reserved for Christmas parties or team-building outings. In Thailand, in contrast, it is quite common for co-workers to go out for lunch together or go out on a Friday night to a karaoke bar or restaurant. Whereas Western reluctance to see colleagues outside of work hours perhaps stems from the feeling that enough time is spent on that carpet as it is, the general thinking among Thai colleagues is that socializing together makes for a more harmonious, happy and ultimately better team. Managers or bosses will rarely attend these social gatherings, but if they do they will be expected to pick up the *check bin* (bill).

Refusing to go out with colleagues, even if your dog did eat your hairdryer, will translate badly in Thailand and further serve to divide the workplace.

MY EXPERIENCE AS BOTH MANAGER AND EMPLOYEE

I've worked as both a manager and employee while living in Thailand. Almost immediately after completing my Masters in the UK, and full of ideas, theories and strategies, I returned to the comparatively sleepy island of Phuket where, after a few months working as a sub-editor for a fortnightly newsmagazine, a death at the publication thrust me unexpectedly into the editor's chair.

Unaware and unversed in the Thai way of doing things, I proceeded to alienate almost the entire office within a week or two. This was done by making what I thought were perfectly legitimate and reasonable requests and suggestions—be punctual, don't eat smelly fried chicken in the office, work harder, answer questions. The requests themselves were not necessarily the problem, it was how I made them.

In an almost all-female office, my brusque, sullen, no-nonsense northern English ways, combined with belligerent, arrogant youth meant that my requests, with glorious hindsight, could definitely have been delivered with a touch more *wan* (sweetness). A close Thai friend recommended that I either go easy on them or continue using a more Western managerial style and accept that people would not like me. As I had come back to Phuket to enjoy the beaches and the laid-back lifestyle, I opted for the former. Things gradually got better, at least with regards to the office environment.

I've also worked as an employee for a huge company in Thailand. There my duties involved working with both Thais and foreigners. As I had only worked for large foreign-owned companies in the past, where the ethos and style were international, joining a Thai-owned company and working for Thais instead of managing them was a huge culture shock. How divided and segregated the departments were, how unquestioning, blinkered and browbeaten the staff, both foreign and Thai. It was like walking into an alien world or being thrust into a play where I was required to assume a role that I knew I could do better.

For the first few months I tried to take with a pinch of salt what my foreign colleagues said with regard to the often negative work environment because I had worked with smaller Thai companies where Thais and foreigners

had worked together to make a better product and where everyone was aware that at the end of the day this was the main reason we were walking around the same carpet every day.

Working in a huge Thai company with an established history and way of doing things, with *phu yai*, egos and a bunch of cultural differences was a totally new ball game. It took me a while, but I finally realized that I could bang my head against the proverbial wall all day, wailing that this was not the way it should be done, but nobody would listen to me and no amount of smiling, calm talking or sweetness would be of any use.

I knew that as a mere cog, and a *farang* (foreign) one at that, it would be extremely unlikely for me to bring about any tangible change or even be granted a willing audience to present my suggestions. Yes, a lot of the staff were hopeless and many *phu yai* were out of their depth and unable to manage the culturally diverse team. As a result, the work environment was often toxic, but I did my job, I did exactly what was asked of me, no more, no less, and I smiled. It's all experience I told myself, experience that can be used if the time ever came for me to be a *phu yai* in Thailand again.

Small and provincial, huge and national, foreign or Thai-owned, the minefield that is the multicultural Thai workplace can be a challenge.

SUCCESSFUL FOREIGNERS IN THAILAND

The Thai word *farang* is an umbrella term for someone of European ancestry regardless of where they come from. Many Westerners are uneasy about the use of the term, believing it to be insulting and racist in the way that ethnic slang terms are reserved for slurs, but on the whole it's a neutral word. Whether it's an insult or not really depends on the context in which it is used.

While being referred to as a *farang* in restaurants, shops and even some formal situations in Thailand can become tiresome, this is often because some foreigners read more into the word than they should. That is not to say the term cannot be used in a negative, offensive and alienating sense at times. *Farang khi nok*, which translates as 'foreign/white bird shit', for example, is often used to describe backpackers or low-spending foreigners. As *farang* is also the Thai word for a guava fruit, this has given rise to numerous foreigner jokes.

Etymologists suggest that the word originates from the Thai pronunciation of 'Francais', one of the first European mission groups to visit, while others believe it derives from the Persian word *farangi*, meaning 'foreigner'.

Over the last decade or two, Westerners have become more visible in Thai society and popular culture. From foreign writers to businessmen and monks, many foreigners are now quite well known and even admired.

FOREIGNERS WHO HELP

There are many foreigners in Thailand who champion charities and contribute financially to various causes, whether through the opening or furnishing of schools, the financing of orphanages, volunteering or donating money to Thai wildlife foundations or, in the case of Englishman John Dalley, caring for Thailand's *soi* (street/stray) dogs.

Dalley opened the Soi Dog Foundation (SDF) in Phuket in 2003. The SDF's chief aim is to care for Thailand's abused and neglected *soi* dogs and cats. As well as providing shelter and medical treatment for the stray dogs on the holiday island and the surrounding region, the SDF also sterilizes dogs and reached the impressive milestone of 85,000 sterilized dogs in 2015. The SDF also arranges for *soi* dog adoption, and sends hundreds of Thai street dogs to new homes in Europe, America and Australia every year. Much of the work is carried out by volunteers.

BANGKOK'S FREE AMBULANCE

There are few foreigners, however, who get their hands as dirty as New Zealand-born Marko Cunningham. Cunningham is one of Thailand's very few foreigner-registered rescue

BILL HEINECKE

AN AMERICAN ENTREPRENEUR TURNS THAI

American-born billionaire Bill Heinecke has spent most of his fascinating life in Thailand. At the early age of 17, and a keen go kart driver, he became Bangkok World's advertising manager after persuading the editor to let him sell advertisements in exchange for contributing a regular article on go karting. From those early days as a salesman, Heinecke pursued a diverse and hugely profitable career that included everything from luxury hotel chains, luxury brands and, most profitably, franchises in American fast food brands.

In 1991, Heinecke gave up his American passport to become a Thai citizen, enabling him to own businesses and take advantage of many opportunities not available to foreign businessmen. In 1999, he launched the hugely popular pizza brand and business, The Pizza Company, which went on to dominate Thailand's fast food pizza market. He is also credited with introducing Thai-style pizzas to the country, with such flavors as Tom Yung Goong (spicy prawn with lemongrass).

The Bangkok Free Ambulance is just one of many ambulance crews that serve the greater Bangkok area.

workers and is one of the founders of Bangkok Free Ambulance. He was inspired to start volunteering in 2000 after seeing volunteers helping flood victims in Saraburi province.

A typical night for Cunningham involves tending to those injured in motorcycle and car accidents in the Sukhumvit area of Bangkok. But fires, snakes, floods, terrorist bomb threats and attacks (including the August 17, 2015 bombing), tsunamis, coups and mass demonstrations are often part of the work. "If it helps someone, we will do it!" says Cunningham. He also assists in translating and helping with every stage of the body collection process for foreigners who die in Thailand. Unlike some other ambulance crews, all emergency services are provided free.

Marko received medals from both the Thai and New Zealand governments for his work in transporting bodies in the aftermath of the 2004 tsunami.

John Dalley with friends for life, along with staff from the Soi Dog Foundation.

The English Monk

Vince Cullen is a recovering alcoholic who has been associated with the Wat Thamkrabok monastery since he made his first visit to the Saraburi province temple near Bangkok in 1998. The Briton became an ordained monk shortly after, and has represented the temple abroad on many occasions, teaching Buddhist-oriented drug and alcohol recovery through total abstinence.

"Thailand has a huge alcohol problem, but people here just pretend that it doesn't exist," says Cullen.

As well as regularly helping people from the UK visit Wat Thamkrabok to get treatment, Cullen also travels around the world giving talks on how Buddhism and knowledge of 'the hungry ghosts' can aid in recovery.

Thailand's Face of English

Andrew Biggs is a fluent Thai-speaking Australian who has been living in Thailand since 1989 and is well known among both the expatriate and Thai population. Expats in Thailand know him as a national newspaper columnist, who shares his musings and foreign observations on Thai culture and life from a *farang* resident's unique perspective.

To Thai audiences of a certain age, Biggs is better known as a television personality who probably helped them with their first words in English. Since appearing on Thailand's first English talk-back radio program in 1995, he has continued to appear on TV programs as well as produce content on his YouTube channel. Biggs has also written various books, in both English and Thai, and has a Bachelor's degree in the Thai language. In 2004, he was the first Westerner to be awarded the highly prestigious Petch Siam Award for excellence in using the Thai language.

ANDREW BIGGS

JOBS FOR FOREIGNERS

If you ask foreign residents how they came to be living in Thailand, the chances are that the answer will be much the same. Many foreigners who choose to live in the kingdom will have visited on holiday, fallen in love with the country, culture or a particular Thai citizen, and then taken steps to return to live and work in Thailand.

Visitors can choose to live frugally, Thai style, or enjoy a more indulgent, hedonistic existence. The choice is up to them. So too is how they wish to sustain themselves when they're there.

Popular places for foreigners to live and work include Bangkok, Phuket, Pattaya and Chiang Mai, although the countryside and rural parts of Thailand, such as Isan and the north of Thailand, are also becoming increasingly popular, especially with retirees who are likely to get more bang for their baht.

Those who do decide to take the leap quickly find out that it is not as simple as just moving here and getting a job. As well as restrictions regarding the purchase of property, there are also certain occupations that are barred to foreigners, including laboring work, wood carving, driving for commercial purposes, hair cutting and garment making. A general rule of thumb is that a foreigner cannot do a job that a Thai could do.

Even if a job is deemed to be 'foreigner friendly', labor laws and rules and regulations are quite strict, and there are various loops that an applicant must jump through in order to get the necessary work permit and visa.

The average monthly salary for a foreign worker is around 30,000 baht (US$950). Although the Labor Office stipulates that the minimum salary for a foreign worker must be around 50,000 baht, in reality this is more like a suggestion and companies tend to pay a lot less.

TRANSLATING THAI

A highly prized and sought after skill in Thailand is fluency in both Thai and English, and if you are able to find work as a translator it can be quite lucrative. Translators are needed in many sectors, from tour companies and newspapers to large corporations. Opportunities exist for translating Thai to English, English to Thai and, increasingly, Chinese and Russian to Thai and vice versa. As well

TEACHING ENGLISH

One of the most popular jobs for foreigners, at least initially, is as an English teacher. Thailand has a number of companies and schools offering training in TEFL (Teaching English as a Foreign Language). After qualifying, it is relatively easy to find work. With the TEFL qualification, teachers are able to teach English classes at private English language institutions open to both adults and children. Average salaries are around 20,000–25,000 baht for a five-day week, eight hours a day.

After a few years' experience, TEFL teachers are able to teach in state schools for more money. If the teacher also has a teaching qualification from his/her own country, they should be able to work for an attractive international salary at an international school.

PLAYING THE FOREIGNER ON TV

You don't necessarily need to look or indeed act like Brad Pitt to find work as a model or actor in Thailand. It's unlikely that you will be cast as the star, or earn much money, and you are likely to play a rather two-dimensional version of a foreigner, but it can be good fun and an interesting way to meet lots of new people and see different parts of Thailand. Again, work is typically available on a daily basis for around 2,000 baht a day. Those who are serious about finding work in an advertisement, a soap opera or even a movie, may want to seek out an agency, where an agent will charge a commission of 30 percent for every job he manages to find.

WORKING UNDERWATER

Many foreigners also choose scuba diving as a vocation while living in Thailand. Because of the many great dive spots and a thriving dive industry, there is rarely a shortage of jobs for qualified instructors, especially during the high season. Instructors must, of course, be scuba certified and, as with English language teaching, there are many dive centers in Thailand that offer dive master courses to get to scuba instructor level. Once divers have received a certificate and qualification, most either find work full time at a dive center or work freelance at a number of centers.

as long-term contracts, work is also available on a daily basis and translators can expect to get paid around 2,000 baht per day.

HOLIDAY-MAKERS

The tourism sector is another popular industry to work in, with many foreigners with the relevant hospitality qualifications and training able to get

extremely well-paying but demanding jobs as General Manager or Food and Beverage Manager in hotels around Thailand.

THE THAI P.I.

A thoroughly interesting, albeit potentially dangerous, job is as a private investigator. Although it sounds rather glamorous, in reality the work itself

boils down to little more than stalking distrusting men's girlfriends. But if the idea of hanging around in a bar all night to see if a girl goes home with another man in order to substantiate or disprove a man's fears is appealing, then work is there for the foreigner, who has the advantage of blending easily into the background.

LIVING THE THAI DREAM

A common job for many older foreign man, especially in the more touristy areas of Thailand, is as a bar owner. As many quickly find out, however, it is a notoriously difficult market to succeed in. They discover that 'Living the Thai dream' is more complicated than simply opening a bar where they and their mates can hang out and drink. That may be the case initially but, as with every business, competition and the waning novelty factor kick in. Location is key, and unless a bar is situated along a busy thoroughfare or comes equipped with an existing clientele, it can be notoriously difficult to do well. Some bar owners end up becoming little more than pimps, who prostitute their bar staff, and the Thai dream very quickly becomes a Thai nightmare.

CHAPTER 4

The country's official slogan, 'Amazing Thailand', encapsulates the many cultural assets, activities and situations that contribute to the unique experience that is Thailand. Local pastimes and entertainment, ranging from bullfighting and karaoke to kickboxing and ladyboy cabaret shows, are just that little bit different and, well, not quite what they seem.

AMAZING
THAILAND

WEIRD AND WONDERFUL THAI PASTIMES

Although the younger generation of Thais are now more likely to go to coffeeshops and shopping malls and watch American movies and English football matches, a sizable number, especially in the rural areas, still indulge in traditional Thai pastimes.

Men line up with their birds to find out whose bird can sing the loudest.

KNOW WHY IT SINGS

One of the strangest but most endearing hobbies enjoyed by Thai men is bird-singing. Competitions are held regularly up and down the kingdom, not just in the countryside. It is quite common to see a Thai expertly steering his motor-cycle with one hand while holding a birdcage with a blanket draped over it in the other on their way to an event.

Sometimes competitions are separated into different categories according to bird species, at other times it's a mixed event. The aim, however, is always the same—to see whose bird can sing the loudest. There are subtle differences in judging. In one particular event, a bird needs to 'trill' a certain number of times, while in another the winning bird is decided on how often it jumps up and down in its cage.

Birdcages are arranged in two rows, with each cage facing another. Owners must keep their distance but are allowed to scream and call out to their bird as much as they like, which invariably they do. Often the owners are much louder than the birds! This curious event can attract up to hundreds from the neighborhood and is well worth looking out for. It is a serious pastime, with sometimes money at stake.

THE BEAUTIFUL FIGHT

A slightly less well-known traditional Thai game is fish-fighting. Yes, fish-fighting. Fish-fighting typically takes place in the countryside as it is not allowed within the city limits.

The Siamese fighting fish is a species of the gourami family. It is popular as an aquarium fish but is aggressive towards its own species. Called *pla kad* (biting fish) in Thai, it is a beautiful, flamboyant, multicolored fish native to the Mekong River.

The irony is that the beauty of the Siamese fighting fish and its full array of colors can only be seen when it is agitated and preparing to fight. When the two agreed upon fish are placed in a tall, narrow jar and come face to face, their fins and gills extend in size and their colors become deeper and more vibrant. The fish bite one another, often locking their mouths together, while they wrestle and flip around inside the jar. Once one fish retreats, the match is over. Only the males fight and are often bred specifically for the purpose.

THE SPORT OF GAMBLING

Although gambling in Thailand is restricted to the state lottery, horse-racing and a few select Muay Thai stadiums, all of the above activities as well as the English Premier League are common fodder for betting. Indeed, viewing the frenetic pace with which gamblers place bets and exchange information is part and parcel of the intoxicating atmosphere at a Thai sporting event.

BULLFIGHTING THAI STYLE

Thai bullfighting is without the pomp and ceremony you might see at a bullfight in Spain. There are no matadors, spears or red rags, just a simple arena with two bulls in the middle surrounded by jeering spectators. Thankfully, very few bullfights result in death. Much like Thai cockfighting, a match is usually brought to an end when one of the animals gives up and runs away. There's more snorting, horn-locking and hoof-scraping than there are collisions between the two 1,000-pound (450 kg) animals, so it's a lot like sumo wrestling of the animal world.

Cock of the North

A slightly darker event involving birds, which is also popular throughout Thailand, is cockfighting. From the countryside of Phetchaburi to the city of Bangkok, men in their hundreds turn up every week to these events. It's illegal to gamble in Thailand apart from state lotteries and at government sponsored events, so unless the event is organized by the government, such as the Festival for the Preservation of Thai Cock Fighting in Samut Prakan, any gambling that is done in the arena is technically illegal.

A typical cockfighting event begins with the owners weighing their respective roosters in order to find suitable opponents. Sometimes blades are attached to the ankles, sometimes not. In Thailand there is a no 'fighting to the death' rule, so when a cock either sustains a serious injury or runs out of the ring twice, the match is called off.

If visitors to Thailand want to learn more about this ancient traditional sport and see what goes into training the cocks, there is a Cockfighting Learning and Exhibition Center in Chiang Mai.

There's an Amulet for That

Thai males wear amulets with the same exhibitionism and pride that disco lovers wore medallions in the 1970s. Amulets differ in appearance, size and shape and can be purchased at temples or in designated amulet alleys or stores. The price of an amulet depends on which monk it is blessed by, where it is from and how old it is.

Different amulets are available depending on what type of fortune, protection or power the wearer wishes the amulet to bring. Amulets depicting Buddha, gods or revered monks, in particular, are known to bring luck and provide protective powers to the wearer. Whether for luck with love, money or school exams, a suitable amulet will be available.

A typical amulet can sell for around 100 baht (US$3), but there are some that can be as expensive as 1 million baht (US$32,000). The amulet business is not to be taken lightly and there are magazines, forums and communities dedicated to the trade.

Love charms (*koo*) blessed by sorcerers can also be purchased in Thailand. A *koo* charm may depict a couple having sex and is supposed to give the wearer untold powers of attraction to the opposite sex. Another is *palad khik*, which is a phallus charm made of wood. In the past, it was worn around the neck to ward off evil. Nowadays, specific symbols are crafted onto phalluses and mean different things. For example, a monkey carved on a

Shoppers peruse the latest amulets at a market in Bangkok.

An array of Buddhist amulets.

phallus represents quickness and agility, while a naked lady carved on a phallus attracts love and kindness.

Talismans

Shopkeepers also keep all manner of talismans and trinkets in the hope that they might bring prosperity to their business. Many of the talismans have their origins in traditional folklore and are of Buddhist, animist and Chinese god characters. A popular talisman seen hanging on walls is a spider, which is believed to help trap customers.

It is also quite common to keep amulets and images of monks in money boxes. Some shopkeepers, especially those from rural areas, keep *palad khik* in money boxes or on prominent display in their store. Another popular talisman for businesses is *nang kwak* (Beckoning Lady), which takes the form of a beautiful Thai woman kneeling and beckoning with her hand. As you can imagine, this 'household divinity' is also meant to bring wealth and good fortune to a business. On rare occasions you can see hybrid talismans, for example, of a beckoning penis.

A *palad khik* necklace to attract luck, prosperity and probably a few glances.

A karaoke customer serenades
all who are willing to listen.

Left Karaoke is a
popular after-work
pastime.

Below A Thai karaoke
hostess ready to sing
for you.

THAILAND'S KARAOKE CULTURE

**Karaoke is incredibly popular in Thailand but, like many other
pastimes in the kingdom, it is just that little bit different. While the
karaoke bar experience elsewhere is centered around the vocal
skills and often exhibitionism of the customer, in many Thai karaoke
bars most of the singing is done by karaoke hostesses.**

BOOTHS AND BARS

In Thailand, there are three different
types of karaoke establishment: karaoke
booths complete with individual karaoke
machines, which can be found in many of
the shopping centers around the country;
more reputable and larger open-plan
karaoke bars in hotels and upscale
entertainment venues; and dark, dingy
traditional Thai karaoke bars.

WOMEN'S WORK

As with most service industries in Thailand, the bulk of the entertainment lies
on the shoulders of women. The duties
of karaoke hostesses include serenading
punters on a stage or perhaps performing a duet with a customer. In general,
if customers want to sing, a microphone
and song book will be brought to their
table. Thai songs predominate, with a
limited number of English numbers.

These karaoke bars can be found on
the outskirts of major towns and are
very 'local' establishments; some are
little more than driftwood and corru-
gated iron shacks that contain a cheap
sound system, a computer screen to
display the lyrics and a basic assortment
of drinks. They are often decorated
outside with multicolored hanging lights
and inside with red lights.

If visiting alone, you can pay for
'company' from one of the Thai hostesses, which means just that. She will
chat with you, laugh at your jokes, pour
your drinks and may even perform a
duet of 'Islands in the Stream' with you.
In some places, the service is charged by
the hour, while in others it is expected
that you will buy your hostess drinks.

BRINGING FLOWERS

In some karaoke joints customers can
show appreciation for the hostess by
buying a garland of flowers and placing
it around her neck while she belts out a
number. The implication is that either
the customer is a fan of her vocal skills
or that he'd like to get to know her
better. The latter is more likely, so after
she finishes her performance she will
come to the customer's table to chat
and share a drink.

Many of these establishments, especially those where hostesses sit outside
in wait, are places where women are
also available for providing a more
euphemistic form of company.

For many Thai men, these types of
karaoke bars are definitely a cheap
form of entertainment, especially when
indulging in the Thai practice of 'bring

a bottle of whiskey' and soda form of refreshment, but not necessarily cheerful places. Because of the low prices of alcohol, late (illegal) opening hours, male posturing and, invariably, the possibility of irritating other customers with abysmal singing, it is common for disagreements to escalate into fights. Guns or knives and, in one case in Samut Prakan in 2007 a grenade, may be pulled out to put an end to an argument.

Friends in life and song, karaoke is a popular pursuit for Thai men.

SINGING FOR MONEY

The proliferation of pirated goods in the markets and streets of Thailand may lead one to think that in the ramshackle local karaoke bars there is a similarly lax approach to playing music in a public place using un-licensed versions of songs and instrumental numbers. But this is not the case. Even the smallest and dingiest of karaoke bars is constantly raided by one or all of the 15 agencies in Thailand that sell copyright licenses on behalf of copyright holders.

Representatives regularly visit venues to check computers and music collections to see if the owners have the right to play a particular song. If a representative finds that their clients' music is being played illegally, then the bars are subject to a fine. In reality, what tends to happen is that bar owners are either fined anywhere up to 200,000 baht (US$6,000) or given the option of buying a 12-month license on the spot.

Early morning visits are also carried out by the police who drop in on karaoke bars to ensure that they are complying with rules and regula-tions concerning the operation of a public bar and entertainment venue. Again, if the owners are found to be without a correct license or are play-ing music after the 1 am deadline, they will be fined.

From Karaoke Screen to Big Screen

The karaoke bar industry in Thailand has been the subject of a number of local films and documentaries. *Sao Karaoke* (Karaoke Girl) is perhaps the most powerful and memorable. Part documentary/part film, *Karaoke Girl* is about a 15-year-old from the countryside who decides to come to Bangkok to support her family. After a few years of working in a factory, and realizing that she cannot earn enough money to send home, she finds work in a karaoke bar. Cast as herself, 23-year-old Sa shares her memories of her childhood in the countryside and of working as a young sex worker in the city before finally giving it all up.

Of the inspirational film, Sa says, "I would like this film to touch the many people who watch it. I would like them to see that anyone can start over. It's never too late."

Much more lighthearted is the 1997 film *Fan Ba Karaoke* (Dream Crazy Karaoke). The English running title is *Fun Bar Karaoke*, but the Thai translation is a much more accurate description of the content of this fast-paced story of a man who falls for a karaoke hostess with links to the Mafia.

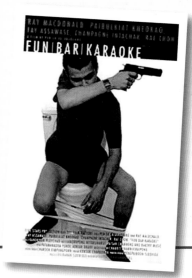

Left Many Thai spas are designed to act as mini retreats where people go to forget their worries, aches and pains, at least for a few hours.

THE JOYS OF THAI MASSAGE

Thai massage has become a huge industry and many of the nation's spas and massage techniques are revered around the world.

Right There are all manner of massage treatments to choose from, each designed to provide specific restorative properties, such as this coffee scrub massage.

Thai massage is also one of the staples of Thai tourism, with many visitors believing that no trip to the country is complete without at least some sort of pampering. No country boasts as many massage and wellness facilities in all price ranges, from streetside traditional massage parlors to luxury hotel spas.

HEALTH BENEFITS
To call Thai massage pampering is to do it a disservice, or at least that's what many Thais believe. Having a massage, while certainly pleasurable and generally relaxing, is also seen as essential to the physiological health of the body. It's a necessity, part of the restorative and healing processes and, as such, most Thais will have regular or at least monthly massages. Thai massage is one of the branches of traditional Thai medicine, and as a medicinal discipline is recognized and regulated by the Thai government. Thai massage is widely used in hospitals.

THE POPULAR FOOT MASSAGE
A foot massage is one of the most popular types of Thai massage as the client merely has to sit in a comfortable chair, sometimes on the sidewalk, which also provides an opportunity to people-watch or chat with a friend. Foot massages usually come in one- or two-hour sessions. Prices range from 200 to 800 baht (US$6 to $24) depending on the location and type of establishment. For spa treatment prices, expect to pay at least double. If the masseuse is trained, however, it doesn't matter whether it's performed by the roadside or at a luxury spa, or (like here) topped off with a pedicure, the principals and basic execution are very much the same.

Thai foot massage usually begins with the washing of the feet followed by rhythmic massaging, focusing on the different pressure points of the feet. Quite often in parlors and spas there will be diagrams of the different 'energy' sections of the feet and how these relate to the internal organs of the body.

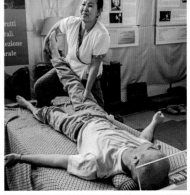

One can also have a Thai massage on a beach, by a roadside, at an airport, in a small shop with a partitioned back room or in some of the most luxurious spas and wellness centers in the world. A haircut may sometimes begin and end with a head and neck massage.

Testimony to their regard for the benefits of massage, Thais playfully squeeze friends' biceps and regularly massage their partners as it is seen as a way of showing love (and traditionally speaking 'transferring the spirit') to their partners, families and friends.

Not surprisingly, Thailand won the *Guinness Book of World Records* record for the biggest mass-managed Thai massage in 2012. Organized by the Ministry of Public Health to promote Thai massage, 641 people were massaged simultaneously in Bangkok.

Above It is quite common, especially in the tourist areas of Thailand, for masseuses to sit outside a parlor clutching a massage menu, and literally grab customers off the street. Right Often described as a form of passive yoga, Thai massage can sometimes feel like a real workout and leave your body quite sore, but eventually relaxed.

ORIGINS OF THAI MASSAGE

Thai massage incorporates elements of yoga, Aryuvedic treatment and Chinese massage or Tui Na. The masseur/masseuse makes use of almost every part of his/her body to manipulate, stretch and massage the muscles of the client.

There are many different forms of massage. Here are some of the more common forms:

Traditional Thai Massage

Traditional Thai massage is without a doubt the most popular form of massage and also one of the cheapest because no oils are used. This is the classical form of Thai massage that has remained largely unchanged throughout Thai history. It works by focusing on the particular 'energy lines' within the body, including the arms, legs, hands, shoulders, back, feet and, to top it off, the tip of the head.

This type of massage is not for the faint-hearted, and despite the small size of many masseuses, it is worth knowing beforehand that the pressure applied is sometimes rather strong. Don't be embarrassed to ask for a softer (*bao bao*) massage. Prices range from 200 to 800 baht (US$6 to $24) depending on the establishment.

THE WINK WINK MASSAGE

Part of the Thai massage industry, of course, revolves around the seedier side of the business, with some parlors merely acting as fronts for practitioners to offer sexual services. Much like karaoke bars, it's quite easy to tell the difference between a genuine massage parlor and a sex trade one. Bear in mind the location of the parlor. If the neighboring businesses are bars, then there is a good chance that the massage parlor will be offering services that are not on a typical menu. If the name of the establishment is suggestive, for example, 'Naughty Noon's', then it might not be the best place to go for a relaxing foot massage and a chat with a friend. These types of parlors can also be identified by their layout. Quite often the masseuses will be seated behind a plate glass window, what is known as a fishbowl, which allows for a less awkward selection process. A customer can point or discreetly gesture to which one of the available women he would like.

There are few Thai people more aware of the delicate balance between the law and the oldest profession in the world than former massage parlor owner turned politician Chuwit Kamolvisit. This colorful and controversial character was once Thailand's biggest massage parlor owner and at one point owned six 'luxurious' massage parlors in Bangkok alone and employed over 600 women.

After an arrest in 2003, he claimed that he had paid millions of baht in bribes to police officers. He subsequently sold many of his parlors, denounced his ways and launched his own political party that aimed to end corruption in Thailand. In 2004, he ran, unsuccessfully, for Bangkok governor. He is still in politics and once remarked that he prefers the label of pimp to that of politician.

SNIFF IT TO ME

The sight of a Thai man or woman walking around with a *yaa dom* (inhaler) jammed up his/her nose can initially bemuse foreigners. But Thais think nothing of conducting their everyday business with one of these in their nostril. The aromatic nasal inhaler does serve a purpose, however. With increasing levels of pollution and unpleasant smells, the inhaler not only masks odors but also clears nasal passages.

THE THAI SPA INDUSTRY

Growing concern for overall health is a worldwide trend and more and more people, foreigners included, are seeking health, relaxation and detoxification at massage, health and spa centers. Thai spas regularly feature in Asian and Global awards and, in fact, Thailand has its own Thailand Spa Awards that reward spa products, creative spa designs, spa menus and many other categories of the spa experience and industry. Thailand also has its own Thai Spa Association, set up to preserve the 'Thai spa experience' and establish a worldwide standard of service, training and spa operations in Thailand. As well as being a hugely popular exported practice, Thai massage generates around 30 billion baht (US$980 million) in revenue for the country each year.

Massage is also a great way in which blind people in Thailand can be self-sufficient, with many large towns in the country having Blind Massage parlors. It is believed that the 'unsighted' have a better understanding of touch and are therefore more intuitive in manipulating muscles.

Thai massage is even used as a rehabilitative discipline, with many prisons in Thailand (Chiang Mai Women's Prison Massage Center being one), offering female prisoners the opportunity of learning the discipline and then being allowed to offer massages to members of the public. The money the masseuses earn is returned to them when they are released from prison.

There are various schools where visitors, both local and foreign, can learn the ancient art of massage. Perhaps the most famous and respected school is the Thai Traditional Medical and Massage School located within the Wat Pho temple complex in Bangkok. This center for teaching traditional Thai massage was opened in 1962. Hundreds of ancient plaques and paintings of the human body on the walls of the center form the basis of the instruction.

Herbal Compresses

A massage with herbal compresses is much like a traditional Thai massage but the pressure is applied via a heated herbal compress. Special cotton bags are filled with various herbs and spices (tamarind, lemongrass, etc.), heated and placed on various points of the body. This type of massage is slightly more expensive and is thought to purify the body of harmful toxins. The average price for a two-hour herbal compress massage is around 1,500 baht (US$47).

Oil Massage

If a customer opts for this particular type of massage in a spa, the first step is usually a consultation. The spa staff will often give the customer a body diagram with which to mark the areas that he/she would like the masseuse to focus on or omit from the massage. The staff will also ask which particular oils they would like to use, based on the medicinal and physiological benefits of each one. Popular oils include extracts of lavender, sandalwood and natural plants. An oil massage is believed to boost the immune and nervous systems by stimulating the lymphatic system and blood stream.

MUAY THAI PAST AND PRESENT

Muay Thai (Thai boxing/kickboxing) is a hugely popular sport in Thailand, with a rich and long history dating back hundreds of years.

Unfortunately, as with many aspects of Thai history, its origins are sketchy because of the lack, loss or destruction of historical documents. What is known, however, is that the 'Science of Eight Limbs', so-called because it makes use of eight points of combat—fists, elbows, legs and knees—evolved from the battle-fields and over the centuries has become a highly respected sport and skill enjoyed by every strata of Thai society. Muay Thai can now be seen during festivals, in schools and in the largest stadiums in the kingdom.

During the Ayutthaya period (1350–1767), the best Thai fighters formed part of the prestigious Muay Luang or Royal Boxers. They were the king's personal guards, charged with protecting king and country. Throughout Thai history, staged fights were often used as a way to solve political problems or national issues.

Above International Muay Thai events are popular, glitzy and well-attended affairs. **Left** A Muay Boran fighter prepares to do battle.

The Sport of Kings

During the reign of King Luang Sorasak (1703 –9), also known as the Tiger King, *muay* (boxing) was to take an even more prestigious turn. King Luang was a highly respected fighter who apparently used to visit villages around the country to compete incognito at various events and competitions.

During the reign of King Rama V (1868 –1910), winners of Muay Thai fights were awarded military titles from the king. Even today, one of the nation's most respected competitions, the annual Kings Cup Super 8 Tournament, is held to honor the birthday of King Bhumibol, which continues the Thai monarchy's long lineage of patronage of Muay Thai.

MUAY THAI'S ORIGINS

Muay Thai is believed to have origi-nated from Muay Boran, which is a generic term for all ancient (*boran*) martial arts practiced in Thailand. Muay Boran fighters typically adopted a much lower stance than Muay Thai fighters and also fought with bare knuckles, although over time they began to bind their forearms and fists with hemp rope.

Muay Boran bouts were fought within a rough circle of spectators, and there was no limit on the time or number of rounds. Instead, a hole was hollowed out of a coconut, which was then submerged in water. When the coconut sank, the fighters had a break. Muay Boran was gradually replaced and superseded in popularity by Muay Thai during the 19th and 20th centuries.

The style of Muay Boran was intro-duced to a larger audience in the 2003 smash hit movie *Ong Bak*. There are other references to Muay Boran and Muay Thai in movies, such as the Jean Claude Van Damme film *Kickboxer*. However, the practice of applying glass to the fists or forearms, as seen in the final fight scene in the movie, was rarely used in competitive fights and was more likely to be used during times of war.

MAINTAINING THE PAST WHILE LOOKING AHEAD

In the 1920s, Western-style rings, boxing gloves, rounds, and rules and regulations were introduced. Despite the standardizing of Muay Thai, many of the traditional aspects of the sport are protected by the World Muay Thai Council and have remained the same.

Therefore, in a Muay Thai bout, every fighter, whether Thai or not, must perform the *wai khru*, a ritualistic dance in order to show respect to the teacher. During the performance, they must also wear the *mongkhon* (headband), which can only be removed by the teacher after a fight.

Each fighter must also wear *prajiad* (armbands) and, like the *mongkhon*, these can only be handled by either the fighter or the teacher lest they lose their special powers.

A large part of the Muay Thai experience has always been the music or *sarama* that accompanies the fights. It is performed by four musicians who play traditional Thai instruments: the *pi*

A MUAY THAI SUPERSTAR

Perhaps one of the most popular and successful Muay Thai fighters in modern history is Buakaw Banchamek, a two-time K1 World Max Champion and two-time Thai Fight Champion. He stopped competing in Muay Thai fights in Thailand in 2012.

When he was active as a Muay Tha fighter, he was known as Buakaw Por Pramook, but after breaking his contract with the Por Pramook gym in 2012 over allegations of exploitation, he could neither continue to use his original 'ring name' nor, under Thai law, fight in Thailand. Buakaw, therefore, decided to open his own gym.

There are legal ramifications when a fighter leaves a gym but continues to fight in Thailand. This happened to Buakaw

in 2012, when after leaving the Por Pramook gym he decided to compete and subsequently win a Muay Thai tournament. He gave an impassioned post-match speech, saying that although he would have to go to jail as a result of contravening his Por Pramook contract, he had to fight as it was his duty and responsibility and that he fought for his father, his fans and for King Bhumibol. Buakaw has still to be officially punished for competing and breaking his contract.

Buakaw went on to work as a trainer at his own gym and to compete in mixed martial arts divisions K1 and Pride. He also performs at exhibition matches and shows around the kingdom.

(Thai oboe) and Thai drums and cymbals. The tempo changes with the pace of the fight, encouraging the fighters to hit and kick harder.

Every March, Muay Thai fighters from all over the world travel to Ayutthaya to take part in the World Wai Kru Muay Thai Ceremony. The five-day event, involving a tournament and demonstrations from the world's best fighters, is also an opportunity for Muay Thai fighters to pay respect to their teachers and also homage to the legendary Nai Khanamtom.

FIGHT FOR YOUR LIFE

Muay Thai bouts still garner a lot of interest, with larger championship fights often attended by high-ranking police officers and governors, and held to honor members of the royal family. The social status of Muay Thai fighters, however, has dramatically declined since the days of the Royal Boxers and has become more an occupation and way out of impoverished circumstances for Thai men, women and, more controversially, children.

Quite often, a young aspiring Muay Thai fighter will join a Muay Thai gym and be trained, fed and provided with shelter. The agreement is that when they are ready to fight at a competitive level, they do so in the name of the gym, which then receives a substantial percentage of the prize money.

THE END OF AN ERA

Without a doubt the most famous Muay Thai boxing venue was the original Lumpinee Boxing Stadium in Bangkok. Opened in 1956, the multistoried stadium, run by the Royal Thai Army, was the place to go to experience the sounds, sights and atmosphere of a

A LEGENDARY THAI FIGHTER

After the fall of the Ayutthaya kingdom in the 18th century, Burmese troops rounded up thousands of Thai prisoners and transported them to Burma. At the time, the king of Burma, who was a huge fan of fighting, organized a seven-night Buddha festival. As part of the festivities, the king wanted to see how Muay Boran compared to Burmese boxing. The Thai fighter Nai Khanamtom was selected to fight the Burmese champion at that time.

Before the bout, Nai Khanamtom performed a traditional *wai khru* dance, after which he proceeded to pummel the Burmese fighter. The referee, however, declared the fight invalid on the grounds that the 'dance'—believed at the time to be black magic—was distracting. Nai Khanamtom then apparently fought nine other Burmese champions, one after the other, without a break. After the ninth fight, no one else dared to challenge him.

The king awarded Nai Khanamtom his freedom along with the choice of either money or two beautiful Burmese wives. He chose the latter, as he believed that money was easier to come by.

Muay Thai fight. Unfortunately, the stadium closed in 2013, to be replaced by a state-of-the-art venue in northern Bangkok, but with the same name.

DIFFERENT BELTS

Despite the billboards and loudspeakers, foreigners don't really know the importance and prestige of 'championship' fights. Unlike traditional Western boxing, Muay Thai has no standardized sanctioning bodies and, instead, each stadium holds it own championships and awards its own belts.

The two most prestigious stadiums in Thailand, and therefore the ones that carry the most credentials, are Lumpinee and Rajadamnern. But as they rarely pit champions from different stadiums against one another for fear of exposing a stadium as having an inferior 'champion', it is almost impossible to work out who the real Muay Thai champion is.

A fighter also has to defend his belt quite regularly, say every 3–4 months. Unless he has the financial means or is based near a stadium, he is often forced to give up the sport, meaning the belt often lies vacant until a new champion can be found.

There are also regional championships and annual tournaments, such as the Toyota Cup and the most prestigious Muay Thai tournament in Thailand, the Kings Cup Super 8 Tournament, all of which have their own belts.

"You see Muay Thai, you see Thailand"

Announcements made over loudspeakers mounted on traveling trucks often profess "You see Muay Thai, you see Thailand". While that might be a slight stretch, there is a grain of truth in it. The covert gambling, the shouting, the atmosphere, the graceful movements and displays of athletic prowess, and the fiercely protected history and traditions of the cultural practice all make for a truly authentic slice of Thai culture.

A Muay Thai fighter performs a *wai khru* before a bout.

A FIGHT FOR FREEDOM

A reality show that has yet to happen but may well do so one day is one in which prisoners who learn Muay Thai fight for their freedom by competing against visiting foreign fighters. Although such an idea sounds far-fetched, in October 2013 Bangkok's Klong Prem Prison offered inmates the opportunity to fight against foreign Muay Thai fighters for cash prizes, and, most importantly, the chance to bring honor to the prison and, at the same time, shave some time off their sentence. The concept of Thai Muay boxers fighting for their freedom has a precedent, of course, in the legend of Nai Khanamtom.

EVERYTHING BUT THE FIGHT

Those who learn Muay Thai will often also learn to perform a *wai khru*, a gentle and systematic form of dance done in the ring before the commencement of the bout to honor and show respect for the gymnasium and trainer.

A large part of the modern Muay Thai fight experience are the sounds of the fight itself and the music (*sarama*) accompanying the fight performed by four musicians playing traditional Thai instruments. The tempo of the music, which sounds somewhat like snake-charming music, changes according to the pace of the fight and goes some way to urging the fighters to fight harder.

MUAY THAI TOURISM

Paralleling the increased popularity of Muay Thai abroad, the country has seen a surge in the number of Muay Thai gyms springing up aimed predominantly at foreigners. Muay Thai tourism is huge and the Tiger Muay Thai gym in Phuket, for example, sees hundreds of young foreigners attend month-long courses all year round. The reasons for attendance vary, with some doing Muay Thai as a way of keeping fit while others harbor dreams of competing at a semi-professional level.

Opponents of such Muay Thai expansion argue that foreign interest and the commercially motivated creation of gyms to accommodate them has led to a watering down of the traditional ancient art.

THE LADYBOY CABARET SHOW

To many, the ladyboy cabaret show has become synonymous with Thai tourism. In most tourist areas, there are huge, glitzy and glamorous cabaret shows, which wouldn't look out of place in Las Vegas. There's singing, there's dancing, there's costume changes and there's more singing. The only difference is that all of the entertainment and all of the characters' parts are performed by *kathoey* (ladyboys).

The raunchy glamor show has also gained international recognition over the years, with a few groups, such as The Lady Boys of Bangkok, touring the world to titillate and fascinate the masses in equal measure. The shows tend to pay tribute to the ultra feminine ideal and the contemporary concept of woman in all her wonderful forms. These include Hollywood starlets of yesteryear and R&B bootylicious songstresses, along with Oriental mythical archetypes of femininity.

BEST HIGH-HEELED FOOT FORWARD

If an aspiring *kathoey* manages to get through the strict selection process and is deemed pretty and ladylike enough, the grueling process of becoming a ladyboy cabaret performer begins. For many, this means weeks of practicing songs, (even though often the performers just mime) and dance steps and perfecting routines before they are even allowed to grace the stage of a cabaret show. Most recently in Phuket, owing to a dramatic shift in the tourist demographic, it has even meant learning a foreign language or two.

As the Korean and Chinese markets are now huge on the island, many of the performers also learn a few songs in the audience's native language. In fact, the shows are constantly being updated to include numbers and routines that are in vogue. In 2012, for example, the hugely popular *Gangnam Style* routine was performed nightly at Aphrodite. Shows are made up of songs and the odd bit of slapstick comedy, routinely involving comically large 'ladies' attempting to grope an 'unwilling' member of the audience.

By and large these cabaret shows are not overtly sexual and, in fact, it is not all that uncommon to see a child or two in the audience.

FLAWLESS PRODUCTIONS

In the larger tourist areas of Thailand—Bangkok, Chiang Mai, Pattaya and Phuket—the shows are big budget affairs in huge venues with awesome acoustics and seating for up to 900 people. Two new productions were launched in Phuket in 2012, bringing the total number to three ladyboy cabaret shows on the small holiday island.

The two new venues on the block—Aphrodite and Simon Star Cabaret—both throw huge shows that attract hundreds of tourists every night, but the oldest and most established is still Simon Cabaret.

Aphrodite, situated in a former microbrewery, is, however, a bigger venue with an even a bigger cast of 80. In high season, it is open seven nights a week and puts on three shows a night.

Performers typically do two shows a night, combined with a meet-and-greet at the end of each performance. At this, the ladyboys, complete with feathers and sequins, line up, either outside or inside the venue, and invite audience members to have their photo taken with them, for a fee of course.

INSIDE THE DRESSING ROOM

Gan is a 37-year-old dancer from Isan in the north of the country. In fact, a disproportionate number (70 percent) of dancers at Aphrodite come from Isan. Gan says that she knew she was a ladyboy when she was as young as 10 years old.

Prior to working at the Aphrodite Cabaret show in Phuket, she worked for 12 years at the Golden Dome cabaret show in Bangkok. Before that, she was paid to travel around Thailand competing in ladyboy beauty pageants.

"I like being a ladyboy mainly because I like dressing up and being on stage. My current favorite song is called 'Mae Hwon', which is about a Chinese flower."

Gan says that although she has to work hard, she likes her job and her lifestyle, and believes that life for a ladyboy in Thailand is much better than it used to be. When she retires from the cabaret industry, she wants to open a beauty salon in Phuket with her boyfriend.

Top right Gan chooses her costume in the dressing room of Aphrodite.

Right A traditional Thai dance is performed by the cast of a big budget cabaret show.

NO SEX PLEASE, IT'S CABARET

The performers work hard and must practice the new songs and routines every day. They typically have just two days off a month and work every night, sometimes appearing in two shows a day, but they are, by Thai standards, very well remunerated.

Life after being a ladyboy cabaret performer is usually pretty good. Having hopefully managed to amass a significant amount of money during their career, many will open up a business, often in their hometown. They will also have probably provided for their family throughout their career and can therefore return to the village a true Thai heroine.

Many, of course, stay in the industry and become trainers or choreographers in the shows once they have finished treading the boards themselves. A popular post-performer occupation is to work in quality control. Here, an ex-performer will observe the dancers and performers with an eagle eye and fine them for minor infractions, like, for example, not wearing earrings.

There are also ladyboys, who, for whatever reason, whether not vocally or rhythmically skilled enough, are unable to find work in a cabaret show. If they still harbor dreams of becoming a showgirl, they will often find work, again in the tourist areas, in bars, where their job is to dance outside to entice revelers in. These are invariably dark and dingy establishments where they will also perform shows, but these are most certainly not for children.

THE JOYS OF THAI FOOD

There's more to Thai cuisine than green curry. Whether at roadside restaurants or in top-class restaurants, Thailand has an endless selection of delicious sweet, sour, salty and, of course, spicy dishes, treats and snacks to satisfy everyone's palate. Take a tasty trip around the cuisine of the different regions and learn about the all-important ingredients. What's a meal without a drink? There are certainly more than enough bars, pubs and quirky huts. Know when, where and how to drink Thai style.

FOOD IN THAILAND

Eating and snacking are central to the Thai way of life. If Thais are not talking about what they are going to eat for lunch, they will be enquiring how breakfast was. Thai people even eat on the way to a meal. A traditional and still popular greeting, especially in rural Thailand, is "Gin khao rheu yang?" (Have you eaten yet?)

It is only fairly recently that the Thais have started, sort of, to adhere to the conventional three/four-meal-a-day eating schedule. Before Prime Minister Field Marshal Luang 'Plaek' Phibunsongkhram's campaign to both Westernize and instill nationalistic pride in the Thai nation, Thais used to eat whenever they wanted.

In sharp contrast to the Western way of wolfing down sandwiches whilst hunched over an office computer, Thais in general tend to take breaks en masse, especially at work. Regardless of the impact on productivity, at precisely midday chairs are pushed back, exclamations of intent are made and lunch is eaten. How the 12 noon lunchtime became so ingrained in Thai culture considering the centuries of lackadaisical gastronomical time-keeping is quite remarkable.

With the availability of roadside vendors, restaurants, fruit stalls, food markets, convenience stores and cafes, there is no shortage of places to eat in Thailand. Each offers a different yet thoroughly authentic experience in Thai culinary culture.

Thai food has gained enormous international recognition in recent decades thanks, in part, to the huge Thai food brand Blue Elephant, which, alongside the Thai Ministry of Culture, has taken successful steps in promoting Thai food abroad. In 2001, London-based Nahm became the first ever Thai restaurant to be awarded a Michelin star. Today, most international cities have at least one Thai restaurant, usually several.

THAI CUISINE AND CUTLERY

The Thai cutlery of choice is a fork and dessert spoon. The fork is held in the less dominant hand, most often the left, and used much like a shovel to guide food onto the spoon held generally in the right hand. Overcome your cultural aversion to using a spoon to eat hot food and dig in. It's a much more logical eating implement than a fork by itself.

In addition to the introduction of standardized eating times, Phibunsongkhram also promoted the use of forks and spoons, first introduced by King Chulalongkorn in the early 20th century, again as a bid to appear civilized in Western eyes. Before the advent of cutlery, the Thais used their right hand to eat. In the days before toilet paper became common, the left hand was reserved for performing toiletry duties. Some Thai dishes still require the use of hands, for example, eating glutinous (sticky) rice. Diners ball up rice to soak up sauce or as an edible implement for scooping up morsels of food.

Central to Thai cooking, the wok is used to prepare almost every dish, from stir fries and noodles to curries.

THAI DINING ETIQUETTE

Unless you're eating alone at home or at a food court or 'mom and pop' style place, and having a one-dish rice meal (a single serving of rice, typically with one serving of curry or vegetables on the same plate), you need to be aware of certain dining conventions.

Depending on the establishment or the people you're with, Thai dining etiquette can be as complex as the carefully chosen ingredients that make up its cuisine. Although, as in many cultures, strict enforcement of etiquette evaporates according to how friendly you are with your companions, there are still general rules to follow when dining with Thais or in a Thai restaurant.

The most striking difference between the Thai and

Western style of dining is the communal aspect of the experience. Unless you have an allergy or aversion to a particular type of food, it is recommended to just let the host or the most senior member of the party do the ordering. You can, of course, order hamburger and fries,

but after you've polished off your fast food, you will likely be left with little more than a smear of ketchup on your plate and a longing in your eyes as your Thai dining companions graze away at the seemingly never-ending stream of dishes.

Thai dishes arrive when they arrive—in a haphazard, non-uniform way. So don't be surprised if you receive your spring rolls towards the end of a meal instead of the beginning. The exception is desserts, which will typically be ordered and received after the main courses.

A serving of rice is either brought out on separate plates or in a big communal bowl, which is placed on the table. Do not just serve yourself. It is best to either wait for somebody to start dishing out the different rice helpings and dishes or take on the task of serving everybody before yourself. The commencement of feasting usually begins after the eldest or most senior member of the table announces "Gin khao" (Eat rice).

LET'S BEGIN

If the taste of the food is not to your liking—perhaps not spicy enough or needs salt—do not despair as there is usually a wonderful array of sauces, spices and condiments on the table.

If you want to attract the attention of a waiter or waitress, it is quite acceptable to beckon them over. Simply stretch out your arm with the palm of your hand down and flap your fingers up and down. Address the waitress as *nong* (younger brother/ sister) for both male and female staff if they are younger or about the same age as you, and *pee* (older brother/sister) for those who are older.

Above In Thailand, sharing a meal is always a great way of getting to know each other.

Left Street vendors selling the most delicious fruit, snacks and meals are everywhere in Thailand.

AFTER EATING

Somehow the English hybrid of 'Check bin' has entered the Thai lexicon and is the most commonly used phrase when asking for the bill. Thais think nothing of scrutinizing the bill to check if it is correct before paying, so feel free to do the same.

It is quite common for the most senior or oldest member of the group to pay, but if this happens don't forget to *wai*. Among the younger generation of Thais and in mixed Thai–foreign company, it has become quite normal to split the bill.

In recent years, and especially in tourist areas or more upmarket establishments, tipping has become quite common, but it is not expected, nor will you receive angry stares if you don't do it. Leaving the spare coins that are returned to you is usually the way to go.

The Four Corners of Cuisine

The subtle difference in the cuisine of Thailand's four main regions is largely a reflection of their geographical location and the availability of raw ingredients.

NORTHERN Owing to the slightly cooler climate of this mountainous region and its abundance of vegetable crops, northern Thai dishes typically contain a lot of fresh produce and are quite sour and bitter. Many northern dishes share similarities with Burmese cuisine. Spicy sausages are particularly popular, especially the local favorite *sai ua*, a blend of pork, chili, garlic and lemongrass.

NORTHEAST Foods from the northeast of Thailand are heavily influenced by neighboring Laos. This rural area favors a simpler, rawer diet and sticky rice in preference to boiled white rice. The cuisine is widely regarded as one of the healthiest in Thailand because of its fresh food and numerous salads (*som tam* being the best known) and use of water instead of coconut milk in many of its cooked dishes. Barbecued meat (*nam tok*) with spicy sauce and lime juice is another northeast local favorite that is more sour than sweet.

CENTRAL Central Thai cuisine (Bangkok and the surrounding areas) is heavily influenced by the so-called subtle and delicately balanced Royal Thai cuisine. Nothing is too spicy, nor too sour or strong. With central Thai food, no single flavor is overbearing. The most famous dish originating from the central region is the coconut milk-based *kaeng khiao wan* (green curry.)

SOUTHERN Like the northeast, the spicy, sharp taste of southern food has been influenced by its neighbor Malaysia. In the past, merchants from India and Indonesia would trade herbs and spices at the various ports along the coastal areas of southern Thailand. Nowadays, the coconuts that grow in abundance all around the region feature in its many delicious yet fattening milk-based curries, of which massaman curry, which often ranks as one of the world's tastiest meals, is the best known. The proximity to the sea means that there are also lots of seafood dishes.

NORTHERN SAUSAGES

PAPAYA SALAD

GREEN CURRY

MASSAMAN CURRY

ROYAL THAI CUISINE

Royal Thai cuisine is not so much a type of food as a method of preparation and presentation. Ingredients are cut delicately and elegantly to ensure that everything fits neatly on a dessert spoon. With Royal Thai cuisine, attention to detail is paramount. All fruit is seeded, the bones of fish are removed and vegetables are peeled. The dishes are also lightly cooked to preserve freshness and flavor. With a green curry, for example, pieces of chicken are poached briefly in coconut milk before being added. Because the monarchy of the last few centuries has spent much of its time in the central region, Royal Thai cuisine is mainly composed of dishes from this area.

It was once customary for members of the royal Thai family to have their own array of dishes, usually seven, which would typically not be shared. The reason for this was to ensure that the diner had enough of each particular dish in order to achieve the intended culinary balance. This dining style is often replicated in restaurants, especially in Bangkok, that purport to provide royal Thai cuisine today.

WHAT'S GOOD TODAY? SERVE YOURSELF

Another style of restaurant that is extremely popular among locals is a *khao rad gang*, a sort of buffet-style restaurant. These are restaurants that have an assortment of pre-cooked dishes in large metal trays behind a glass screen. This allows the diner a look at what's available and, in some places, a whiff of what's good on that particular day. Some places issue you with a plate of rice on arrival and then you help yourself to side dishes. Most people choose two portions and are charged accordingly.

ALL IN TOGETHER

Communal dining areas containing long tables are popular in busy thoroughfares, markets or anywhere where space is at a premium. Here, people share vegetables that are placed in little plastic bowls in the center of the table. The vegetables are typically free and are eaten with the main meal of choice purchased from a nearby stall or other eatery.

THE BLUE ELEPHANT STORY

A true ambassador of Thai cuisine who is perhaps most widely credited with being the chief exporter of the traditions and marketing of elegant Thai food and the traditional Thai dining experience is Nooror Somany Steppe, the founder of the Blue Elephant Group. Born in Chachoengsao on the outskirts of Bangkok, Chef Nooror's origins and introduction to cooking resemble those of many other Thai women. "My mother and sister used to sell rice and noodles, and I learned to cook from them."

Ever since the first Blue Elephant opened in Brussels in 1980, the group has been synonymous with high-end Royal Thai cuisine served in lavish and authentically Thai surroundings. There are now Blue Elephant restaurants in many of the major cities in the world, including London, Paris, Dubai and, of course, Bangkok.

The Blue Elephant Group offers fine dining cooking courses at its many sites and also sells its products, including curry paste and all manner of Thai herbs and ingredients, in hundreds of outlets worldwide.

Nowadays Chef Nooror is kept busy flying around the world promoting Thai food on behalf of the Ministry of Culture and the Thai Tourism Authority. She has cooked for world leaders, including George Bush, Vladimir Putin and former Thai prime minister Yingluck Shinawatra, but it is quite often the average Thai who is the hardest to cook for and the severest critic. "Thai people are very particular when they go to restaurants, so at Blue Elephant they have very high expectations because, of course, their mother and sisters cook so well. It needs to be something 'else'."

Chef Nooror has seen huge changes in the three plus decades she, along with her Belgium husband Karl Steppe, have been operating the Blue Elephant Group. "Nowadays there is no discernible difference between Thai food for foreigners and Thai food for Thais as foreigners are getting more used to Thai flavors and how dishes should taste and what is acceptable."

KAFFIR LIMES

GALANGAL AND CHILI

TURMERIC

CORIANDER LEAVES

GINGER

GARLIC

WHAT MAKES THAI FOOD THAI?

There is no single ingredient that gives Thai food its unique and distinctive flavor. It is not the *nam prik* (chili sauce) nor the *raak pak chee* (coriander root). Rather, it is the subtle and complex mixture of a wide variety of herbs, spices and sauces and ways of preparing food that form a delightful harmony of taste that is at once spicy and sweet, sour and rich and unmistakably Thai.

Nam Prik Chili (*prik*) is at the cornerstone of most Thai dishes, and thus a serving of *nam prik* in a mini saucer accompanies many Thai dishes. Although there are over 100 recipes for making different *nam prik* sauces, the basic ingredients are ground chilies, lime juice, garlic and shallots.

Kra Tiem Garlic brings an intense flavoring to many Thai dishes. It is sometimes added raw but is quite often chopped finely and fried, along with black pepper, which makes for a wonderfully sweet flavor.

Ton Hom Spring onions are milder than other types of onion and when added to a dish give a subtle and sweet kick. *Ton hom* are also served raw as they're great for clearing the palate and cooling the taste buds after a spicy mouthful.

Ma Krood The skin, the leaves and the citrus juice of kaffir limes are all used in Thai cooking. The skin of the lime is used in curries, while the leaves and squeezed juice are used to add flavorings to a variety of other Thai dishes, including soups.

LEMONGRASS

Ta Krai Lemongrass is another vital, incredibly popular ingredient in Thai cooking. The plant adds a zesty, sweet flavor that is also very aromatic and so is used to neutralize conflicting scents in curries, spicy soups and salads. The Thais also strongly believe in the health benefits of consuming lemongrass.

Khing Ginger is added to Thai dishes, either raw or fried, to give it a spicy yet mild taste that perfectly complements the more rambunctious kick of shallots. *Khing* is a popular Thai herb used in traditional Thai medicine and is often administered by Thai doctors for its health benefits.

Kha Galangal is often used in Thai dishes to refresh the taste buds or provide balance to dishes. From the same family as ginger, *kha* is milder, more aromatic and with a slight citric taste.

Kamin Turmeric root is used as a spice in northern Thai curries, and also provides the yellow coloring in many Thai dishes. Its mildly bitter properties produce a very warm and pleasing taste, and alongside lemongrass it is one of the main ingredients in the healthy *tom yum* soup.

Ma Kham Rich in calcium, tamarind is used in many of Thailand's Muslim-style curries, such as massaman curry. It is also used in a variety of more savory Thai dishes to give extra sweetness.

Pak Chi Another ingredient essential to *tom yum* soup is coriander. Both the seeds and the leaves are used in Thai cooking to garnish a dish and add a freshness and tangy component to the meal.

Nam Pla Thai fish sauce is used liberally with most Thai dishes either as a marinade, condiment or vital ingredient. It is made from fish (usually anchovies), salt and water. It is used, alongside chili and shallots, to make the popular *prik nam pla* sauce. Bottles of it can be bought in most supermarkets.

Mortar and Pestle Cooking

No Thai kitchen is complete without the humble and indispensable mortar and pestle. Made from clay or often granite, the pestle pounds, grinds and mixes everything from herbs to chili, coriander and lime to release the natural fragrance and flavors in a way that blenders can't. No oils or ingredients are lost in the process. No electricity is needed, allowing street vendors and roadside restaurants alike to prepare bowls of *som tam* or delicious curry paste in the traditional way of generations of Thais.

I'M SWEET ENOUGH

A special mention must be made of sugar. As Thailand has always had a thriving sugarcane industry, there has never been a shortage of sugar. Before refrigeration, meat was preserved with copious amounts of sugar and hung outside on the corners of roofs to dry. Thai taste buds thus very quickly became accustomed to a certain level of sweetness in their food. Some would maintain Thais are addicted to sugar. From drinks to snacks, they like their food sweet. Many even sprinkle it on their fruit.

According to the Ministry of Health, a typical Thai consumes around three times the recommended intake of sugar per year. Combined with the gradual inclusion of Western fast food into the Thai diet and a more sedentary lifestyle, this means that about 21 million of Thailand's 67 million population are now overweight.

FRESH VEGETABLES

THAI STREET FOOD

With so many tempting roadside restaurants, street vendors, night markets and convenience stores, it's hard to be hungry for long in Thailand. Thai street food delights every sense. Indeed, walking along a busy Thai street in a town or city with a hungry stomach and an open mind is quite an experience.

Shouts of street vendors extolling the virtues of their food, the smoky smells of barbecuing sausage, the colorful collections of artistically arranged fruit, the eye-watering chili that lingers in the air and stings the eyes, and, of course, some of the most delicious tastes of Thailand make for a wonderful culinary treat.

With their increasingly busy lifestyle, many Thais eat on the go. They may choose to sit and eat on plastic chairs scattered around mobile carts, or have skewers of barbecued chicken or polystyrene bowls of *som tam* packed in

plastic bags, along with plastic cutlery and little bags of herbs, spices and sauces, to take away to their car or motorbike to, literally, eat on the go.

Although many street food restaurants, which are little more than a small group of plastic tables and chairs and a propane stove, minus refrigerator, sink or running water, would probably not pass a health and hygiene test, the sanitary conditions are probably better than most foreigners think as the meat, vegetables and fruits are usually bought and sold on the same day.

MOBILE STREET FOOD

Apart from vendors who occupy set stalls at markets or the same stretch of road, there are also mobile street vendors who hitch up their mobile cooking station to their trusty moped and bring Thai street food to the different roads, offices and intersections around the country. They tend to specialize in one type of food, whether it be Isan sausage or *som tam*.

Mobile street vendors can be identified, much like ice cream trucks in the West, by the particular sound they make as they travel about. They contribute to the almost non-stop soundtrack to Thai street life, whether it be the honk of a sweet corn vendor or the tinkling bell of the ice cream man.

There are also vendors who get around by foot. They typically carry two rattan baskets connected by a bamboo pole that balances on the vendor's shoulder. Each basket doubles as a cooking station with potentially lethal hot plates and coals used for cooking simple snacks, such as grilled bananas, sweet potato and boiled eggs.

NOT ON THE MENU

Reflecting Thai people's easy-going nature is the presence of vendors, typically doe-eyed youngsters, in restaurants who sell food, fruit, peanuts or mini snacks. Despite the obvious business conflict, most restaurant owners allow them to walk around the restaurant plying their wares. Don't like what's on the menu? *Mai phen rai*, just wait to see what comes along.

Right A street vendor prepares a serving of *Pad Thai*.

Right below A mobile street vendor waits for a client to order.

The Som Tam Lady

In the early years of the 20th century, *som tam* (papaya salad) street vendors would typically drive to construction sites around Thailand to make this Isan staple for the mainly Isan workers who, at the time, made up the majority of the labor force. The *som tam* vendors' routes have since extended across the country and into even the most upscale of Thai dining establishment menus, but *som tam* has retained its popularity as one of Thailand's most loved street food dishes.

Sayan is a 45-year-old woman from Phetchabun who now lives and works in Phuket as a mobile *som tam* street vendor. She goes to the fresh market at 5 am every day and returns to her home at 6 am to prepare and set out her mobile cart. She then rests until midday, when she takes to her bike and drives throughout the day to four different locations around the area.

Sayan is typical of many *som tam* vendors in that she has a particular spot outside a massage parlor where she spends most of her day. The other locations on her route are only visited at lunchtimes outside offices or at certain times when she knows that passing trade will be strong.

She sells around 90 servings of *som tam* a day at 25 baht (US 80 cents) a bowl.

Clockwise from top left A tourist stops to read the menu of a street food vendor. Eating can be a communal activity, even with strangers. If it can be put on a stick, it can be eaten.

SOM TAM PAPAYA SALAD

MAENG FRIED SNACKS

HERE ARE MY TOP TEN STREET FOOD DISHES YOU SHOULD TRY!

Som Tam Papaya Salad This is a great example of the sheer number of spices, condiments and ingredients that are added, pounded, sliced and diced to make a Thai dish. Witnessing a *som tam* street vendor at work is an experience. The speed with which the complex combination of papaya, tomato, garlic, chili peppers, salt, sugar and oyster sauce is mixed is incredible. A dash here, a sprinkle there, all at breakneck speed. The salad itself is usually served in a bag, with a handful of lettuce, bean sprouts and sliced cucumber on the side to clear the palate. It is often sold with sticky rice and barbecued chicken.

Moo Satay *Moo* (pork) or *gai* (chicken) satay is basically just meat on a stick. It is the accompanying sauce that gives this quick and easy Thai food its delicious flavor. The two most

popular sauces are either peanut or the sweeter vinegar sauce made from onions and chilies. Little slices of cucumber are often served alongside, again to clean and clear the palate. You can also buy fish balls, squid and even deep-fried crisps on sticks.

Kanoom Krock Pancakes These mini coconut pancakes are delightfully sweet, tasty and perfect to eat on the go. They are typically made in a large iron plate, around 20 at a time, but don't worry, you are only likely to be served either six or eight. The base is uncooked rice, coconut milk and flour and comes in many variations. It can be stuffed with all types of ingredients, from spring onion to fruit.

Sai Krok Pork Sausages Although sausages probably don't strike you as being a particularly Asian food, foreign influence combined with the migratory

SAI KROK PORK SAUSAGES

habits of Isan people from the north, who love a spicy sausage, means *sai krok* has become one of the most popular snacks for Thai people, especially in the evening. There are many types of sausage in all shapes and sizes, from large bullet-shaped morsels to long curly strips. As to be expected, the Thai sausage is renowned for being spicy and often contains the usual Thai flavorings—turmeric, lemongrass, kaffir lime and curry paste.

Guay Teow Rice Noodles Fancy noodle soup in the middle of the night? Well, your chances of finding it, wherever you are, are pretty high in Thailand. Mobile noodle stands come out at night and often occupy the same stretch of pavement. At the stand, first choose whether you want rice noodles or egg noodles, then if you want chicken, pork, fish balls or beef. The noodle soup comes with a raft of vegetables and is prepared with plenty of peppers and fish sauce.

Pad Thai Thailand's effortlessly endearing stir-fried noodles is one of the best-known dishes. It is typically served

MOO SATAY

KANOOM KROCK PANCAKES

PAD THAI

GUAY TEOW RICE NOODLES

CHAR YEN ICED TEA

with shrimp or seafood and was one of the dishes championed by Thailand's nationalist prime minister Luang Phibunsongkhram to reduce domestic rice consumption, in order to be able to export the surplus, hence the name. Ironically, it is nowadays most popular with foreigners, with Thais preferring other variations of stir-fried noodles.

Maeng Fried Snacks What was once simply a snack for rural Thai farmers has since turned into a protein-rich treat enjoyed across Thai society, which also even attracts the odd foreigner who dares to sample 'genuine' Thai fare. Insects (grasshoppers, beetles and crickets) are oiled and then fried, but all retain their shape and remain distinctively insect-like.

Pon La Mai Surveying the rows of carefully placed tropical Thai fruits and their awesome array of colors is like looking at a beautiful work of art. Whether along roadsides, at semi-permanent market stalls or on sidecar-motorbike contraptions, it's easy to pick up the freshest and most delicious fruit. The vendor will expertly chop and slice the fruit and put it in a small bag with a wooden stick to skewer the pieces. Often the fruit will come with a small sachet that contains a mixture of sugar, salt and—believe it or not—chili. Again, fruit is typically eaten on the go but can, of course, also be bought and eaten

elsewhere. Beware, however, that if you pick up the notoriously pungent *durian* you may not be able to enter your hotel, as many Thai establishments have banned this odorous fruit.

Char Yen Iced Tea Despite the proliferation of convenience stores that seem to be on the corner of almost every Thai street, many Thais still like to buy their cold beverages from mobile drink vendors. Most popular soda drinks are available, along with a selection of sweet cordials, to be sipped through a straw from a bag full of ice. Many of the mobile stalls also sell *char yen* (iced tea) and *cafe yen* (iced coffee). Both drinks are prepared in the same way, with the tea leaves or coffee granules strained through what is commonly referred to as a sock. Once the hot water has been filtered through the strainer into a small glass, condensed milk and sugar are usually added. It is then poured into a plastic bag or a paper or plastic cup, which is filled with ice. The final step is to place in a bag with wings, so it can be carried away or dangled upon handlebars and driven away.

Kao Tom Mud Packets Wonderfully symbolic of the Thai attention to detail are these banana leaf-wrapped goodies. Sticky rice is boiled with coconut milk and sugar and then molded around an ingredient, usually banana or bean. It is then wrapped in banana leaves and either steamed or grilled. They come in different shapes, sizes and packages.

FRESH FRUIT VENDOR

KAO TOM MUD PACKETS

A GUIDE TO POPULAR RESTAURANT DISHES

Choosing a meal from a menu in a Thai restaurant can be a bewildering experience, especially when you don't know your *prik* (chilis) from you *phad* (fried dishes). So where do you begin?

The safest bet and a dish that is perhaps most suited to the Western palate is the humble but nonetheless delicious *khao pad gai* (chicken fried rice). Stir-fried rice with onion, tomato, garlic and a broken egg, it is usually served with a slice of *minaow* (lime) to squeeze over and add a touch of tang. Others add *nam prik* (chili sauce). As with many other 'one-dish rice' options, you can order a fried egg on top.

Unlike the typically Western way of eating Asian food, where everything is dished out and mixed together at the beginning of a meal, in Thailand small portions of meat, vegetables or curry from the various side dishes are added to the separate rice plate with every mouthful. This allows diners to tailor make every bite and, to a certain extent, create their own harmony of taste. Once you've conquered the fried rice, it's time to embark on more bold culinary adventures.

Tom Yum Goong This spicy shrimp soup is one of Thailand's signature dishes but is definitely not for the faint-hearted. The combination of many of Thailand's key ingredients, including lemongrass, kaffir lime leaves, galangal and crushed chili peppers, gives it a unique hot and sour punch that catches in the throat. Although commonly referred to as a soup, *tom yum goong* is often served with a side order of rice and comes with a small plastic spoon for scooping the soup, in small quantities, onto the plate of rice. *Tom yum goong* can also be slurped like a soup from the bowl.

Khaeng Khiao Wan Gai The traditional preparation of green curry, normally with chicken, is a time-consuming process, which is why in many Thai restaurants today curry paste is used instead of fresh paste. Fresh green chilies, shallots, garlic, lemongrass, galangal and coriander root are pounded together in a mortar to make the paste. Fresh coconut milk is then combined with the paste and fresh Thai basil and green chillies to give it its creamy green coloring. Other ingredients added to the curry include aubergines and peas. Green curry is typically eaten with either a side serving of rice or roti bread.

Gai Phad Met Mamuang Himmaphan Chicken with cashew nuts is another delicious Thai dish that is an easy and relatively risk-free introduction to Thai cuisine because of its mild and non-spicy flavoring. Chicken is mari-

TOM YUM GOONG

GAI PHAD MET MAMUANG HIMMAPHAN

POR PIA TOD

YAM NUA

PLAH KAH PUNG NEUNG MANOW

MASSAMAN CURRY

KHAENG KHIAO WAN GAI

PHAT KAPHRAO

nated in soy sauce and added to a frying pan along with cashew nuts, large dry chilies, onions and mushrooms. Seasoning sauce, containing a delicate mixture of soy sauce, fish sauce, oyster sauce, water, sugar and pepper, is then added to bring all the different elements together.

Yam Nua Be warned, Thai salads are spicy and *yam nua* (spicy beef salad) is one of the spiciest, but is also very delicious. Like many Thai dishes, *yam nua* contains the usual ingredients, including onions, chilies, tomatoes and cucumbers, but it is the combination with the sauce (fish sauce, lime juice ginger, sesame oil) that gives it its special spiciness. Tender strips of beef are added to complete the dish, which is often eaten with sticky rice, perfect for soaking up the sauce.

Phat Kaphrao Although easy and quick to make, chicken with basil remains one of the most popular Thai dishes thanks to its unique and sharp taste that harmonizes with the ever-present chili and sweet basil. This national dish is one of the most popular 'one-rice dishes' and is often served with a fried egg on top. Although minced chicken meat is the most popular, other meats and seafood are also options.

Por Pia Tod Spring rolls are not technically Thai and are available in other Asian countries, but the delicious accompanying serving of sweet Thai

chili sauce (rice vinegar, fish sauce, sugar, garlic and crushed chili) makes it unmistakably Thai and unforgettably delicious. Spring rolls are available both fresh and deep fried. The Thai chili sauce is also a perfect match with grilled chicken.

Massaman Curry This Malaysian-inspired creamy and coconut-based curry has been voted one of the world's most tasty and popular dishes by various travel sites, dining guides and governing bodies in recent times and it's easy to see why. The King of Curries has a subtle yet distinctive taste that blends the sweet, the salty and the sour in a perfect creamy blend. A close second for delicious Malaysian-inspired Thai curries is *Penang gai.*

Plah Kah Pung Neung Manow It would be such a shame to visit Thailand, especially southern Thailand, and not try some of the fresh seafood. While king prawns, whether boiled or fried, are a staple of most foreigners' culinary journeys in Thailand, the spot for the kingdom's most delicious seafood dish must go to the wonderfully indulgent whole steamed snapper with lime. Typically served in a metal tray, often fish-shaped, with a candle underneath to keep it warm, the snapper is placed among raw cloves of garlic, chili sauce and plenty of lime juice to provide its lip-smacking zing.

Khao Niew Ma Muang Although it is technically a dessert, sticky rice and mango deserves an honorable mention. Sticky rice and mango (and technically crushed nuts and creamy sweet coconut milk) can be purchased everywhere, from mobile fruit markets and fruit stands to high-end restaurants.

KHAO NIEW MA MUANG

THAI BAR CULTURE AND ETIQUETTE

When strolling around the entertainment districts of Thailand on a Friday or Saturday night, you may think that Thais have a very serious drinking problem based on the sight of the nation's men walking along clutching bottles of whiskey. Fear not. They are probably heading for a bar or nightclub and are acting in line with the local culture of 'bring a bottle to the bar'.

In Thailand, rather than pay high prices for beer, wine and spirits at entertainment venues, many choose to bring their own. Which bottle you bring depends entirely on the image you wish to project. Although you can, of course, bring a bottle of the cheap local Sang Som whiskey, the most common and popular brand is the imported Johnnie Walker Black.

If you bring a bottle, it is customary to order a few bottles of soda water and coke along with a bucket of ice, though these are sometimes automatically provided. Everything is placed on a side table with caster wheels. Profit margins are, of course, huge with sales of coke, ice and, especially, water, much larger, in fact, than the highly taxed bottles of spirits.

MIXING WITH THE LOCALS

The subtle intricacies and complicated hierarchy of Thai society is sometimes hard to pick up on, but it is ever present and never more apparent than during the curious and fascinating forms of Thai drinking scenarios.

Although many opt to have the waiter or waitress pour, mix and keep everyone's glasses topped up, some choose to participate in the potential cultural minefield themselves. This may be out of respect for their guests or to find out more about a drinking companion. Despite there being only three elements to the Thai equivalent of the Japanese tea ceremony—whiskey, soda and coke—there are subtle differences in the preparation that speaks volumes.

THE THAI WHISKEY CEREMONY

As one's own full glass is tantamount to admitting a drinking problem, you should theoretically fill everyone else's before filling your own.

What do you do if you're unsure whether your companions drink whiskey with coke or with soda, or take one ice cube or two? If you don't know, is it rude to just twiddle your thumbs and wait to have your glass filled, while making no attempt to fill any of your group's glasses? The answer again lies in the complex protocol deemed by Thai social hierarchy—which is again adhered to more ardently the more formal the occasion.

Above Leave the neon-emblazoned tourist areas, the heckles and the placard-holding touts to discover some real Thai entertainment.

Right A beer tower, also known as a portable beer tap, is a popular and affordable choice (around 400 baht/US$12) for groups at outdoor markets and beer gardens.

Anything Europe Can Do....

In continental Europe, it is common to have beer served in chilled or frozen glasses. In Thailand, many go one step further and drink beer with ice. Some Thai bars also offer beer towers, which hold around 5 pints (3 liters) of liquid, with columns of ice in the middle to keep it chilled. This also allows Thai drinkers to participate in the important ritual of sharing, which is at the heart of the Thai drinking and eating culture.

For many, a visit to the country's numerous strip clubs is an essential part of their holiday experience.

In general, it is the younger or lowest-ranking member of the party that undertakes the task. After making mental notes of how the waitress prepares the drinks for each of the guests, one should then keep the glasses topped up, starting with the most senior/oldest/highest-ranking member. There is a trust issue at play here, so if somebody mixes you a drink, even if it contains perhaps a dash too much coke, accept it, drink it and keep an eye out for later in the evening when you may be able to repay the favor.

THAI WHISKEY CEREMONY

GOING OUT, THAI STYLE

There is no shortage of places to eat, drink and have a good time in Thailand. Thailand's tropical heat means that Thais tend to eat late in the evenings and therefore arrive at bars or nightclubs from 10 pm onwards. In Thai bars, the waitress or bar steward writes out receipts each time a new drink is served and usually places it in a wooden cup on the table. At the end of the night, the slips are counted and paid for. It is, however, getting more common for bars in the tourist or busy nightlife areas to charge on a drink-by-drink basis.

In local establishments, it will be assumed that you will be either splitting the bill or the oldest/most senior will be settling it. In more Western Irish-style pubs or in tourist areas, a waitress will often ask if you would like to pay separately or share the bill.

HOW DO YOU LIKE YOURS?

How do you wish to portray yourself at this crucial time? Only tough guys drink whiskey neat. For those on the second rung of the macho ladder, it is common to have whiskey and ice with a dash of soda.

At the other end of the scale, be aware that if you request a touch of whiskey with plenty of coke and ice you will likely appear as a lightweight. Do you wish to come across as 'hi-so' (high society) at a swanky Bangkok lounge? Then whiskey with a little coke, a little soda and a little ice is the way to go.

The pouring and estimating of the type of drink your companions may want is a great way of finding out more about them. According to Thai bar legend, if you pour a stiff drink (lots of whiskey, very little mixers) for a woman you like and she drinks and accepts it, then the implication is that she is attracted to you and thus entrusting herself in your care. Either that or she has a drinking problem.

Signs, promotions, touts and converted Volkswagen vans, you're never too far from a bar in Thailand.

Above Authentic Thai bars and clubs can be both intimate and insular social experiences.

Left Western-style clubs are increasingly popular.

Ships That Pass in the Nightclub

There is a marked difference between Thai nightclubs and the more Western-style ones in the tourist areas of Phuket or Bangkok. Thai nightclubs are basically a much bigger and predominately standing-room-only version of the Thai bar, with tables for different groups.

In traditionally Thai drinking environments, there is very little communal space for dancing, which allows very few opportunities to mingle. By and large, Thai parties tend to stick to their individual tables and drink, chat and shimmy around it.

Many Thai nightclubs eschew having a dance floor for mainly monetary reasons; the owner of an establishment with a dance floor must pay for a specific license. A common way around this is to have a wide web of tables around which people dance. In Thai bars and nightclubs, therefore, your table is your island. This does not mean that you need to be marooned at your table, it just means it's more important to capitalize on the precious glances and moments when revelers do leave their tables—to smoke, make a song request or visit the bathroom. After a few glances, try to strike up a conversation away from the respective tables or outside the club.

If somebody does want to talk to somebody at another table, they must invariably break the ice with the whole table. Or they could, although it may seem rather corny and James Bondesque, raise their glass to a young lady, or gentleman, across the bar. Competing and catching strangers' attention is increasingly difficult among the smartphone generation.

HITTING THE TOWN

As Thais are quite conservative, it's necessary to make an effort when you're going to a bar or nightclub to socialize. Although it might seem logical and therefore acceptable to wear flip flops and shorts 24/7 whilst living in the tropics, it is considered quite rude to turn up at a decent or, especially, an upmarket bar or nightclub in anything other than trousers (or at least jeans) and shoes (or at least trainers). Thai women go to great lengths to dress up and look *suay* (beautiful), so it is only fair to make an effort to prise oneself out of the baggy shorts and vests when socializing.

Many Thai establishments favor live music over DJs and typically have either a full-piece band or, at the very least, a guitar-strumming singer providing musical accompaniment to the evening.

In the more Western-style nightclubs, complete with dance floor, DJ and drinks promotions, many Thai traditions have given way to paying at the bar, dancing with strangers and worshiping the DJ. At some of these nightclubs, there is a cover charge that usually includes a drink. Dress code is casual but smart.

In Go Go bars (strip clubs), however, where the majority of patrons adopt the staple tourist style of beer-logoed vests, shorts and flip flops, and the waitresses wear, at the most, skimpy underwear and high heels, a dress code is not apparent. Anything goes.

Whether you're in the entertainment zones of Patpong in Bangkok, Bangla Road in Phuket, Walking Street in Pattaya or Loi Kroh Road in Chiang Mai, you need to know some 'rules' before visiting a Go Go bar. Although many Go Go bars, especially those advertising ping pong/sex shows, profess to not having a cover charge, the prices of drinks are sometimes highly inflated. In less reputable places, visitors are sometimes prevented from leaving unless they have bought an incredibly expensive drink.

A GUIDE TO THAI BEVERAGES

Thai people like to drink, with alcohol often acting as a social lubricant to smooth the way and flow of the occasion. Upon arrival at a social event with Thai friends, it is quite common to have a glass of an expertly prepared whiskey-based drink ready to clink before you've even managed to *wai* everybody present.

As well as sponsoring events up and down the country, Singha corporation also brews a delicious lager.

The average Thai male, aged 15 and over, drinks around 12.5 pints (7 liters) of pure alcohol per year, the equivalent of around 25 bottles of whiskey.

Thanks to lucrative sponsorship deals and partnerships with world-class brands and companies, including English Premier League giants Chelsea, Manchester United and Everton, many of Thailand's beers and beverages have gone global, deservedly so.

Chang (meaning 'elephant' in Thai) is a full-bodied, almost fruity dry lager and by far the most popular in Thailand owing to its low cost and high alcohol content (6.4 percent). These factors has led to the less than favorable 'Chang-over' description of the morning-after effects of drinking copious amounts. Chang is also a keen sponsor of many local festivals and events.

Named after a mythical lion, Singha comes a close second in terms of popularity. Slightly more expensive, it has a crisper and more bitter taste. It is 5 percent abv. Unlike Chang, however, it is slowly and surely making its mark in the overseas market and is available in a number of supermarkets in the UK and other parts of Europe.

The same brewery that makes Singha, Boon Rawd, also brews the non-premium beer Leo. This is a smooth, clean lager targeted at the budget consumer. For this reason, you are not likely to find it on the drinks menu of the more high-end Thai establishments.

In 1986, Thai brand Siam Winery launched Spy Wine Coolers as a supposedly healthier and more sophisticated alternative to beer and spirits. Relatively low in alcohol content (5–7 percent), it comes in a variety of flavors, all of which are approximations of rose, white and red wines. They can be found in most Thai convenience store refrigerators.

The two most popular Thai whiskeys are Sang Som and Mekong although, strictly speaking, both concoctions could more accurately be described as spiced rum. A brave man or woman would drink these cheap spirits straight, which explains why it is almost always consumed with lots of soda, ice and coke.

Herbal Moonshine

Still popular in the Thai countryside and among the rural classes, but dying out among the middle class and urban Thais, is the Thai equivalent of moonshine—the homemade herbal drink Yaa Dong. These whiskey-based beverages come in many varieties depending on the herbs and ingredients added. Popular 'secret' ingredients are usually ginseng, basil and tree bark. Some Yaa Dong concoctions are said to aid digestion, keep the drinker alert, provide strength or help the drinker sleep. For many people, especially those who visit fortune-tellers and witch doctors, these potions are seen as medicinal and even magical and can bring a myriad of benefits to the consumer, including sexual virility and superhuman strength.

With so much competition in Bangkok, bars do what it takes to stand out.

Sang Som often forms a vital part of the heady mix of the Ko Pha Ngan Party Bucket. Stalls set out along the beach or in tourist areas sell cheap plastic buckets containing a small bottle of alcohol, a can of coke and a bottle of energy drink. Ice is added, as is a colorful straw.

Another common Thai cocktail to enjoy (perhaps enjoy is too strong a word) is Sabai Sabai (Well Well or Happy Happy), which is a mixture of Thai whiskey, lime juice, sugary syrup, soda and a pinch of Thai basil.

WHAT ARE *YOU* DRINKING?

A popular, but highly illegal drink is Kratom 4x10, so-called because of its four ingredients—

Whether in a park, on a beach or by a waterfall, Thais love their picnics.

WHY NOT **HERE?**

Thai people are extremely resourceful when it comes to socializing. Indeed, all it takes is the rolling out of a reed mat and you have a perfect picnic or party spot. Sunsets in Thai parks are popular places for impromptu gatherings. The reed mat party can also be held almost anywhere, including at beaches, outside houses and on roadsides.

Although many politicians have tried to enforce a ban on drinking in public places, for obvious reasons, they have failed. The sight of shirtless men gathered around a bottle of whiskey on cement seats outside family-run convenience stores is not a pleasant one. Of more concern is the huge loss of tax that would otherwise be made from sales in licensed venues.

Reed mat gatherings remain the most popular drinking spots for Thai men of a certain income bracket. The younger generation and those with more disposable income favor bars, lounges and nightclubs.

kratom leaves, cough syrup, coke and ice. This sweet, sickly drink is popular with both teenagers and laborers because of its energy-giving properties, ease of manufacture and availability. Lao Khao is an incredibly strong white liquor made from glutinous rice. It can be bought from convenience stores or made at home if you have the patience and know-how.

WHERE AND WHEN

Apart from specially designated entertainment zones, like Silom in Bangkok or Bangla Road in Phuket, where selling of alcohol is permitted until 2 pm, alcohol sales are generally only permitted until midnight. Thai beers and a few imported brands (Heineken, Tiger) are sold in both 330 ml and 500 ml bottles and cans and can be bought from convenience stores, supermarkets and 'mom and pop' stores.

Sales of alcohol are therefore prohibited from midnight to 11 am, although, in reality this is sometimes up to the seller's discretion. Another more curious time slot ban is from 2 to 5pm. This law was believed to have been introduced to prevent school children buying alcohol on their way home from school. You can, however, buy alcohol in restaurants or bars during this time.

Sales of alcohol are prohibited on election days and most religious holidays. At these times, most bars close and those that do dare open tend to serve only apple juice that looks suspiciously like whiskey.

ENERGY IN A BOTTLE

Thailand, the country that gave the world perhaps its best-known energy drink, Red Bull, has a thriving energy drinks industry that includes several other products, such as M150, Shark and Caraboa Dang. Although Red Bull is commonly used as an aid in Europe and America to keep people partying all night long, its caffeine and taurine properties and low cost (10 baht/US 30 cents) make it extremely popular with the Thai labor force. In Thailand, therefore, you're more likely to see a builder than a clubber consuming these tiny bottles of energy drinks.

Reasons for the modern-day popularity of stimulant-based aids among the Thai workforce requires a look into Thailand's history of *ya ba* use (pills containing a concoction of methamphetamine and caffeine) among field laborers, rice field workers and long-distance lorry drivers. Up until the 1970s, when the Thai government officially made it illegal, *ya ba* was sold in petrol stations and by roadside flower sellers who placed the pills in the eyes of their flowers.

Ya ba and its much stronger cousin, *ya ice* (methamphetamine), is still used, albeit illegally, by teenagers and others wanting an abundance of energy to help them stay awake for long periods of time.

The sale of alcohol is prohibited for those under 20 years of age, but again it is rarely enforced, and unless a lad is wearing a school uniform or a girl with pigtails skips into the convenience store, they are rarely asked to show their ID. Locations where drinking is banned include public parks, temples (unless drinking is part of the ritual), educational institutions and hospitals.

THAI BEER GIRLS

On the lower end of the 'Pretty' job scale is that of Beer Girl/Promotion Girl. Attractive young women dressed in tight dresses bearing a particular beer logo are employed by breweries to walk around bars and pubs looking gorgeous and making customers thirsty. The idea is that, perhaps subliminally, the customer's longing and focus on the Pretty Young Thing will be transferred to the beer of choice.

CHAPTER 6

THAI MUSIC, MOVIES, ART THEATER, TV AND BOOKS

SpokeDark.TV

Although Western culture is becoming increasingly popular in Thailand, the country's rich and proud traditions of music, movies and theater are still taught in schools and performed at prestigious events. Discover Thailand's incredible and vibrant, yet woefully unheard of, artistic scene and some of the finest pieces of classic literature from Thailand's libraries. Lose yourself in the Thai pop culture of animals, gods, kings and myths.

Left A production of the *kinnaree* dance.

Above Dancers perform *fawn lep*, the fingernail dance.

TRADITIONAL THAI DANCE AND PUPPET THEATER

The elegant, slow and mesmerizing movement that characterizes traditional Thai dance is unique, otherworldly and enchanting. It's unfortunate, therefore, that the few times most tourists get to see such performances are as part of a sanitized snippet at a theme park or cultural show.

To the uninitiated, the 100 or more forms of traditional Thai dance (*ram Thai*) may seem indistinct and repetitive, but they all have subtle differences in choreography, rhythm and meaning. Each dance is also performed in a specific costume or to a particular piece of music. *Ram Thai* is a form of interpretive dance and is often performed to honor or pay respect to the nation's agricultural methods, elders, religion, spirits and festivals associated with a specific region and culture.

Central Thailand is home to *sri nuan*, the most popular of traditional Thai dances. Its gentle, angelic-like choreography is invariably accompanied by a *pi-phat*, a traditional Thai wind and percussion instrument ensemble.

A curious and unique form of traditional Thai dance, native to the northeast, is *serng krapo*, or the rather descriptive 'coconut dance' in English. In this, young girls take to the stage clutching two halves of a coconut shell and proceed to shake, clap and move them around to the music.

There are also dances, like *ram dab* (sword dance), native to the north of Thailand, that are performed to demonstrate the dancer's athletic and martial arts ability.

KHON AND LIKAY

Like *ram Thai*, traditional Thai dance dramas such as *khon* and *lakhon* also originated in the palace courtyards and were almost exclusively performed for royal entertainment. The most popular and well known of the forms is *khon*, which features non-speaking dancers and performers who wear colorful costumes and masks and mime the action while a narrator recounts the story, usually an episode from the *Ramakien* (The Glory of Rama), derived from the Hindu epic *Ramayana*. Popular characters include monkeys, demons and celestial beings.

Queen Sirikit has been hugely influential in keeping *khon* and all of the Thai arts it encapsulates—music, dance, costume and culture—alive and in the public consciousness. Every year, the Support Foundation's Khon Performance puts on a grand spectacle that typically runs for a month and attracts a huge attendance in Bangkok.

While *khon* was once reserved almost exclusively for the royal court, *likay*, historically considered a sort of folk opera, emerged as entertainment for the working class. *Likay* is characterized by a combination of elaborate costumes, minimally equipped stages and vague storylines that often give way to an actor's particular propensity for improvisation. *Likay* performances are still regularly put on at village fairs and festivals.

ART IN THE SHADOWS

Nang talung (shadow puppets) and *nang yai* (big shadow puppets) are other Thai art forms that are, unfortunately, becoming increasingly difficult to see. Like *khon*, many of the plots are based on episodes from the *Ramakien* epic.

Nang yai translates loosely as 'big skin' as the puppets, sometimes as tall as 7 ft (2 m), are fashioned from cowhide. The puppets are held up behind a huge white screen and their silhouettes illuminated by a glowing fire or, more commonly these days, a hanging lamp. The puppets' movements are performed in time to the narration and traditional Thai music.

BEHIND THE THAI MASK

Benjamin Tardif discovered his love of traditional Thai arts, in particular the ancient art of *khon*, as a 17-year-old exchange student in the historical city of Sukhothai.

At the end of his year of studies, Tardif returned to Canada and gradually forgot all about traditional Thai dance. A decade later, he returned to Thailand for a holiday and to catch up with old friends. After speaking to his old dance master, Benjamin decided to quit his job in Canada and move to Bangkok to enrol in a two-year course at the Bunditpatanasilpa Institute, and to start what he refers to as fulfilling his destiny.

The 31-year-old Canadian was assigned to specialize in the monkey character from the *Ramakien* epic, mainly because of his short stature but also his 'friendly personality'. Tardif is one of a handful of foreigners studying traditional Thai dance at the Masters level. He is also part of the Sala Chalermkrung Royal Theater and regularly participates in performances at festivals, funerals and other events.

Above Benjamin dressed as the green monkey character from the *Ramakien*.
Above left Benjamin with his dance master Wirod Yusawa.

Why *khon*? What does it mean to you?

For me, *khon* represents one of the traditional dance legacies of the world that has to be preserved for posterity. I was also intrigued by the challenge of dancing while wearing a heavy handmade costume and a mask that covers my entire head while having to express my emotions to the audience through dance.

How do Thai people respond?

Most people can't believe that I'm a *khon* performer because the general perception is that it's a very difficult dance for Thais, so they can't imagine what it would be like for a foreigner. It is often the older Thais who show their appreciation when they see a foreigner studying *khon* and contributing to the preservation of traditional Thai arts. Some think that a foreigner could not possibly fully understand *khon* and that I should not be allowed to study the 'sacred' dances. Many were concerned about what I would do with my *khon* knowledge and whether I would disrespect the ancestors. Over time, I believe I have been able to prove them wrong and that I have *khon* at heart as much as my fellow Thai performers.

PUPPET THEATER

Thai puppet theater (*hun luang*) was performed only at royal functions when it was first introduced during the Ayutthaya period. As time went by, it began to gain nationwide and even international popularity, which led to a great number of traveling *hun krabok* (bamboo puppet) troupes in the late 19th and early 20th centuries.

Owing to competition from contemporary Western forms of art and entertainment, the popularity of Thai puppet theater has waned with each successive generation. Working tirelessly to keep the tradition of Thai puppet-making and *hun krabok* alive is Niwet Waevsamana, a former advertising executive who became interested in the art of puppetry as a business venture. Although his initial plan was to merely export the puppets outside of Thailand, he became fascinated with the very delicate technique and started making them himself.

Now Nivet's home—Baan Tookkatoon Hun Krabok Thai—in Bangkok, is home to the country's largest collection of Thai puppets. He also holds an annual puppetry workshop where he teaches participants how to make puppets and also how to put on a traditional show.

Right Niwet Waevsamana with one of his puppets.
Left Dressed in black, the puppet master brings the puppet to life at Baan Silapin.

THE THAI MUSIC SCENE

Music appears to be everywhere in Thailand, from the latest American pop hits blasting from cars at traffic lights to the tinkling tin pot sounds issuing from the wireless radios that dangle from street vendors' vehicles. Indeed, even in Thailand's martial arts, Muay Thai, *sarama* music played during bouts is a vital part of the proceedings.

Above One of Thailand's biggest bands, Paradox, entertains the crowds at the annual Chang Fest.

Left A girl plays the traditional *saw duang* stringed instrument.

BANDING TOGETHER

Traditional Thai orchestral music dates back to the palace courtyards of more than 800 years ago. Nowadays, this ensemble music still carries much of the prestige of the past and, as such, can be heard in five-star hotel lobbies and at festivals, perhaps providing the musical accompaniment to a traditional Thai dance. Although no longer mandatory in school curriculums, many Thai children still choose to learn a traditional Thai musical instrument and join a musical ensemble in after-school classes.

The three different styles of Thai musical ensembles are *pi-phat* (wind and percussion instruments), *khrueang sai* (bowed string instruments) and *mahori* (bowed string instruments mixed with *pi-phat*).

PLUCKED FROM THE GODS

Both the distinctively sweet sound of the *sueng*, a four- or six-stringed hardwood fretted lute, or the larger *jakhae*, which sits on the floor, play an important role in any musical ensemble.

Made of hardwood and with 42 strings, the string instrument *khim* is struck by two flexible bamboo sticks tipped with leather to create a very peaceful and graceful sound. The *phin* is the Thai guitar/lute of choice for folk music (*molam*) musicians. It is immediately recognizable as it has just two or three metal strings and quite often is decorated with a mythical dragon headstock.

JAKHAE

KHAEN

KHIM

CHILDREN OF THE FIELDS

Many of Thailand's most popular musical genres from the 20th century originated in rural parts of the country. In fact, *luk thung*, widely considered the Thai equivalent of country music, translates as 'songs from children of the fields'. Although contemporary *luk thung*, accompanied by electric guitars and drums, sounds dramatically different from the easy swaying sounds of songs from what many consider the 'golden era' of the 1960s, the crooning style, the subject matter of unrequited love and the gentle rhythm remain largely unchanged.

It was quite common for Thai orchestras to tour Europe and America in the latter part of the 19th and early 20th centuries. This gradually died out when it came to be considered 'backwards' and 'old fashioned' during Thailand's nationalistic World War II period.

MUSIC AND DANCE

The most common Thai ensemble and the one that tourists are most likely to be exposed to is the wind and percussion *pi-phat*. Principal instruments include the *ranat ek* and *ranat thum* (Thai xylophones), the *kong wong* (a circular set of differently shaped gongs that are hit with two beaters) and the lead instrument, the highly characteristic *pi* (Thai oboe).

Traditional Thai percussion is often provided by a combination of the *thon*, a goblet-shaped, bongo-like drum, typically played alongside the small, shallow-framed *rammana* drum, which produces a comparatively much lighter and softer sound.

BAWDY, YET CULTURAL

Thai folk music, known generically as *molam*, also has rural roots. The *molam* singing style is much faster paced than *luk thung*, and is generally accompanied by a melody provided by the *khaen*, a mouth organ made from bamboo. *Molam* subject matter is considered rather risqué for Thai audiences, with the lyrics often relying upon Thais' love of puns and double entendres.

In 2012, the Jim Thompson Farm in Nakhon Ratchamisa province, which cultivates mulberry bushes for silk production, initiated a project to preserve Isan culture, including *molam*. In 2014, the farm launched an exhibition, 'Joyful Khaen, Joyful Dance', in Bangkok and other provinces in the northeast. Dubbed Molam 101, and now located at the farm, it included information on the different types and uses of *molam*, including how it was used in the political arena to disseminate anti-communist and pro-democracy lyrics.

RESURGENCE OF INTEREST

While traditional Thai music genres like *molam* and *luk thung* are becoming less popular with younger Thais as more choose to shake their bodies to either Western or carbon-copy Thai versions of Western music, there are still groups, such as the Paradise International Molam Band, that are helping to keep the traditional torch alive.

The slightly odd-looking band, often described as a sort of Oriental Rolling Stones, consists of two young Bangkok-born Thai indie rockers, two older Isan-born *molam* stars, a British percussionist, and the man who put it all together, DJ Maft Sai.

The Paradise International Molam Band sounds exactly like it looks, but there are times when it does all come together in a wonderful and, most importantly, experimental way, with familiar driving Western bass rhythms side by side with idiosyncratic snake charm-like Thai melodies.

In some of the more hispter areas of Bangkok, *molam* and *luk thung* have now gone full circle, becoming niche, almost counterculture, with bars like Studio Lam attracting an international audience alongside young Thais, who turn up to listen to the exotic songs of their grandfather's era.

Down the same Sukhumvit side lane where Studio Lam is situated is DJ Maft Sai's record store Zudrangma, which contains an awesome collection of original and reissued classic and modern *molam* vinyl records.

MR MOLAM DJ Maft Sai spends most of his time promoting old Thai music, in particular *molam*, through three inexplicably linked areas—a music label that reissues *molam* hits; his experimental *molam* band, The Paradise International Molam Band, which once opened for Damon Albarn; and Studio Lam, a bar that plays and hosts regular *molam* events.

Although born in Bangkok, DJ Maft Sai left Thailand at the age of 11 and moved between the UK and Australia. It was in London, when he was in his twenties, that he started being a DJ, but back then he was focused more on music from Africa or reggae, or Middle Eastern music, in fact, most genres other than Thai. That all changed when he moved back to Thailand in 2007. Visiting a record store in search of some vinyl records, he picked up a few *molam* and *luk thung* record sleeves, and so began a discovery of traditional Thai music that led him from the hip Bangkok lounges to the Isan rice fields and back again.

When were you first exposed to molam? I first heard it when I was a kid, but nothing that really made me feel connected to it. When I moved back to Thailand I started listening properly, and was more open-minded. I had no expectations but when I found it, it was wow, especially the 1970s experimental music, when each band was trying to get its signature sound and rhythm. There were lots of influences in 1970s *molam*, including disco and Western rock. I realized that nobody from Europe or even my friends from Bangkok had heard this kind of music before. People were generally negative about it and asked me why I was into taxi driver music.

So you decided to put on an event? We—British percussionist Chris Menist and I—said we should do a party that showcased all this great music. It wasn't a business plan, we just thought "If it works, great, if not, no problem." Our first party was in 2009. It had very little promotion. About 200 people turned up for it, two-thirds foreigners and about a third Thais.

After working on the *The Sound of Siam—Leftfield Luk Thung, Jazz & Molam in Thailand 1964–75* compilation record, where I had to source old photographs, conduct interviews and get information from the artists themselves, I started wanting to see these artists play live, so I went to Isan to knock on some doors and ask them to come to the capital to play. Some of the artists were difficult to get hold of. Many had retired or gone back to the rice fields. Some thought I was joking: "You're going to pay me to come down to Bangkok?"

How did molam veterans take to performing in Bangkok? After I booked one of the artists, Angkanang Kunchai, a huge star from the 1970s, and showed her the venue in Ekamai, an upmarket area in Bangkok, she said she couldn't believe foreigners or even Bangkok people would dance to her music, but they did. Networking with other artists started from there.

So how did your own band, Paradise International Molam Band, start off? I always dreamt of forming a more experimental *molam* band. I talked with a lot of artists but many asked me why I wanted to change *molam*, because in Thai culture you don't break the rules or do things your teacher has not taught you. But, for me, it's better than having the culture frozen. The band has two main groups of guys really, the young Bangkok guys, the drummer and guitarist, who had zero *molam* experience, and the older Isan guys, a 75-year-old *khaen* player and a mid-50s *phin* player. There's also Chris on percussion. In 2012, when we first started, it was very hard and there were arguments, but the more time we spent together, the more we gelled. After our first gig in Vietnam, there wasn't a division any longer, it was a big bonding experience.

What countries have you played in? We've done two tours in Europe. The first time we went for 11 days and did nine shows in six countries. In Poland, we were the stand-in for Solange, so it was the main stage, at prime time. We got a great response. People danced and even crowdsurfed to a *molam* show.

What's next? We want to do 21st-century *molam*, so we're focusing on more reinterpretation projects and remixes. We want to do dub and reggae versions and also some electronic remixes. A lot of the time we're working with *molam* musicians and they're poor. When they're struggling to find food for the family, they're not thinking creatively. They get a gig and they have to do what is asked of them to get paid. This is a platform for them. All entrance fees for the nights go to the musicians, so at least they have a platform to be creative and they get to keep all the sales of the vinyl records that we cut.

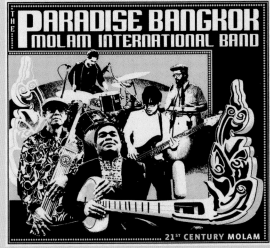

THE FOREIGN FACE OF THAI MUSIC

It is surprising, considering the very traditional and rural roots of the genre that two of *luk thung*'s biggest stars from the turn of the century were foreigners. Fluent in Thai and masters of the subtle nuances of pronunciation, the blonde and blue-eyed Jonas Anderson of Swedish descent, and Christy Gibson, of English and Dutch descent, grew up together in the Isan countryside.

Jonas and Christy now regularly perform together up and down the country. Both admit that when they first began performing, many Thais regarded it as 'slightly weird', but they were quick to change their minds when they actually heard them sing.

CHRISTY GIBSON

JONAS ANDERSEN

SONGS FOR LIFE

Thailand in the mid-1970s will forever be remembered for its student protests, which found political expression in both the arts—Art for Life—and music—Songs for Life. In 1976, students flocked to the campus of Thammasat University, founded by pro-democracy activist and former prime minister Pridi Banomyong, to protest against the return of controversial former prime minister and army general Thanom Kittika-

chorn. On October 6, the military was deployed, alongside right-wing Thais who feared that the students were, in fact, protesting for communist rule. At least 46 students were killed according to official accounts, but other reports that say it was more like 100.

Pleng pheua chiwit (Songs for Life) is a sort of musical hybrid of folk, blues and rock. One of the most famous groups in this genre was Caravan, a four-piece band of former Ramkhamheang University students. Caravan used traditional Thai musical instruments like the *phin* and *wut* (panpipes), alongside guitars. As well as songs with a strong political commentary, Caravan also sang many that romanticized rural Thai life. Their most famous hit, *Khop Kap Kwai* (Man and Buffalo),

told of the special bond between the Thai rice farmer and his buffalo, but also contained various anti-Thanom regime messages.

A band from the early 1980s, Carabao ('buffalo' in Tagalog) was to take the genre of music and run with it, bringing electric guitars and more musically complex scores and rhythms to it. The message remained the same, however, of protest and of giving Thai people, especially the disenfranchised Thai farmer, a voice.

There are few Thai bands nowadays that have managed to captivate the nation's imagination and represent them as a whole like the student bands of the 1970s and 1980s. Contemporary bands like Slur are controversial for the sake of it and carry confused, sensationalist messages, such as in their song *Hitler*, which is apparently about the sheep-like way music companies produce songs.

TAKING A BITE OUT OF THE MUSIC INDUSTRY

Yellow Fang, an all-girl band who play instruments and sing, is a great example of young Thai sisters doing it alone. Without a record label or manager, Yellow Fang promote themselves through social media and YouTube and attract sizeable crowds to the gigs they play in Bangkok and the surrounding areas. Their solid sound and their resistance to cutesy love songs in favor of more meaningful and deeper lyrics have earned them a loyal following at home and also in Japan.

There are many more Thai bands, singers and artists who, through the power of pirate radio shows, Internet radio shows and indie music clubs and pubs, are able to produce music that they, and by extension Thai youth, want to hear. Just don't expect to hear or see them on mainstream Thai TV, radio or concert stages.

With its cacophony of bells, honks, barks and songs, Thailand is a country that never sleeps. It's way too noisy for that.

THAILAND: THE NOISIEST COUNTRY IN THE WORLD

Thailand is perhaps one of Southeast Asia's noisiest and yet most melodic countries. With beeps, barks and all manner of bells, the noise never seems to let up. Even at a suburban home, a peaceful afternoon is quite often interrupted by a passing truck with a loudspeaker mounted on its roof crawling through neighborhood streets advertising the latest condominium, car or beauty cream. There is also a smorgasbord of different street vendors that take to Thai suburbia to plug their wares, whether food, brooms or toys, each of whom has its own particular honk or horn.

Leaving the safe confines of the home, you'll be ushered, warned and beckoned through shrill whistles from car parking attendants to security guards. Even an aimless and innocent stroll around a shopping center is likely to include a verbal assault by a 'Pretty' clutching a microphone extolling the virtues of the latest car oil. Out in the carpark, there will be little respite as you encounter an aerobics class, music at full blast.

Noise continues throughout the evening with TVs blaring from roadside restaurants and music from karaoke bars competing with live music from nightclubs and bars.

When all that dies down, there's just enough time to grab a few hours' sleep before the morning chants from the Buddhist temples or Islamic morning calls to prayer begin at sunrise.

When communicating with Thai people, noise levels are often used as a barometer of familiarity. Whereas the first few encounters are likely to be conducted in little more than a whisper, when you do make a Thai friend, voices are raised to an eyebrow-raising level. Whether this is a device with which to bypass or knock down walls of restraint or to let the whole world know you are friends, it can be quite startling. So when the barista at your local cafe begins shouting her greeting in the morning, you know that you've made a friend, perhaps for life.

BLIND BUSKERS

As Thailand has a woeful welfare system, many of the country's disabled or impaired are either taken care of by their families or undertake the task themselves. Two common lines of work for the nation's blind or visibly impaired are as masseurs and buskers.

Often operating in twos, but sometimes on their own, the blind trawl through markets or busy thoroughfares with a microphone in one hand crooning popular *luk thung* hits, and a plastic cup for donations in the other.

DANCE COMPETITIONS

Although the risqué lyrics of legendary *molam* singer Ken Dalao have been replaced by the likes of Katy Perry, and the *khaen* has been swapped for digital decks, Thai youth still like to dance and take every opportunity to do so in Thai nightclubs and football stadiums and, of course, at festivals.

There are all manner of dance competitions held throughout the year, ranging from B-Boy to synchronized street dance competitions. One of the most popular annual dance competitions is the Seacon Square Cheerleading Championships.

Vanquish, a group from Dhurakij Pundit University, won the 2014 championships in which 21-year-old Oum stood atop the collective's human pyramids of 24 students—nine women and 15 men—and generally got flipped and spun any which way. Although she studied traditional Thai dancing when she was young, Oum found that she was more drawn to jazz and contemporary Western dance. "I love dancing. It makes me feel happy and healthy. I decided to practice cheerleading because I saw it at my university and it looked so much fun and I realized I could also use my gymnastic skills." Her favorite part of the routine is always the same— the stunts.

Despite wearing an American cheerleading outfit and performing American dance moves to American music, Oum believes that Thai dance is a valuable part of the unique identity of Thailand that should be maintained. An identity, she believes, echoing more and more Thai artists, shouldn't necessarily be imprisoned in the past or left to stagnate in the present. "Whatever the dance, whether jazz or hip hop or anything else, we should try to bring the unique Thai aspects to it. This is a good thing and is sure to ensure its popularity in the future."

COUNTERPART COPIES

The Thai music industry invariably releases Thai replicas of pop stars or hits currently doing the rounds in the international market. Thai superstar hip hop group Thaitanium is a great example of this, but there are also Thai versions of R&B divas and a large number of boy bands modeled and piggy-backing on the success of various K-Pop bands.

Because the Thai music industry views counterfeit bands as a surefire way to make a hit, it is difficult for genuine, authentic Thai bands to succeed or even reach a wider audience. This is further exacerbated by the popularity of TV talent shows like *The Voice* and *Thailand's Got Talent*. Some do make it though and manage to carve out a niche in the burgeoning indie scene.

MY CAR IS LOUDER **THAN YOURS**

A curious and surprisingly legal form of entertainment up and down the country are the makeshift parties formed from huge numbers of cars and trucks that meet and park, usually in the same place and time each week. Here, trucks with gaudy lights and monstrous sound systems complete for the loudest vehicle in the lot.

Some of the promoted, sponsored, marketed and arranged events feature coyote dancers who take to the car roofs (hopefully minus heels to prevent paintwork damage) to perform sexy dances. In reality, most events are comprised of car owners in their thirties who stand around with what appears to be the sole aim of impressing young teenage lads.

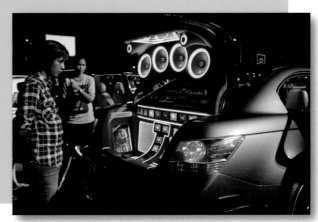

@johnwinyu

@fuxsuxlux

No mentions. No one, I guess.

SpokeDark

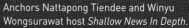

Anchors Nattapong Tiendee and Winyu Wongsurawat host *Shallow News In Depth.*

THE BEWILDERING WORLD OF THAI TV

From the perspective of a non-Thai, there are few things as perplexing as the nationwide popularity of Thai TV variety/game shows. These studio-based productions are filmed in front of a live studio audience and are on virtually every night. They feature bad costumes, worse acting, poor sound quality and the kinds of games and activities that would have been deemed too lowbrow and childish for a 1970s kid's TV show.

In true Thai fashion, the shows are also incredibly loud. Presenters, actors and guests shout, scream and exclaim, perhaps to compete with the insane number of special effects. Whoops and honks and tinks and tonks are used for everything, from the sitting down of an overweight person to a double-take of somebody who has just said something 'outrageous'.

One of the best-known stars of the Thai TV variety show is Petchtai 'Mum Jokmok' Wongkamlao, who started out as a comedian in the Bangkok club scene. These clubs are, in fact, more like dining establishments with stages, which put on various forms of entertainment throughout the night. The Thai TV variety show is basically a celebrity-enhanced televised version of these live entertainment shows that includes a mix of music, games, stand-up comedy and dancing.

Although the popularity of these clubs has dwindled in recent years in proportion to the increased popularity of the TV shows, the themes, the exaggerated comical characters (dwarves, fat people, *kathoey*), the worshiping of celebrities, the audience integration, and the 'fun' and games have remained the same.

SUSPICIOUS SOAPS

Another incredibly popular TV program is the soap opera, both foreign (mainly Korean) and home-grown. Korean soap operas and dramas tend to be highly aspirational, with perfectly groomed, beautiful men and women with flawless white skin in high-powered jobs in the city, and the eternal struggle associated with finding the right partner.

Although Thai soap operas are called *lakhon*, after the traditional dance drama of the same name, they are certainly not as highbrow. They are incredibly stylized and very melodramatic, with cameramen

often given more than liberal license to use the camera zoom. Characters are two-dimensional. They ham it up, overreact and even talk to themselves for purposes of exposition. Much like its highbrow namesake, Thai soap operas rehash stories from the *Ramakien*, with the classic characters of good, evil and silly made up for the modern era and represented as Bangkok businessmen, doting beauty queens, foolish friends, cackling *kathoey* and evil elders.

Recurring themes include lovers overcoming obstacles to finally come together. Usually the obstacle takes the form of a 'bad' woman who tries to seduce and wrest the man away from the 'good' woman. Another theme is righting a wrong and solving injustice. At the end of a drama, which usually lasts about 30 episodes, everything is resolved, all conflicts have been dealt with and everyone lives happily ever after.

POLITICS ARE NO JOKE....

The political situation in Thailand and its never-ending string of scandals, military coups, protests, riots and killings lends itself to a real-life *lakhorn*, and is certainly nothing to laugh at unless, of course, you are the writers or anchors

Left Thai soap operas often come under fire for romanticizing rape.

Above There was nothing much to watch on Thai TV in the latter part of 2014.

MUAY THAI TELEVISION

While Thai women have their TV soap operas and variety shows, the equivalent for the Thai male are televised fights of Muay Thai. Although there is the odd televised fight during the week, the majority of match-ups occur at the weekend, when it is a very common to see crowds of Thai men huddled around a TV screen shouting obscenities and encouragement in equal measure.

Whether at restaurants, taxi stands, bars or homes, a large number of Thai men stop whatever they're doing to watch the local fight or, better still, a big national fight. With gambling being illegal in Thailand, many are, of course, just watching it for the sport.

of the YouTube comedy sensation *Jor Kaw Teun* (Shallow News In Depth). The news show is described as having a Western-style biting humor because its scripts, written by a Thai-American brother and sister, are heavily laced with satire and sarcasm. Although the show has been running since 2009, it became more popular at the onset of the 2014 protests, when an increasing number of Thais tried to make sense of the nonsensical happenings in their country.

Episodes tried to decipher how blocking voting booths was democratic, how a corrupt billionaire could be the champion of the poor, and many other such contradictions amid the chaos of life. The feeling of the people was, if you can't laugh at the political situation in Thailand, you'd have to cry.

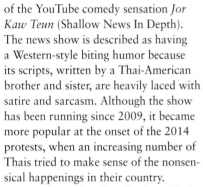

Petchtai 'Mum Jokmok' Wongkamlao prepares to get a pie in the face on a Thai variety show.

THAI TV, A REAL TURN OFF

In 2014, as in the 2006 military coup, the army seized all TV stations, effectively shutting down the channels that had been broadcasting political speeches. Once again, producers of Thai TV programs had a strict mandate of what could and could not be shown, the latter basically any content that was deemed defamatory of the military's mission to restore order, peace and, most importantly, happiness, to the people of Thailand. TV schedules were thus dramatically altered until the latter part of the year and many channels simply ran an image of the NCPO logo.

The Internet and users of social media also came under similar scrutiny and restrictions. As part of the NCPO's aim of restoring order, a ban on gatherings of more than five people was introduced. Protesters therefore found new and weird ways of expressing their opposition to the coup, including eating sandwiches in public, reading a copy of George Orwell's *1984* in public and giving the *Hunger Games'* three-fingered salute. In June 2014, the performing of that movie's signal of silent dissent was also banned in public.

THAI FILM

It is of little surprise considering the Thais' fascination with myths, folklores, spirits and love stories that the most successful Thai movie of all time is *Pee Mak*. Indeed, the one genre that is almost guaranteed to capture public interest is the Thai horror movie.

Pee Mak (Brother Mak) is a romcom based on an old legend in Thai folklore. It follows the story of male protagonist Mak who, upon becoming a soldier, has to leave his pregnant wife (Nak) at home in the country. During the war, he makes four good friends and at the end of the skirmish, takes them back to his village only to find that his wife is now a ghost, or rather his four friends discover that. The rest of the movie is about his friends trying to convince Mak of the fact. Many movies, cartoons, books and even musicals have been made based on the tale of *Mae Nak Phra Khanong* (The Lady of Phra Khanong) and a shrine to Mae Nak on the outskirts of Bangkok in Phra Khanong attracts hundreds of visitors every day.

When released in 2013, *Pee Mak* captured the imagination of the country and the box office, and became the highest grossing domestic film of all time, earning over one billion baht (US$33 million). This unprecedented success

earned it the honor of gracing the cover of the motion picture industry magazine *The Hollywood Reporter*.

CAMERAS ROLLING

The first cinema was opened in Thailand in 1905 by a Japanese company and was therefore called the Japanese Cinematograph. In those days, Japanese films were almost exclusively shown, which led to all moving pictures being referred to as *nang yipun*, with European and American movies bearing the collective term *nang farang*. Such productions were called *nang* after the shadow puppet plays *nang yai*.

Thailand's home-grown movie industry is believed to have begun in 1927, with the Hollywood co-produced silent movie *Nang Sao Suwan* (Miss Suwanna of Siam), about a beautiful young woman who attracts many men but is ultimately unable to find her soulmate. Unfortunately, this movie, like many early Thai films, has since been lost.

PEE MAK

Silent movies, shown in cinemas with ensembles and narrators, only lasted for a few years in Thailand. By the late 1920s, many 'talkies' were being imported, which ultimately superseded the silent movies in popularity. Silent movies were translated live, on the spot, by an expert dubber who read the dialogue of both the male and female characters into a microphone at the rear of the theater. Many of the Thai dubbers had quite a following and often shared equal billing on movie posters.

Foreign Films Shot in Thailand

Thailand's beautiful natural landscapes and relatively low movie production costs make the country a natural choice for foreign film-makers.

Some of the more famous international movies set and filmed in Thailand include *The Big Boss* (1971) starring Bruce Lee; the James Bond movie *The Man with the Golden Gun* (1974); and *The Deer Hunter* (1978). *Rambo: First Blood Part II* (1985) starring Sylvester Stallone was set in Vietnam but filmed in Thailand. The 1990s saw another James bond movie, *Tomorrow Never Dies* (1997), filmed in the country. The hugely popular *The Beach* (2000), which catapulted Leonardo DiCaprio's career, was also filmed in Thailand. In *Star Wars III*, the Wookie kingdom of Kashyyyk was filmed in Krabi and parts of Phuket. *The Impossible*, *Hangover II* and *Only God Forgives* are other hugely profitable movies made in Thailand in recent years.

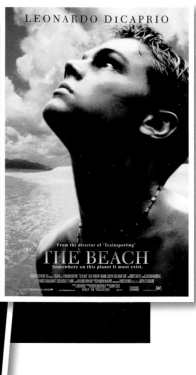

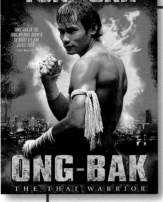

In the 1930s, many Thai movie production companies could not afford to make sound movies and therefore just made silent films with the intention of getting them dubbed at the theaters.

CENSORS AND SENSIBILITY

Much like TV, the Thai film industry is heavily controlled and censored and must pass a series of rules regarding sex, violence and other things that can and cannot be shown. The rules and regulations have, since the 1930 Film Act, been enforced and monitored by civil servants, members of the aristocracy and police officials.

THE 'NEW WAVE'

From the late 1990s, a new wave of critically acclaimed Thai films were released. They included *Jan Dara*, an erotic drama based on a novel about an unloved young man who uses sex as currency in which to control his life and those around him. A few years later, the controversial *Blissfully Yours* by Apichatpong Weerasethakul was released. The ostensibly Thai romance went on to win the Un Certain Regard prize at the 2002 Cannes Film Festival, an awesome achievement by a Thai film that was only bettered when Apichatpong released *Uncle Boonamee Who Can Recall His Past Lives* and won the Palme d'Or at the 2010 Cannes Film Festival.

Up until 2005, the national police force was responsible for vetting and approving every Thai film made. This changed when the Ministry of Culture took over. Every year, many Thai and international movies are banned in Thailand.

THE THAI FILM MUSEUM

For those who are interested in learning more about the Thai film industry, its cinematographers, actors, actresses, writers and directors, a visit to the Thai Film Museum on the outskirts of Bangkok, in Nakhon Pathom, is well worthwhile. Founded by Thai film historian Dome Sukwong, information is in both English and Thai. Movie buffs can wander around a replica of the now demolished Sri Kung Talkie Company to get an idea of how and where classic Thai movies were made. They can view authentic working equipment from the early days of film production, and also see how films were projected.

The Thai Film Museum also showcases many vintage movie posters, stills and props from old sets.

THE FATHER OF THAI FILM

Although he began making movies with his first short film *Tang* in 1937, Rattana Pestonji's long and influential career, up to his untimely death in 1970, was to earn him the title of 'Father of Contemporary Thai Film'. His first movie, about a young Thai girl, was much lauded and won the young Thai-Indian film-maker the Alfred Hitchcock award.

THAILAND'S POSTER BOY

Rather appropriately named, Santi (Movie) Tuntipantarux has been collecting movie posters for the last 18 years, and professes to have more than 3,000, the largest collection of movie posters in Southeast Asia. He traces his love of the memorabilia back to when, as a young artist, he used to draw movie posters by hand.

Santi's shop in Bangkok is tiny but is never short of customers. "Many foreigners come and visit my shop. Some phone ahead to order posters. I have posters of Thai movies and American and Asian movies. Old Thai movie posters are the hardest to find."

The price of the posters depends on how rare they are, and ranges from 100 to 100,000 baht (US$ 3 to $3,000). Those for the original *Star Wars* movie are the most popular purchases, but it is the *Godfather* poster that is Santi's favorite, and the one he is most unwilling to sell because it bears the signature of the director, Francis Ford Coppola. He also keeps hundreds of posters in his small Bangkok apartment, protected by plastic coverings, that he says he will never sell as they are too rare.

The most expensive poster he currently stocks is the 6.7 ft x 6.7 ft (2 m x 2m) poster for the original 1966 *Batman* movie. This is on sale for the princely sum of 100,000 baht (US$3,000).

For Santi, working with movie posters is a labor of love. As well as being in his shop all day every day, he is often online until late each night searching for new acquisitions.

In the early 1950s, Rattana formed his own film studio, Hanuman Films Company, where he often alternated between cinematographer and director and on some occasions worked as both. Unfortunately, few of his films became commercial successes. After making his last movie, the romantic *Nahmtaan Mai Waan* (Sugar Is Not Sweet) in 1965, he retired.

Rattana continued to support the industry, however, because he believed it very much needed it. He co-founded and was the head of the Thai Film Producers Association and would often give talks and lobby government bodies to get involved and promote the Thai film industry. Indeed, Rattana collapsed and shortly after died of a massive heart attack while giving a speech to Thai film producers and government officials aimed at rousing government support for the industry. His final words were reported to be: "I've spent every baht I

ever earned on my productions and now I have to make adverts just to survive. The foreign film distributors have been preying on Thai cinemas…."

A few days after his death, the government set up the Thai Film Promotion Board, but to this day there is no

government aid or support given to the Thai film industry. The Hanuman Films Company is still run by his surviving family members. It no longer makes films, but instead provides equipment and technical assistance to visiting foreign film-makers.

GOING IT ALONE

As a way of encouraging and incentivizing the Thai movie industry, in the 1970s huge import taxes were imposed on foreign movies. As a result, many Hollywood film studios boycotted Thailand, meaning that Thai film studios had to pick up the slack. This they did, making a record 150 films in 1978 alone. Stand-out 1970s movies include the 1979 release *Plae Kao* (The Scar), a tragic love story set in an old and nostalgic Bangkok, which made a name for the protagonist, Sorapong Chatree, who to this day is an actor who is never too far from a *lakhon* or two on Thai television.

This era of the Thai film industry is also remembered by many for the death of Mitr Chaibancha who was the lead actor and director of the Thai superhero movie *Insee Thong* (Red Eagle). Mitr died when he fell from a helicopter while shooting the final scene. In the initial release, the footage was left in.

KONG'S TOP FIVE

Ong Bak Martial arts movie about a country boy who travels to Bangkok to retrieve the stolen head of a sacred Buddha statue.
"It's a silly film, but it's well made and clear as to what it wants to be."

Uncle Boonamee Who Can Recall His Past Lives By the same director as *Tropical Malady*, this film once again weaves Thai myth and folklore around a plot, which this time is of a man who, on his deathbed, begins to look back at his past lives.
"Nobody thought a Thai film could win a Palme d'Or, so when this movie won, nobody could quite believe it."

PEE MAK

Pee Mak Romantic horror comedy about a returning soldier who fails to realize that his wife has become a ghost.
"It made such a huge amount of money and commercial success. It made Thai people feel confident in their own cinema. If the viewers are confident, then the industry can carry on."

Tropical Malady Praised by Quentin Tarantino, this film by Apichatpong Weerasethakul about a same-sex romance between a soldier and a country boy, with a seemingly unrelated folk tale tagged on the end, got mixed reactions when released.
"It's an art film. Some art films are bad, but this is very good. It touches viewers in a powerful way."

Phrae Dum (Black Silk) Shown at the 1961 Berlin International Film Festival, this crime drama about a mobster falling in love with a widow was Thailand's first film noir ('dark' film).
"One of the best of Rattana Pestonji's movies. He was one of the pioneers and visionaries and very much paved the way for modern Thai cinema."

UNCLE BOONAME WHO CAN RECALL HIS PAST LIVES

TROPICAL MALADY

BLACK SILK

CRITICALLY SPEAKING

Kong Rithdee is Thailand's foremost film critic and a regular at Cannes, Berlin and an assortment of Asian film festivals. He is also a Chevalier dans l'Ordre des Arts et des Lettres (Knight in the Order of Arts and Letters), an award bestowed upon him by the French Ministry of Culture for his contributions to film.

Kong started writing film reviews at the *Bangkok Post* in 1997, a key year, he says, in the history of Thai film. This was when Nonzee Nimibutr's *Dang Bireley's and Young Gangsters* was released, a pivotal movie by an influential director, both of which are often credited as instrumental in the ushering in of the 'New Wave' of Thai cinema.

What are the main differences between Thai and US films? Content-wise, there's more variety in the US. We are good at horror films, comedies, action films, but not at social issues or challenging people to think. I don't want to say that's a good or bad thing, that's just the way it is.

For Thai people, we regard film as entertainment, but elsewhere it can be culture or it can be something else, but in Thailand, when a film tries to be something else, the audience feels like this is not right, so people don't respond to it with the same passion or level of understanding.

Do you see this changing? Slowly, yes.... *Pee Mak* is a good example. It's a quality film that also entertained people. We need consistency to keep Thai films going.

Besides *Pee Mak*, why do you think so few Thai films have been successful internationally? The quality of the film is the main thing. We can argue about culture, taste, sophisticated stuff like that, but it's the quality of the film that is the main factor.

We often try to compare Thai film to Korean cinema, but Koreans can export their films very easily. You know what Korean film is. It's a brand and you can sell it easily, but with Thai cinema there is no brand.

What do you think of the way Thailand is often portrayed in international movies? It's always the same exotic stuff. One of the first films ever made and shown in Thailand, *Chang: A Drama of the Wilderness* (1927), was about an elephant attacking a village in the 'Jungles of Northern Siam'. That was 80 years ago, and even today it seems that every film shot in Thailand must have an elephant in it. International perception has not changed that much.

I think there's a tendency by most film-makers to simplify everything, to see things in the extreme, because that's the easy way to understand things—from the spiritual and calm, the Buddhist temples to the other side of Thailand, Patpong and the colorful debauched amusement park industry. These two extremes are true and both exist, so to include them in films is OK, but it also means that if you are simplifying things then you are also ignoring the nuances.

What do you hope to see from the Thai film industry in the next 10 years? We need more diversity. We've proved ourselves with horror films. Now we need drama films and historical and political films. We need films that reflect the social situation.

Censorship needs to be relaxed, and the attitude of the state towards culture should be modernized and opened up. The Thai government needs to decide how it sees the film industry, and then adapt its policy.

Are you optimistic? Not really, at least not for the next five years or so.

HAND-DRAWN POSTERS TO ATTRACT AUDIENCES

Whether for their retro appeal or as a reverent nod for Thai tradition, hand-drawn movie posters are still used to advertise the latest films.

This is not only the case in the rural areas but also in the larger and wealthier cities of Bangkok and Phuket, for example.

In the past, and to a lesser extent today, this artistic route was quite common for aspiring Thai artists from working-class backgrounds who were unable to go to art colleges and would instead try and find an apprenticeship at a company specializing in movie posters.

An apprentice would be responsible for everything, from mopping his master's brow to coloring in the less detailed sections of a poster.

With each release, numerous versions of the same poster are created, enough for every roving movie van.

THAI ART AND ARTISTS

Thailand has a wealth of exceptionally talented artists producing unique and wondrous works that have, unfortunately, not received the same international acclaim or recognition as other Asian artists.

BUDDHIST AND ROYAL ART

Historically speaking, Thai art has its origins, both in terms of subject matter and purpose of creation, in either the temples (Buddhist art) or the palaces (Royal art). Sculptures, for example, were almost exclusively of Buddha's image, while paintings and murals were reserved primarily for decoration of palaces and temples.

Up until the mid-19th century, perspective drawing was rarely used in Thai art. Rather, the size of a work denoted its importance. In the Sukhothai kingdom, for example, Buddhist sculptors used metaphors as inspiration, explaining why many Buddha statues of the time had shoulders 'as large as an elephant's head' as described in various Pali texts studied at the time.

MODERN THAI ART

Ironically, it is Italian citizen Corrado Feroci, who later became a naturalized Thai citizen called Silpa Bhirasri, who is referred to as the 'Father of Modern Thai Art'. Bhirasri was invited to Thailand in 1923 to teach Western sculpture at the Fine Arts Department of the Ministry of Palace

Prateep Kochabua's *Luang Ta Ma* (Traditional Thai Music).

Thawan Duchanee was almost as recognizable as this 'Untitled' artwork.

THAILAND'S FIRST CELEBRITY PAINTER

In the early 1960s, Thailand's first artist superstar burst onto the scene. Thanks to his long, flowing beard and flamboyant personality, Thawan Duchanee (1939–2014) was instantly recognizable and one of the few Thai artists to receive acclaim in the international arts arena. The Chiang Rai-born artist was once a student of Silpa Bhirasri. Right up to his death, he traveled around the world creating and restoring murals and putting on exhibitions containing his unique and striking paintings in bold red and black tones.

As many of his works, which deal with the darkness within humanity, were created using traditional Thai Buddhist art techniques, some of his early pieces were considered blasphemous and were even attacked and defaced in exhibitions. Some Thai intellectuals, however, including renowned author and former prime minister Kukrit Pramoj, were quick to defend him: "His art is to be understood as giving life to myth."

Affairs, and it is this significant date that many regard as the beginning of modern art in Thailand, and the beginning of an era when artistic focus broadened somewhat.

With the ending of Thailand's absolute monarchy and its complicated involvement in World War II, modern Thai art took on new forms and a new purpose. It was during this constantly changing, turbulent political landscape that the Thai government first latched onto the idea that cultural pursuits and arts could also be used as effective tools by which to promote a national identity and establish a sense of pride, unity and the concept of 'Thai-ness'.

Throughout the 1950s, many private galleries opened to showcase and sell art, but it was only after King Bhumibol took up painting in 1959 that art was legitimized as a worthy and noble pursuit that served to solidify the nation's acceptance and love of art.

In the 1970s, politics entered Thai art and it was from here on that artists began using art as a platform to convey messages. During a decade rocked by political instability and student protests, works from the artistic movement Art for Life often dealt with issues of poverty, social problems and political suppression.

Preecha Thaothong in his studio.

Right *The Shape of Light in the Emerald Buddha Temple.*

ART FIT FOR THE KING

There were also many artists in the 1970s and 1980s who never courted controversy and kept Thai art, subject matter and style traditional and pure and thus received recognition and acclaim. Bangkok-born Preecha Thaothong, for example, is currently Assistant Professor in the Thai Art Department at Silpakorn University, which he also attended as a young man.

Preecha was one of seven artists commissioned to provide images for King Bhumibol's book *Mahajanaka* in 1997. Although his work deals with Thai temple forms and design, he is also well known for his exceptional shading to create realistic shade and shadow effects.

THAI ART GOES POP

The 1980s and 1990s saw the establishment of various art groups and an emerging interest from both popular culture and commercial enterprises as magazines rushed to carry articles and interviews with the star artists of the time.

Reflecting the emerging commercial market's interest in the arts and the opportunities it created was the career of Prateep Kochabua who, after graduating from Silpakorn University in the early 1980s, worked for six years as an art director for an advertising agency.

Not for everyone, Prateep's work has been described as grotesque, violent and weird. Indeed, his work would not be out of place on a rock album from the 1970s. It is, in a word, surreal.

Prateep focuses on a variety of subjects and sources of inspiration, including what he sees as the different duties that Thai people are bound to according to where and how they choose to live. His work is thought-provoking and deals with existential and mythical matters, encapsulating this belief, along with frustration that

his work does not get the recognition it deserves. Prateep once told me, "Sometimes I think I should die to paint for gods and the angels. It would be better."

A RETURN TO TRADITIONAL THEMES

It was also during the 1970s, 1980s and 1990s that artists started returning to Buddhism, folklore and tales from the *Ramakien* as subject matter for their art. Popular themes for what was later to become neo-traditional Thai art were scenes of a perfect and traditional bygone era of rural Thailand, a yearning for a lost cultural heritage and the glorification of monarchical leadership. A leader of this form of Thai art is the much-celebrated Chakrabhand Posayakrit, another Silpakorn graduate, who creates serene, peaceful and contemplative 'otherworldly' pieces with mythical characters like Kinnaree.

A true champion of Thai culture and arts, Chakrabhand has also worked on a number of traditional Thai royal puppet restoration projects and created new puppets for his own troupe. Nowadays, the Bangkok-born artist spends much of his time helping to preserve the Thai artistic heritage through the Chakrabhand Posayakrit Foundation, which was established in 2002. Two of the foundation's current projects are the creation of mural paintings in the ordination halls of Wat Tritho-sathep in Bangkok and Wat Khao Sukim in Chantaburi.

LOOKING BACK TO MOVE FORWARD

Like many artists of his generation, Chalermchai Kositpipat began painting movie posters, although he later went on to study Fine Arts at Silpakorn University. Much like Thawan, his early work, murals from the late 1970s, were initially controversial because they combined contemporary scenes and images with traditional Thai temple Buddhist art techniques.

A keen sculptor and designer, Chalermchai was also the architect for the visually stunning Wat Rong Khun (White Temple), built in his native Chiang Rai province. His love of combining the past with the future and the traditional with the contemporary is apparent in his design of the temple, where visitors can see images of Superman and Neo from the *Matrix* among many of his murals. Started in 1997, the temple is scheduled to be finished by 2070. Not one for being shy about extolling his own virtues, he once remarked he was perfect.

Art and Graffiti

Although relatively new, graffiti is an emerging art form in Thailand, especially in the urban areas of Bangkok. Some murals have been commissioned while others, on walls of boarded up and dilapidated buildings, have not. Subject matter is varied and includes monkeys, *manga*-inspired cartoon characters and English lettering. Except for a few odd pieces, it's all unconventionally Thai, which is perhaps the whole point.

Left Veerachab's *The Creator of the Universe*. Below Watcharin with one of his huge artworks. Bottom Romadon creating art on TV.

LIVE ART: FROM THE STREETS TO THE GALLERY

The holiday island of Phuket is home to a tight-knit community of painters, sculptors and photographers.

Former street performer Romadon Suriyan found national fame on TV talent show *Thailand's Got Talent* in 2012 and even made it to the final. The Thai Muslim's live art performances, which included pouring paint over himself and throwing himself at the canvas, dealt with issues of a divided political nation, love, life and death. The fact that he managed to get so far in the competition is indicative of how far Thailand has come as a nation that appreciates art. He now sells traditional Thai coffee, tea and roti bread from his working studio in Phuket.

Another great young artist working in Phuket is Bangkok-born Isara Thaothong, Id8 for short. His work, although created entirely with a simple black marker pen, is incredibly detailed and well thought out but, at the same time, is cartoony, abstract and, perhaps most importantly, lots of fun.

TATTOO ART

Tattoos in Thailand do not carry the same stigma as they do in the West or in other Asian countries. A particular form of tattoo popular in Thailand is *sak yant*, which are typically designs of animals, Buddhist teachings, or spiritual subjects created for the purpose of bringing strength, peace, protection or prosperity to the recipient.

The intricate, distinctive, black-dotted designs are often administered by either monks or shaman with a long bamboo stick or metal spike. *Sak* means 'to tap' and *yant* is short for Yantra, a Sanskrit term used to describe a geometric design that aids in meditation or worship.

Various festivals and mass tattoo ceremonies are held throughout the year, the biggest one being the annual Wai Kru ceremony held at Wat Bang Phra, which attracts around 15,000 people. Here,

Receiving a *sak yant* tattoo can be a serene and spiritual experience.

it's common to see young men become 'possessed' upon absorbing the power of the tattoos. These tattoos are also favored by Thai Muay Thai fighters who get them in the hope it will protect and instill in them an animal-like strength. One of the most popular designs is the *suea* (tiger), a design representing power.

Certain forms of *sak yant* are also popular with Thai women, the most common location being the back of the neck or on the back left shoulder. Famous Hollywood actress Angelina Jolie has a *ha thaew sak yant* tattoo on her shoulder. This is an intricate design of five descending lines that represent different types of success and luck.

Watcharin Rodnit's abstract paintings, which he sometimes creates alongside music at public events, are colorful yet also dark and disturbing. His huge pieces, Watcharin explains, are inspired by the nature of his hometown of Surat Thani. He is the founder of the Chino Art Group, and hopes that one day the local government of the hedonistic holiday island of Phuket will open an art museum. His dream has not yet come true.

Phuket resident, but originally from Uttaradit in the north of Thailand, Veerachan Usahanun's journey to become an artist began rather unconventionally. As the young lead guitarist in a rock band, Veerachan decided to travel to Vienna, Austria, to study music. Discouraged to find out he would need to start from the beginning, Veerachan decided to pursue art instead. He stayed in Austria for 11 years, studying with art professors and helping restore classic paintings in castles scattered around Europe.

After a visit to India, he became fascinated with the origins of the Hindu god Ganesh. When he returned to Thailand, to Bangkok and later Phuket, he embarked on what was to become his largest collection of art, 'The Miracles of Ganesha'. His pieces contain nudity, phalluses, writhing animal/human hybrids, and a dark reimagining of Ganesh, but to Veerachan it is all just fantasy. Veerachan also does commissions and helps crystallize people's visions, dreams and nightmares.

Keep your eyes peeled when examining murals.

Murals of Everyday Life: Moments in Time

Thai murals can be seen in most temples in Thailand. They are often huge in size and typically tell a story or ancient parable from, yes, you guessed it, the *Ramakien*, which tells of Buddha's life before enlightenment. Much like ancient Thai art, the scale and size of murals often relate to importance rather than any kind of accurate perspective. Examples of some of the most interesting and respected murals can be found in Wat Phrao Kaew in Bangkok.

It is usually quite difficult for foreigners to identify a particular Buddhist fable and its characters, but many Thai Buddhists can instantly recognize these. Characters are often repeated within the same piece, and common landscapes include earthy mountains and countrysides, combined with mystical higher planes and mythical beasts. Keep a keen eye out, however, as in some temples, like one recently built in Phuket, visitors are likely to see the odd bit of modern realism thrown into a mural, including love-making couples, drunk foreigners and fighting teenagers.

Murals are often updated or changed when a temple is renovated. In the past, old temples were abandoned whenever a new temple was built, meaning that quite often the murals also fell into disrepair. Nowadays, however, historically significant murals are often restored and maintained.

The Moca Museum

Although there are a number of national museums in Thailand, the most famous and celebrated museum is a privately owned one established by Boonchai Bencharongkul, the 12th richest man in Thailand. The sleek building is a work of

art in itself and looks almost like it has been sculpted from stone. Inside, spread out over five floors, is a wide array of old and contemporary pieces of Thai art spanning several centuries.

THAI LITERATURE

Many of the classic works of Thai literature are believed to have been either lost or destroyed in the kingdom's turbulent years of war.

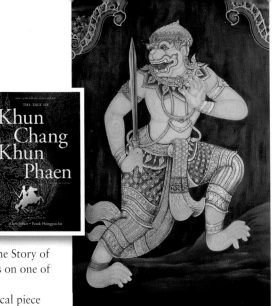

After the sacking of Ayutthaya in 1767, the restoration of Thai literature became the responsibility of Thailand's kings. During the reign of Rama I, and later his son Rama II, a Thai version of the Hindu epic, the *Ramayana*, the *Ramakien* (The Glory of Rama), was written.

Kings Rama V and Rama VI were also writers, who tended to create works that combined Western knowledge and Thai culture. The current king of Thailand, King Bhumibol, has written many books during his reign, including the popular *Mahajanaka* (The Story of Mahajanaka), which focuses on one of Buddha's past lives.

Another important historical piece of Thai literature is the epic poem *The Tale of Khun Chang Khun Phaen*, which was originally a piece of romantic Thai folklore, written down in the early 19th century. Like much of the work until the latter part of the 19th century, it was written in verse form.

THE 20TH CENTURY

In the 20th century, as with most other forms of art, Thai authors began to experiment with style, voice and a broadening of subject matter that dealt with not only royalty and religion. Although much of the emerging literature is aimed at the mass market and deals with the theme of love, there are other authors who tackle more substantial themes and who have had their works translated and published in other languages.

Saneh Sangsuk is, in French translator Marcel Barang's opinion, Thailand's most talented writer working today. Barang has translated a number of Saneh's short stories as well as his widely regarded *Ngao See Khao* (The White Shadow).

Barang avoids the use of computer translations, the scourge of modern-day translation, as he never learned to type in Thai. This means the process is often painstaking as he must translate each Thai word individually before moving them around to form coherent sentences. Although he is almost 70, Barang's ambition is clear: to translate every classic Thai book of note. He believes he is close to realizing his goal. "After my Thai Modern Classics series of 20, I'm afraid there are only second-rate novels left [to translate]."

The playful, yet loyal Hanuman (monkey warrior) is a popular and recurring character in the *Ramakien* epic.

RAMAKIEN'S RUNAWAY SUCCESS

In Thailand, the *Ramayana* was adapted in various ways to infuse Thai culture and context into the stories and was renamed *Ramakien*. The mythology embedded in the tales lent itself easily to the existing Thai belief system of the time, which was a mixture of animism, myths, folklores and Buddhism.

The importance of the *Ramakien* epic to Thailand's literature, arts and culture cannot be overstated. Its stories are, to this day, still recycled and explored in *lakhon* on TV and *khon* on the stage.

Folklore and Its Influence

Folklore and myths have had an enormous impact on the evolution of Thai literature. Perhaps the most important Thai scholar involved in keeping the old stories, oral traditions and folklore alive is Phya Anuman Rajadhon. As well as studying both written and oral Thai folklore, Phya studied Thai sociology and, according to many of his peers and the nation's subsequent scholars, set the foundations for further studies in Thai folklore and Thai cultural awareness in a rapidly modernizing kingdom.

Phya's work included recording the details, names and likenesses of the spirits and ghosts that were reported to have existed throughout Thai villages. Because such records, paintings and writings prior to his work made no mention of particular types of ghosts and spirits, he believed they must have been passed down through oral lore. Phya also studied the different types of amulets and charms used by shopkeepers and local people and the practices of village shamans and witch doctors. Although he had no formal or academic training, Phya wrote many articles, books and research papers on Thai folklore and, thus, he is to a large extent responsible for keeping many aspects of ancient Thai culture alive.

SANEH SANGSUK

Saneh Sangsuk is an award-wining contemporary writer who received the Ordre des Arts et des Lettres (Order of Arts and Letters) Medal from the French Ministry of Culture in 2008 for his contributions to literature. His work has been translated into seven languages. He is perhaps best known for his 1986 semi-biographical novel *Ngao See Khao* (The White Shadow) which, although poorly received in Thailand at the time and deemed scandalous, went on to garner substantial international acclaim and recognition.

Bringing Thai Literature to New Audiences

Frenchman Marcel Barang has been hugely influential in bringing Thai literature to a foreign audience. Since moving to Thailand in 1978, he has translated over 40 Thai novels, short stories and poems into mainly English, but also French. A former journalist, Barang began translating Thai novels out of a love for what he saw as an under-appreciated art form. He has even taken it upon himself to re-translate many Thai books.

Responding to what Barang saw as a "mongrel version in English [of *Si Phaendin, Four Reigns*] in circulation", he set his eyes on one of the most widely regarded Thai classics. Unfortunately, his "complete and faithful translation" was denied publication by the copyright holder.

Barang did, however, get permission to translate many other classic Thai books, although most translations are only available as e-books.

THREE FROM THE SHELF

SRI BURAPHA, the pen name of Kulap Saipradit, wrote from the 1920s to 1960s, and is one of the must-read authors for anyone studying Thai literature. Many of his works have anti-government undertones. Despite this, he is best known for his romantic novel *Khang Lang Phap* (Behind the Painting), a tale of unrequited love and longing shared by a couple who met in Japan while the woman was married to an older man. He wrote much of his anti-government work during the premiership of Phibun-songkhram. As a result, he spent four years in jail and lived his final 16 years in exile in China.

WIN LYOVARIN is best known for writing provocative novels and short stories, but is also credited with encouraging a generation of young Thais to start reading and develop critical thinking skills. He won the S.E.A. Write Award in 1997 for his political novel *Pracha Thippatai Bon Sen Khanan*, which was translated into English in 2003 as *Democracy, Shaken and Stirred*. He won the same award again in 1999 for a collection of short stories.

KUKRIT PRAMOJ has written two accclaimed titles: *Si Phaendin* (Four Reigns) and *Phai Daeng* (Red Bamboo), about royal life and the dangers of communism, respectively. The Thai aristocrat, scholar and politician—he was Thailand's 13th prime minister—focused on writing about contemporary history and various aspects of life. Kukrit was controver-sially accused of plagiarism, with allegations that many of his books followed European literature plots a little too closely, an allegation he vehemently denied.

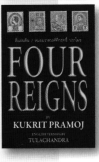

THE RISE OF MANGA

Much like the outside world, the birth of technology and the emerging popularity of smartphones, tablets and apps have had ramifications for the reading habits of Thais. Many read tweet feeds, Facebook statuses and little else. The children and adults who do read, tend to read large type, thin paperback novellas on a range of topics from Hitler to classic boy meets girl or religious tales.

Japanese *manga* translated into Thai is also very popular, with both the young and old being avid readers of these 20 baht (US 60 cents) comics.

Despite the relatively high literacy rate (93 percent), Thailand doesn't have a particularly strong reading culture, and has one of the lowest averages for the number of books read per year per person (five). In 2015, Thais spent just 28 minutes per day reading books.

Most bookstores in Thailand have huge sections dedicated to Japanese *manga*.

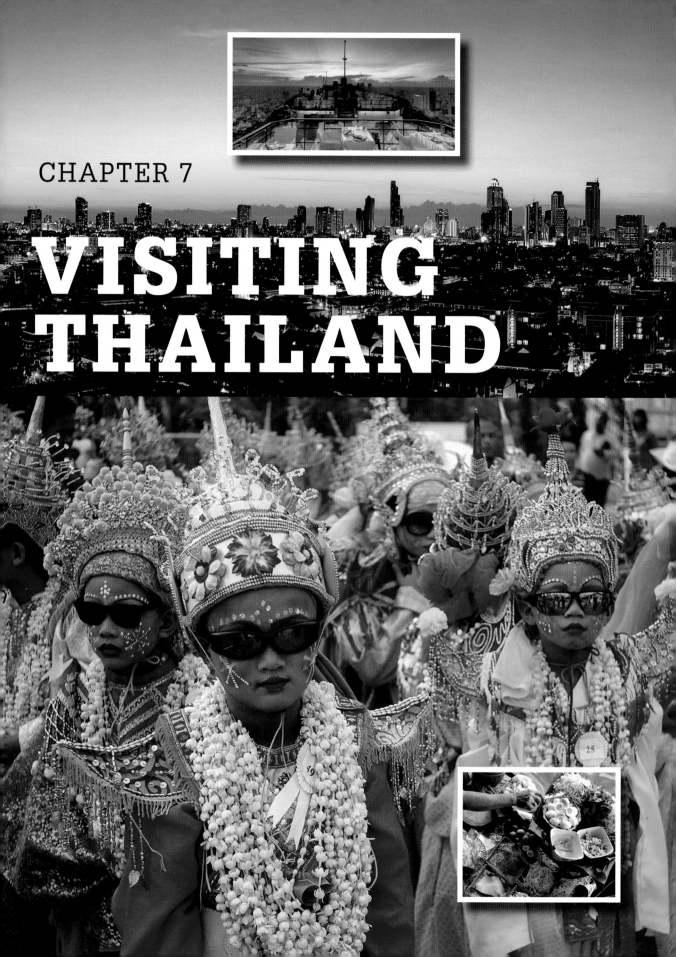

CHAPTER 7

VISITING THAILAND

From the busy metropolis of Bangkok to the idyllic paradise of Phuket, go on a journey that includes the jungles of the north, the beaches of the south and other places of intrigue and interest, such as the culturally rich and artistic center of Chiang Mai. Along the way, learn about the origins of many of Thailand's most colorful, mystical and romantic festivals and what to do and definitely not do whilst in the Land of Smiles.

BANGKOK: THE CITY OF THE FUTURE

Many visitors to the eccentric, chaotic and surprisingly charming city of Bangkok quickly discover why it is often voted best city in the world and also why it remains one of the most visited.

The reasons so many people become enamored with Bangkok are often as long as its original name. When it became the capital of Thailand in 1782, Bangkok was originally known as—take a deep breath—Krungthep Mahanakhon Amon Rattanakosin Mahinthara Yuthaya Mahadilok Phop Noppharat Ratchathani Burirom Udomratchaniwet Mahasathan Amon Phiman Awatan Sathit Sakkathattiya Witsanukam Prasit. That translates loosely as—take another deep breath—The City of Angels, the Great City, the Residence of the Emerald Buddha, the Impregnable City (unlike the City of Ayutthaya) of God Indra, the Grand Capital of the World Endowed with Nine Precious Gems, the Happy City, Abounding in an Enormous Royal Palace that Resembles the Heavenly Abode Where Reigns the Reincarnated God, a City Given by Indra and Built by Vishnukarn.

Thankfully, Bangkok in Thai is known nowadays as simply Krungthep.

In 1767, Thonburi, on the western bank of the Chao Phraya River, was chosen as the capital city of Thailand for its strategic position and convenient geographical location for sea trade. The capital city moved across the river to what is now known as Bangkok in 1782, because it was thought the new location would be more defensible in what was at the time a highly likely Burmese attack.

THE SINKING CITY

Ironically, it is the city's one-time convenient location that is causing geologists to fear that Bangkok is doomed, and will be submerged under water by as early as 2030. The topography and construction of the city, combined with the effects of climate change and a rising sea level, mean Bangkok is actually sinking at a rate of around 1 inch (2.5 cm) per year, with some parts of the city already measuring 3.3 feet (1 m) below sea level.

In the 19th century, Bangkok was known as the Venice of the East, and only the city's temples and royal palaces were on dry land. Homes were either built on bamboo rafts or were, like shops and factories, moored to banks. Over time and to facilitate construction in the city, many canals were built on the city's wetlands and swamplands as short cuts between parts of the city.

The heavy rainfall during the monsoon season (June–October) often results in floods, the worst of which occurred in 2011 when 65 out of the 77 provinces that line the Chao Phraya River were flooded. More than 800 people died and property damage and disruptions to the manufacturing industry caused an estimated loss of 1,425 billion baht (US$45.7 billion). The revenue from tourism was also significantly affected.

Top The Chao Phraya River, 227 miles (365 km) long, flows from the mountains of northern Thailand through the central plains to the Gulf of Thailand.

Far left The BTS Skytrain weaving along Sukhumvit Road.

Left Many high-end hotels act as oases of calm amidst the chaos of the capital.

Issues of dam mismanagement, canals filled with waste that prevents the flow of water, insufficient irrigation infrastructure and disputes over the placement of flood barriers followed. How to prepare the city in the event of future floods continues to be a hot topic during political campaigns.

Plans for large artificial waterways to divert water away from the city have been suggested, along with more regular and efficient draining of reservoirs. But for now, the Bangkok flooding problem seems to be an issue that government officials prefer to manage when it happens rather than solve in the long term.

BANGKOK, WHERE ELSE?

There are certain sections of Bangkok that have remained untouched, and some would argue unspoiled, by the ceaseless modernization of the city. In neglected slums and canal-lined huts, its inhabitants know nothing, or perhaps care even less, about the towering skyscrapers and brand-name stores of Sukhumvit Road.

It is the diversity of the city and the coexistence of so many contrasts that make Bangkok so different and so exciting. It is its familiarity, yet foreign-ness, that gives Bangkok its true identity. Where else can you see barefoot monks collecting alms at daybreak, Louis Vuitton handbag-clutching socialites parading around Siam Paragon in the afternoon and squabbling taxi drivers dotted along roadsides betting on Muay Thai fights in the evening?

It is the coexistence, and in some ways neutralizing effect, of so many opposites that gives Bangkok its true sense of equilibrium and unparalleled freedom. For lunch, you can eat at a makeshift Thai roadside restaurant complete with plastic chairs and a *soi* dog for company, and in the evening dine at one of the city's world-class eateries. It's a city where anything is possible, you just have to have the imagination to make it so.

Bangkok is divided into 50 districts and is home to around 6.5 million people, about 13 percent of the population of Thailand. Owing to its fabulous public transport system, which includes the MRT subway, BTS Skytrain, *tuk tuk*, meter taxis, motorcycle taxis, river boats and water taxis, getting around is relatively easy and cheap.

Silom and the Riverside Because of its strategic and central location along the country's river trade route, the Bangkok Riverside was once the epicenter of all the kingdom's business and industries. Over the years, as the rivers and canals became less vital, most businesses gradually moved inland to the Silom area, which is where Bangkok's financial district is also located.

A visit to the Bangkok Riverside is still essential, however, if only to marvel at how Bangkok city life used to be. There are still plenty of tours and cruises, which are great for seeing many of the city's most beautiful temples, such as Wat Arun (Temple of Dawn). In recent years, certain areas have undergone gentrification, with open-air mall Asiatique, for example, now standing where the docks of the East Asiatic Company used to be.

Silom also contains the infamous Patpong, which was once one of the most famous red-light districts in the world, certainly in Thailand. That rather dubious title has now been passed to the Walking Street in Pattaya. Although Patpong still maintains many of the bars and strip clubs (Go-Go bars) that were opened to accommodate the new wave

of R&R tourism during the Vietnam War, it also shares its space with a generic Thai night bazaar.

A delightful place to spend an early morning or late afternoon when the sun goes down, away from the hustle and bustle of the city, is Lumphini Park. Occupied by protestors for nearly six months during the 2014 protests, the 142 acre (58 ha) park has since been returned to its former lush glory.

Another Silom attraction is the stunning Sri Marlamman Hindu Temple, which dates back to 1860. Colorful and intricately decorated, the temple remains a popular place of worship for visiting and resident Hindus.

Sukhumvit Over the years, the built-up area of Sukhumvit has developed into a mecca for consumerism, with high-rise apartment buildings, shopping malls and the finest restaurants, both roadside and high-end, in the city. Much of the Bangkok nightlife and red-light district scene is also spread around the Sukhumvit-located *soi* (offshoots) of Soi Cowboy and Nana Entertainment Plaza.

There are many different areas and *soi* in Sukhumvit. From the tourist-focused bars, clubs and nightlife of Sukhumvit Soi 11 to the upmarket, fashionable lounges and restaurants in the Ekamai and Thong Lor areas of Sukhumvit Soi 55, there is something for everyone, even a Little Arabia on Sukhumvit Soi 3. All you have to do is explore. With the dedicated Bangkok BTS Sukhumvit Line traversing the most popular areas of Sukhumvit, exploring is easy.

Chinatown Unlike other parts of the city, the charm of Bangkok's Chinatown doesn't lie in museums, palaces or nightlife but in its twisting, turning chaos of alleyways, *soi*, streets and roads. Let yourself become lost in

Bangkok's Chinatown for an afternoon. You will emerge a few hours later tired, clutching exotic spices and beautiful souvenirs after a thoroughly entertaining and enriching cultural experience. It is also, of course, the place to visit if you have a craving for authentic Chinese cuisine.

Bangkok's largest Chinese Buddhist temple, Wat Mangkon Kamalawat, is also located in Chinatown. Dating back to 1872, the beautiful courtyard and entranceway attract hundreds of tourists and worshippers every day.

Little India can also be found near Bangkok's Chinatown. Known locally as Phahurat, it is a great place to visit to soak up the culture, pick up fabrics and souvenirs, and savor the food and drinks.

Bangkok Old City Rattanakosin is the area of Bangkok that has changed the least. Originally used for royal cremations and events, Sanam Luang (Royal Field) has stood at the center of the historic area since the establishment of the capital in 1782. Although its temples, palaces and gardens look much the same as they ever did, they are now dwarfed by Sukhumvit's skyscrapers and apartment buildings.

Khao San Road This relatively short street in the Banglamphu area of the city is known as the backpacker ghetto.

Every square inch of it is crammed with youth hostels, street stalls selling pirated goods, artists, street vendors, hawkers and makeshift cocktail bars. Here is where the world's traveling youth typically head to, congregate and party. Many also leave from Khao San Road as there is a wide range of coaches and mini buses departing for other popular Thai tourist destinations at all times of the day and night.

BANGKOK PUBLIC TRANSPORT

Whether by road, rail or water, there are many ways of getting around Bangkok. By far the most common, and also the cheapest and most convenient, is by rail. Bangkok has three rail links: the BTS Skytrain, the MRT underground service and the Airport Railway Link. Prices are low, starting at around 15 baht (US 45 cents). As well as single-journey tickets, travel cards (separate ones for the MRT and BTS) can be purchased and credited with money for use.

There is also a comprehensive and extensive bus service in the city. Buses cooled only by fans charge just 8 baht (US 25 cents) while air-conditioned buses charge slightly more. Although it is a slightly slower method of getting from A to B, bus journeys are good for

Above and left Although buses and trains are cheaper, *tuk tuk* are still considered Bangkok's most iconic form of public transport.

visitors who want and have the time to see parts of the city they would not otherwise experience.

Getting around by taxi or *tuk tuk* and motorcycle (*motorsai*) taxi is also easy and relatively cheap. Almost all of the 100,000 registered taxis (cars) have meters, but sometimes drivers will attempt to bargain a fare before the journey begins and refuse to take a customer if they deem the journey not profitable enough. This is where motorcycle taxis come in.

There are an estimated 100,000 motorcycle taxi drivers in the city,

clad in recognizable vests, waiting and willing to take you anywhere for a low price. Zipping in and out of traffic, down alleyways and short cuts galore, they will get you where you want to go. *Tuk tuk* are much the same, and exist in the city more for the experience than the convenience, with locals preferring to use trains, buses or motorcycle taxis.

Again more for the convenience than anything else is the city's water-based transport. As well as the independent-operated long-tail boat drivers, there is also the Chao Phraya Express Boat and the Khlong Saen Saep boat that goes along prescribed routes every day. Traveling along the river is a delightful way of getting around, but unless you're familiar with the exact stop, direction and particular color-coded boat that will take you to your destination, it is more for travelers who would like to experience Old World Bangkok rather than those who want to get somewhere as quickly as possible.

WEIRD AND UNUSUAL BANGKOK

Bangkok has more than its fair share of weird and wonderful attractions. The longer you stay, the more *soi* you go down and shoulder-shrugging conversations you have, the more examples you are likely to find.

If you happen to stumble across Cabbages and Condoms, a restaurant decorated with a liberal use of condoms, then you will probably not be too surprised to get a condom with your bill. The restaurant was the brainchild of Mechai Viravaidya as a way of promoting safe sex and the eradication of HIV in Thailand.

One of the most famous examples of Bangkok weirdness is the Phallic Shrine, a garden dedicated to the phallus. Hundreds of wooden and stone statues, both big and small, compete for attention among the

shrine for Chao Mae Tubtim. In Thailand, the phallus (*palad khik*) is believed to be a symbol of good luck and fortune, and women often visit the shrine when they wish to conceive.

Looking for an afternoon with a difference? Then look no further than the Siriraj Medical Museum, also known as the Museum of Death. Located in Siriraj

Hospital, visitors can peruse a range of repulsive collections and exhibits, from weird anatomical anomalies, jars of dead babies preserved in formaldehyde, and the mummified remains of Thailand's most prolific serial killer, Si Ouey.

Restaurants where you get a condom with your bill, gardens decorated with phalluses and a museum full of death are sites that should be on your Bangkok itinerary.

HERE ARE MY
TOP 10 THINGS
TO DO IN BANGKOK

NATIONAL MUSEUM

Popular with both aspiring artists and those with just a passing interest in the arts is Baan Silapin (Bangkok Artist House), a former merchant's house set along the banks of Bang Luang Canal on the outskirts of Bangkok. It is now home to a number of artists who have transformed the area into a place for people to pursue their interests in traditional Thai dance, music, art and performance.

Escape the concrete jungle by taking a trip to a real one. Bang Kra Jao is an unspoiled, smog-free island in the center of the city. Get there by taking a long-tail boat from Khlong Toei Pier and rent a bicycle on arrival to explore stilt houses, fruit trees, exotic lizards and dense jungle. This government-protected area, which is also known as the Green Lung, is a true urban oasis.

Although not as authentic as it used to be, a visit to the Floating Market, the traditional strip of Bangkok shopping, in the nearby area of Ratchaburi is enjoyable nonetheless.

No trip to Bangkok is complete without a ride along the mighty Chao Phraya River. Whether on a small long-tail boat or

on one of the numerous cruise boats, there are few things as awe-inspiring as taking in the sights and silhouettes of the cityscape from the river at sunset.

THAI BOXING

Whether you're a fight fan or not, a visit to a Thai boxing stadium is an excellent night of entertainment. Although the legendary Lumpinee Boxing Stadium closed in 2014 and was replaced by a newer one, it's still the best place to go in Thailand to watch a fight. To experience it at its best, don't get the VIP ringside tickets as you will miss out on the true atmosphere—the music, shouting and gambling that take place in the stands.

Watch the Bangkok sunset and enjoy the incredible city views with a cocktail from a rooftop bar. Relive the *Hangover II* scene—minus the helicopter and guns—at the Sky Bar.

FLOATING MARKET

Shop till you drop at Chatuchak Weekend Market.

Go people-watching on Khao San Road, sink a few cold ones and discover Jimi Hendrix all over again.

Find out about the silk industry at the Jim Thompson House.

A great option on a hot day is the National Museum, which contains the country's finest displays of art and ancient artifacts. The Bangkok Art and Culture Center is another enjoyable and informative way to spend an afternoon.

BANG KRA JAO

JIM THOMPSON HOUSE

BAAN SILAPIN

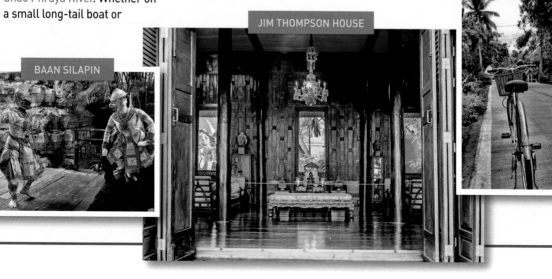

Southern Thailand, especially the islands of Krabi and Phuket, is home to some of the world's most breathtaking beaches and most luxurious resorts.

PHUKET AND OTHER ANDAMAN ISLANDS

Phuket's moniker, 'Pearl of the Andaman', is a slightly saccharine description of Thailand's largest island (210 sq miles/543 sq km) that conveys how important it is for the prosperity of the region.

Although hard to imagine when strolling along its beautiful beaches, Phuket was the hub of Thailand's tin mining industry from the 17th to the 20th century and traded extensively with the Dutch, French and British. In the 20th century, new revenue from tourism coinciding with a decline in demand for tin ultimately led to the mines closing and around 200 tin mine lakes being filled in. Visitors can learn more at the Mining Museum in Phuket.

The island is currently struggling to strike a balance between having an infrastructure capable of servicing an expanding number of hotels and attractions that continue to spring up to entertain and accommodate the 10 million plus annual tourists, without sacrificing too much of what attracted people to the one-time mountainous tropical island of Phuket in the first place.

From the 1970s onwards, Phuket's dense jungles, pristine beaches and, more controversially, areas of national parks have slowly been invaded by five-star hotels, restaurants and tourist attractions.

Part of Phuket's popularity lies in its ability to offer many different things to many different people. High-end tourists come to spend a week at a luxury resort on the island, many of which are located in the Kamala Millionaire's Mile area. They'll go to spas and dine at the finest restaurants. Perhaps they're members of the keen yachting community who moor their luxury yachts in harbors in Phuket, a perfect base from which to explore the stunning Andaman Islands.

While Phuket is no longer as cheap as other Thai provinces, many tourists also come to take advantage of the reasonably priced guest houses, food, drink and entertainment, especially in the hedonistic town of Patong, which has a casual vibe.

Phuket is a place where pleasure-seekers, surfers, backpackers, honeymooners, young families, retirees and, of course, Thais manage to co-exist and have their own unique and distinct tailored Phuket experience.

ENTER THE MILITARY

In the months following the 2014 coup, it took the Thai military just weeks to do what past governments, mayors, and governors had been unable to do on Phuket and other Thai beach destinations—clear the beaches of illegal private enterprise (rental of sun loungers, sales of food and drink). In just a matter of months, hundreds of illegal structures, bars and restaurants were demolished. A substantial effort was also made to regulate the taxi and *tuk tuk* situation in Phuket—the so-called taxi mafia—with drivers who had failed

to register arrested and fined. More meter taxis were introduced, leading many Phuketians and tourists to hope a much-needed fair and structured taxi organization like the one in Bangkok was on the way to the island. Unfortunately, the meter rates were extortionate and it took only a few weeks for non-meter taxis to cotton on to what they were charging and to quickly raise their prices so as not to miss out on the pickings.

PHUKET OLD TOWN

PROMTHEP CAPE

HERE ARE MY **TOP 10 THINGS TO DO IN PHUKET**

Popular with both locals and tourists, especially at sunset, is Phromthep Cape, situated on one of the island's tallest hills. The views of the nearby islands and sands of Phuket's Rawai and Nai Harn beaches are breathtaking.

Quietly emerging as a must-visit destination is the historically rich and significant Phuket Town. Stroll around the town that tin built and enjoy the early Sino-Portugese buildings. There are plenty of great little cafes and art galleries that are perfect for refueling before heading out onto the streets again.

The island's notorious nightlife at Bangla Road is definitely worth a visit. This walking street, complete with numerous *soi* full of little bars, nightclubs and Go-Go bars is always pulsating with energy and people. It's a great place to people-watch those who are people-watching.

Whatever tickles your fancy, Phuket has a wide and wild variety of cultural and cabaret shows, among them Fantasea, Siam Niramit, Simon Cabaret and Aphrodite. Many of the performers are the world famous *kathoey* (ladyboys).

WAT CHALONG

With the advent of medical tourism, many visitors are choosing Phuket for its award-winning spas and beauty treatment and wellness centers.

Go and watch Phuket FC play a game at Surakul Stadium. The Islanders have a faithful and loyal following, which always makes for a great atmosphere.

LEARN MUAY THAI

It's also just 100 baht (US$3) admission.

Although not a particularly popular temple with the locals, Wat Chalong is definitely one of the island's glitziest and grandest, a crash course in ostentatious Thai temple architecture. Big Buddha is also nearby—a 148 ft (45 m) high Buddha statue that dominates the summit of a hill between Kata and Chalong.

Although fewer since the 2014 military clean-up on the country's beaches, Phuket still has some beach bars. One of the oldest and most popular is Ska Bar, a reggae bar built within a huge tree on Kata beach. Another local hangout not particularly well known despite a visit by popular TV show *Bizarre Food* a few years back, is the delightful Mor Mu Dong restaurant in east Phuket, which is set among mangroves.

There are many Thai boxing training camps where you can stay onsite and learn the ancient art of Muay Thai. Or you can simply visit the Bangla Boxing Stadium to see how the pros do it.

Get off the beaten path and explore the jungles and dirt tracks of Phuket on quad bikes with one of the island's many ATV companies. There are also three great go kart tracks in Phuket.

BANGLA ROAD

KATA BEACH BAR

QUAD BIKING

TREKKING AND WILDLIFE

For 200 baht (US$6), the Khao Phra Thaeo Wildlife Sanctuary, located just off the airport road, is a great day out. Explore the 9 sq miles (22 sq km) of rainforest to get a good idea of what most of Phuket used to look like before the bulldozers rolled in. There's plenty of wildlife and plants but not necessarily footpaths, so be careful when trekking. If you want to help whilst learning more about the plight of the island's gibbons or stray dogs, visit the Gibbon Rehabilitation Center or Soi Dog Foundation. They are always looking for volunteers.

PHUKET'S BEACHES

Phuket's best beaches—there are 13 major ones, each distinctive—are located on the western side of the island facing the Andaman Sea. They range from strands several miles long to smaller crescents and are connected by a narrow road. Some of the best are those that have not yet succumbed to mass tourism, among them Laem Ka, about a mile (2 km) north of the popular Rawai

Beach. Don't expect much here except perhaps a coconut vendor and a sleeping *soi* dog. The wonderfully named Banana Beach, situated between Bang Tao and Nai Thorn Beaches, is also better known by locals than tourists.

ANDAMAN ISLAND HOPPING

The Andaman coast also offers a bountiful bevy of secluded, picturesque islands, many of which can be reached by boat from Phuket. The province of Phang Nga and its 42 beautiful islands—James Bond Island to name just one—are nearby and can easily be reached by boat.

Many tour companies offer great island-hopping day trips. For those who want to have an adventure whilst exploring, there are a good number of canoeing and kayaking companies, with John Gray Sea Canoe perhaps the most famous. Take a kayak or canoe around and inside Phang Nga's caves to see monkeys, sea creatures and all manner of beautiful birds in their natural habitat.

PHUKET'S QUIETER COUSIN

Many predict that Khao Lak (just 45 minutes from Phuket Airport), could, in the coming years replace Phuket as the primary destination for visitors to the Andaman region. Much more low key than Phuket, especially during the low season, it offers a wide variety of accommodation, from beachfront bungalows to five-star resorts and everything in between.

Khao Lak, along with Phuket, was one of the areas worst affected by the tsunami of 2004 and although much of the damage has been repaired, with new hotels and restaurants in place of those destroyed, it has not yet succeeded in reclaiming the glory of its past. It is still popular, however, especially with the dive community who tend to use it as the base from which to set sail for the stunning Similan Islands, which are just 30 miles (50 km) away.

PHI PHI, SWIMMING AND SNORKELING

Just one hour by boat from Phuket, Phi Phi Island, a one-time Muslim fisherman's village turned coconut plantation, is now famous the world over as the setting of the Leonardo DiCaprio movie, *The Beach*. Controversially, yet not unexpectedly, the filming, followed by the subsequent party people's pilgrimages, resulted in extreme damage to the island's ecosystem.

Whether by long-tail boat, luxury yacht or canoe, exploring the many caves, islands and lagoons of Thailand is a memorable and magical experience.

KRABI, CATCHING UP

Krabi, located on the west coast of southern Thailand at the mouth of the Krabi River where it empties into Phang Nga Bay, can be reached by road or water, with boat easily the most popular and picturesque option. Krabi is still catching up with Samui and Phuket in terms of being an international destination, but at least for the time being it offers something that Phuket and Samui have all but lost—peace, quiet and that slow-paced tropical island feel.

The island of Koh Lanta is the most popular destination for visitors, especially for its water sports. It is relaxed, chilled and easy to traverse, with a range of accommodation and entertainment options. Like Phuket and its neighboring islands, Koh Lanta has many islands dotted offshore that can be reached by boat tours.

PARTY WITH A BUCKET

The province of Surat Thani, located at the lower southern gulf coast, is home to the islands of Koh Samui and Koh Phangan. Samui, like Phuket, is a huge, popular island and as such has much of the same infrastructure—cinemas, shopping centers and international hospitals—to cater to the millions of tourists who visit each year. As with Phuket, however, mass tourism has taken its toll on the natural beauty of the island and its paradise-like atmosphere. The

busiest beach, Hat Chaweng, is the most popular and has plenty of beachfront restaurants, bars and evening entertainment.

If it is only nightlife you are looking for, then the all-night Full Moon parties on Koh Phangan—just 9 miles (15 km) from Samui—might be for you. Any trace of Thai culture has evaporated from this small island in its complete surrender to international hedonism. Cheap accommodation, with cheap restaurants and cheap bars, serve party people all year round, cheaply. The town sleeps and recovers during the day, and at night young people in their twenties and thirties descend upon the beach, with buckets of alcohol and glow sticks in hand to party all night. Hundreds of

stalls line the beach, typically serving a small bucket containing ice, soda, a bottle of whisky and an energy drink.

These beach parties would once only have takeen place on nights with a full moon, but now beach parties take place every weekend. In high season, about 10,000 people visit for a genuine Full Moon party.

Following a number of documentaries on the nightlife on Koh Phangan, the island has gained a rather negative reputation in recent years, with rising complaints concerning drug-related crime, sexual assaults and the propensity for bringing on mental illness!

Body paint, flip flops and a bucket of booze is all that is needed for the notorious Full Moon party.

The Thai bus (*songthaew*) is predominantly used by locals, with tourists favoring the brightly colored, exceedingly expensive four-wheel *tuk tuk*.

GETTING AROUND

Unfortunately, public transport in Phuket is woefully weak. One of the main reasons for this are the companies and organizations that run the taxi and *tuk tuk* stands around the island. Staunch opposition, regular protests and influential friends have all hampered Phuket's ability to offer a comprehensive public transportation system that the area so badly needs.

A previous attempt to introduce a public bus service around the main tourist sites resulted in a bus driver being beaten up, and so the service was promptly discontinued. In the latter part of 2013, an airport bus service was finally given the green light to take passengers to Patong. It was initially scheduled to also drop passengers off at Kata and Karon, but protests quickly put an end to those routes.

As it now stands, and probably will for at least for another few years, apart from a few *songtaew* (adapted pick-up truck) bus routes that are usually only used by school children and the elderly, Phuket taxis and *tuk tuk* monopolize public transport on the island and therefore are able to charge excessive fares. This 'system' is, unfortunately, replicated in other parts of the Andaman region.

Another reason why fares are so expensive in Phuket and the surrounding regions is that quite often taxi drivers adhere to a strict policy of not picking up passengers from any area other than their own, meaning they have to return to their point empty-handed and the passenger, in effect, pays for the return journey.

The other option for getting around is for the visitor and traveler to hire a motorbike or car, but be warned. Thai roads are extremely dangerous and very few Thai drivers adhere to international driving regulations or are trained to a very high level.

WHERE YOU GO?

Because of the aggressive behavior of many *tuk tuk* drivers and their habit of overcharging foreign customers, the *tuk tuk*, both the three-wheeled traditional version and the more recent four-wheeled one, has become an icon of Thailand for all the wrong reasons.

GETTING OFF PHUKET

It's quite common, and fun, to go to Phang Nga, Krabi or other Andaman destinations by ferry or boat, but the cheapest, quickest and perhaps most convenient way is by long-distance bus.

There are two main bus stations in Phuket and plenty of pick-up points in and around Phuket Town. The old Phuket Bus Station in the center of town still travels to Krabi and Khao Lak, among a few other areas, but the majority of inter-provincial travel is now done from the new bus station, which is located just outside of town.

Prices are relatively cheap, non-negotiable and leave regularly. From Phuket you can be in Khao Lak within two hours. Phuket to Koh Lanta is just six hours away and Samui is also just a six-hour journey. There are also buses to Bangkok, which take around 12 hours.

FUN ON THE WATER

Take a tour boat around the Andaman region, go scuba diving or just explore beneath the waves with a snorkel. Even a short trip to a floating restaurant or a nearby island on the ubiquitous Thai long-tail boat is a lot of fun.

Phuket's west coast beaches, especially Kata and Nai Harn, regularly host surf competitions. Many Phuket beaches offer surfing lessons and sizable surfing communities to get involved with. Other popular water sports include parasailing, banana boat rides and even kite surfing.

Although banned in certain areas of Krabi, jet skis can still be rented on some Phuket beaches. Be warned that although most jet skis in Phuket are now officially insured, this has not prevented the operators from running the infamous jet ski scam unhindered, whereby a slightly damaged jet ski is hired out, and when the renter returns to shore, the jet ski operators, through intimidation, threats and creative interpretation of repair costs, extort up to 30,000 baht (US$900) for 'major repairs' and to cover the time that the jet skis are out of action. Quite often the jet skis are out on the beach the next day. Either don't use them or take plenty of photos of the machine before use.

Chiang Mai is home to over 300 Buddhist temples, including the stunning Wat Phra Singh.

CHIANG MAI AND THE NORTH

A common measure of how long an expatriate has been in Thailand is usually how many times they have been to Chiang Mai, the cultural capital of the country, in the north.

If Bangkok with its industries, companies and businesses is the brain of the country, and the Andaman region with its beautiful beaches, myriad of islands and stunning resorts is the face of the country, then Chiang Mai with its ancient temples, dedication to arts and abundance of wildlife is certainly the heart of the country.

The former capital city of the Lanna kingdom, Chiang Mai and its surrounding area has a distinctive character. It has managed to retain aspects of the old while still moving forward. Indeed, it is the city's ability to balance tourism with a thriving cultural, arts and handicrafts identity and industry that is central to the city's identity.

The province of Chiang Mai has one of the highest numbers of national parks in the country, and even when you are in the city of Chiang Mai its surrounding

mountains rise above buildings, meaning you never really feel as hemmed in as you do in other huge cities.

THE LESSER KNOWN CHIANG

The original capital city of the Lanna kingdom, Chiang Rai, the northernmost city in Thailand, is less known but, much like Chiang Mai, is rich in culture, diversity and natural attractions. Many tourists choose to visit Chiang Rai for

BO SANG UMBRELLA MARKER

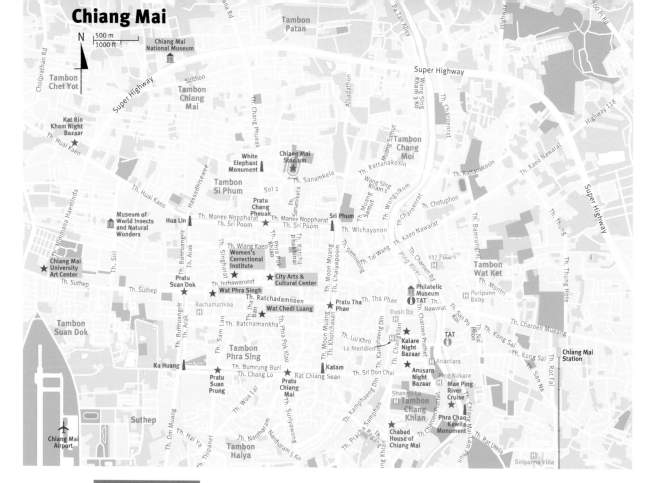

Chiang Mai

N 500 m
1000 ft

WAT RONG KHUN

CITY OF PILLAR FESTIVAL

ANANTARA GOLDEN
TRIANGLE RESORT

its stunning Wat Rong Khun (White Temple), while others make the 2.5 hour trip from Chiang Mai to go trekking or to explore the picturesque mountains, jungles and remnants of its historical past.

THE LIFE OF PAI

It takes around four hours to get to Pai from Chiang Mai, but the journey, involving 762 sharp turns up, down and around mountains, is an adventure in itself. Pai is popular with both foreigners and Thais who visit this sleepy but delightful little town all year round. Rent a motorcycle and explore the town's hot springs, waterfalls, cafes and thriving arts and crafts scene in this quiet and picturesque town.

CHIANG MAI OLD WALLS

HERE ARE MY TOP 10 THINGS TO DO IN CHIANG MAI

It is easy to know when you are in Chiang Mai city center, well at least the Old City center, as it is surrounded by the ancient walls and a moat that date back to the 13th century. This makes exploring its 30 plus temples, city cafes and places of interest inside the Chiang Mai Old City easy and fun. Temples of note include Wat Chedi Luang, and one of Thailand's most visited temples, Wat Phra Singh.

The Chiang Mai Sunday Market Walking Street is consistently voted the best market in Thailand, even beating out the chaotic and mammoth Chatuchack Market in Bangkok. Every Sunday, at around 4 pm, the 1 km long Ratchad-amnoen Road, which runs east to west within the Old City walls, becomes a walking street, and hundreds of stalls are brought out to line it and many of the offshoot streets and roads. Vendors sell everything from handmade arts and crafts to handwoven

clothes, souvenirs and general tourist tat. There is also lots of delicious Chiang Mai street food, an assortment of street music and street performances.

Open most nights, the Chiang Mai Night Bazaar, located in the tourist-centered Chan Klan Road, is where tourists head to for a spot of shopping and street entertainment. It's a great place to go to people-watch, perhaps while getting a foot massage at the same time at one of the many roadside massage parlors.

There's a plethora of day tours and trips that you can take whilst staying in Chiang Mai. One of the most popular places to visit is the Doi Suthep National

Park, situated around 9 miles (15 km) from the city center. The national park contains beautiful peaks, valleys, dense forest and incredible views, including the beautiful Doi Suthep Temple, dating back to the 14th century. An ancient Thai phrase still used today is that you haven't experienced Thailand until you have been to Chiang Mai, nor experienced Chiang Mai until you have seen the view from Doi Suthep. Visitors can either climb the 309 steps to reach it or take a tram up.

Another popular day out is to visit Doi Inthanon, the highest mountain in Thailand with more than a few pictureworthy waterfalls scattered around. It's also home to plenty of nature trails through beautiful surroundings, and most importantly contains the twin stupas (hemispherical relic mounds) built to honor the King and Queen of Thailand. The twin stupas are built within immaculately manicured gardens containing the finest and most colorful flowers and foliage native to this part of Thailand.

CHIANG MAI BAZAAR

CHIANG MAI SUNDAY MARKET

CHIANG MAI WALKING STREET

DOI INTHANON

CHIANG MAI ARTS AND CULTURAL CENTER

WAT PHRA DOI SUTHEP

For those who have an interest in finding out more about the history of Chiang Mai, then a visit to the Chiang Mai City Arts and Cultural Center is a must. The Chiang Mai National Museum is also worth popping by for the same reasons. The area of Nimmanhemin, situated around the Chiang Mai University Art Center, has flourished of late and become a beacon of light for contemporary Chiang Mai art, with many funky little galleries and cafes springing up to showcase the alternative arts scene. The University Arts Center itself is also well worth a visit and contains exhibitions and works by both established and more contemporary artists.

Get out of the city and explore the vast Chiang Mai jungles by going on a Chiang Mai trek. Available throughout the year, treks usually include visits to nearby hill tribes, elephant rides and bamboo raft travel. As previously mentioned, both elephant riding and the visiting of hill tribes is not for everyone, and both activities have, rightfully, come under scrutiny in the past few years.

Chiang Mai has some stunning spas that allow you to experience an authentic Lanna spa in beautiful natural surroundings. It also has an abundance of massage parlors where you can get a rub down for a great price. As with Thai cooking, there are many schools and centers where you can learn about the art of massage. To mix social responsibility with relaxation, why not visit the Chiang Mai Women's Correctional Institute? Wait… yes it's a prison, but all the inmates there are trained masseuses who are doing it to earn money, learn a skill and become sufficiently rehabilitated so that life on the outside may be less daunting.

CHIANG MAI WATER RAFTING

Although Chiang Mai offers an assortment of elephant trek tours in the nearby areas of Mae Hong Song and Chiang Dao, those with ethical objections to elephant tourism may prefer instead to visit the Elephant Nature Park in the beautiful Mae Taeng Valley. Think Jurassic Park but with elephants. Here, elephants that are either rescued or retired from the tourist trade are allowed to roam freely around a vast expanse. Visitors cannot sit on the elephants' heads, but they can bathe them, feed them and observe them in their natural habitat.

Owing to an abundance of Chiang Mai coffee bean plantations in Chiang Mai and Chiang Rai, combined with long-established local government initiatives to replace opium cultivation with coffee crops, the province's reputation for producing high-quality coffee beans and coffee has grown by huge strides over the past few decades. Enjoy a locally brewed coffee at one of the provinces' many coffeeshops. The region has produced some high-quality brands, including Doi Tung and Doi Chaang.

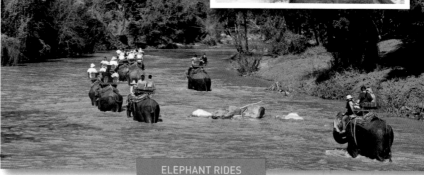

ELEPHANT RIDES

Monks light candles and release lanterns during the Yi Peng festival, which, in contemporary Thai culture is often celebrated and amalgamated into the Loy Krathong proceedings.

MONKEY BUFFET FESTIVAL

COLORFUL THAI FESTIVALS

There is something unmistakably Thai about its colorful, noisy, beautiful and mythical festivals, and also about the way they are celebrated with such abandon, joy of life and hint of danger.

FLOAT YOUR TROUBLES AWAY

One of the most recognizable and romantic Thai festivals is Loy Krathong, which usually takes place midway through November on a full noon night.

Originally a festival to give praise to Buddha and request forgiveness from Pra Mae Khongkhla (the Goddess of the River Mae Khong), the festival has, over time, taken on new meaning and come to represent the washing away of the past year's sins and misfortune.

Preparations for the ancient festival begin a few days beforehand, when the whole family gets involved in making *krathong*, small bouyant boat-like decorations, from a variety of natural materials, including elaborately folded banana leaves, banana trunks, coconut shells and flowers. Traditionally, people used to put nail clippings and hair strands in the boats together with candles, incense and flowers, and sometimes a coin, but nowadays most merely light the candles and incense sticks that are in them, and then float them away in one of the country's major and minor waterways, believing that the bad luck of the previous year will go with the *krathong*.

MONKEYING AROUND

For a sense of what it would be like to have been in the movie *Gremlins*, one should visit Lopburi city in the northeast of Thailand, a city where humans and monkeys literally share the space. Entire buildings and sides of roads have been given over to the monkeys and the city has well-known no-go zones (if you're a human). The best time to visit is during the Monkey Buffet festival in the last weekend of November, when a huge feast is put on, well, for the monkeys. Strange, amazing Thailand.

A DAY LIKE A PRINCE

The Poy Sang Long (Festival of the Crystal Sons), which takes place in the mountainous and islolated northern province of Mae Hong Son, is a rite-of-passage ceremony, specifically an ordination ceremony, that culminates

CELEBRATING THE ARTS

Because of its natural splendor and rich artistic heritage, it is little wonder that so many visually stunning festivals occur in Chiang Mai. The Chiang Mai Flower Festival in the first weekend of February coincides with the blooming of flowerbeds all around the province. A variety of parades and, as usual, beauty pageants, are held in the area.

Every year during the third weekend of January, the Bo Sang and San Kamphaeng villages celebrate the Umbrella Fair and Handicrafts Festival. During the fair, a number of exhibitions, competitions and traditional Thai cultural dances and performances take place.

in a grand, colorful and foot-tapping parade. Held every year in late March or early April, the three-day ceremony is for young boys aged 7 to 14 from the Thai Yai (Shan) community. During this merit-making festival, the novices are carried on the shoulders of male villagers and have their heads and eyebrows shaved. They are also dressed in lavish clothes, jewelry and head-dresses to resemble the first Buddhist novice, Buddha's own son, Prince Rahula. The novices take vows and participate in monastery life for a period of time that can vary from a week to many months.

PUT A PIN IN THE DIARY

The Phuket Vegetarian Festival is another one-of-a-kind festival, but it is definitely not one for the squeamish. This nine-day festival takes place every October, mainly in and around Phuket Town, to honor the town's Chinese ancestors who recovered from a fatal disease by apparently strictly adhering to vegetarianism.

For the entire period, residents wear white and abstain from eating meat, drinking alcohol or having sex. Those who take part in the actual festivities, the *ma song* (mediums), channel evil spirits, become possessed and impale themselves with spikes, swords and all manner of weird implements in order to banish evil from the community. Other sacred rituals include walking on hot coals and climbing bladed ladders.

As with most Thai festivals, sections of the town are cordoned off and made into walking-only zones, and food and clothes stalls line the streets.

POY SANG LONG

ON YOUR BIKES

Phuket Bike Week celebrated its 21st anniversary in 2015, and each year seems to get bigger. Bikers from all over Asia, and even further afield, descend on the island to join in processions, bike shows, parades and mass drives in convoys during the period of Songkran. There are also large concerts, exhibitions, plenty of food and drink and, of course, beauty pageants, with women from the region competing for the honor of Miss Phuket Bike Week.

DON'T FORGET YOUR TRUNKS

Thailand's New Year, Songkran, is either a few days of fun that ends way too soon or a test of endurance that one must survive every year.

Apart from in Chiang Mai, where it goes on and on for a week, Songkran usually lasts a few days every mid-April and is celebrated by all, but in dramatically different ways.

Set at the hottest time of year, typically at the end of the dry season, people traditionally celebrated Songkran by sprinkling water over statues of Buddha and their elders as a way of showing respect.

Nowadays, however, Songkran has evolved into the world's biggest water fight. Thais and foreigners fill huge water pistols, or heap barrels filled with water onto the back of pick-up trucks before heading out and soaking anybody they come

across. Nobody is exempt from the festivities, so if you're in Thailand during Songkran, whether you like it or not, you are going to celebrate it—you will get wet. The party continues into the night, when water pistols are put down and glasses are raised, along with the volume of the music. Each province also hosts a Miss Songkran beauty pageant.

Controversy erupted during Songkran 2011 when video clips emerged of young Thai women dancing topless on a pick-up truck on a Bangkok street. Following a national outcry, a modern-day witch-hunt took place and the women subsequently surrendered, paid a fine and apologized. The Culture Minister was quoted as saying that such images had negatively affected Thailand's image. Netizens took to the web to reveal the government's hypocrisy because, while this was taking place, a picture on the Thai Ministry of Culture's homepage depicted a scene of topless Thai women frolicking.

ADVENTURE OF A LIFETIME

Because of the large number of national parks to roam, cliffs to climb and seas to swim, Thailand is quite the adventure playground. Environmentalists would argue, however, that the outdoors scene is too lively and too thriving, with many of the country's seas and coral reefs having become irrevocably polluted and damaged through excessive tourism and that its forests, jungles and coastlines have also been excessively chopped down and built upon to make way for resorts, restaurants and tourist attractions.

SIMILAN ISLANDS

There is, however, slow progress, or perhaps regress, being made at both the government and private levels amid a general awareness that Thailand's nature needs to be protected, not only to preserve the beauty of the environment but also to preserve a healthy and sustainable tourism industry.

Recycling, beach clean-ups and mass dive-for-trash events are just some of the initiatives that have gained momentum in the last decade or so. There are also very active environmental groups that have managed to keep the government in check over recent years, especially with regards to proposed plans for the building of a number of dams.

EXPLORING UNDERWATER

Visitors to Thailand are spoilt for choice when it comes to diving, with literally hundreds of dive spots, coral reef sites, sunken ships and exotic marine life located along the country's two coasts—the

DOI INTHANON NATIONAL PARK

CRAZY HORSE BUTTRESS

Andaman coast and the Gulf coast. There are also, of course, countless more areas out at sea and around Thailand's numerous islands.

Thailand offers a variety of diving options, including night diving, cave diving, scuba diving, free diving and live-aboard trips. For beginners, most Thai beaches also have facilities where one can rent snorkeling equipment.

The Thai dive industry is worth millions of dollars.

One of the dive sites consistently voted among the world's top places to explore the wide and wild variety

ANGKHA NATURE TRAIL

of exotic marine life, including whale sharks, is at Richelieu Rock near the Surin Islands. The stunning waters of Ko Tao (Turtle Island) off the Gulf of Thailand have also become increasingly popular in recent years for their abundance of shallow reefs and gentle currents, ideal for beginners.

TAKE A HIKE

Keen hikers and trekkers tend to go to the northern part of the kingdom, where Chiang Mai and Chiang Rai's milder climate and numerous national parks make them natural choices.

Some of the best and most rewarding trails can be found among the hills and jungles of Doi Inthanon in Chiang Mai. There are plenty of other hiking trails all over the kingdom, though, from Surat Thani to Krabi, and in fact anywhere where there is a waterfall, there is likely to be an exhilarating trail with wildlife, scenery, temples and perhaps even hill tribes.

Because hiking and trekking are not particularly popular Thai pastimes, some of the lesser-known trails are not very well signposted, and it is not all that uncommon for rescue teams to be deployed to assist a plucky and unlucky hiker or two.

Instead of standing in front of waterfalls and hot springs to take photos, it is much more Thai to take a fully clothed dip in them, and then spend the rest of the visit relaxing, eating, drinking and laughing.

BETWEEN A ROCK AND A HARD PLACE

The mountains and cliffs of Chiang Mai are also popular with Thailand's growing rock climbing community. The limestone cliffs in the middle of the Andaman Sea and around Phang Nga Bay also provide great rock climbing opportunities. The king of Thai rock climbing sites, however, is most definitely Railay in Krabi. Over 600 climbing spots, from beginner to advanced, along with breathtaking views of the surrounding islands and deep blue water, make it a climber's dream.

KING'S CUP REGATTA

SAIL AWAY WITH ME

Testimony to Thailand's ample sailing spots are the number of well-attended regattas held along its seaways. Indeed, King Bhumibol was once a keen sailor himself and, along with his youngest daughter Princess Ubolratana Rajakanya, competed in many regattas. There are plenty of yacht companies and high-class hotels offering both bareboat yacht charters and all-inclusive charters for private hire.

The Phuket King's Cup Regatta is held annually off the shores of Phuket, home to the well-established Boat Lagoon and Royal Phuket Marina. A little further up the Andaman Coast is the Krabi Boat Lagoon.

Up until fairly recently, however, the Gulf of Thailand, at least among yacht owners, remained largely neglected. In 2012, in response to an emerging need from a growing private sailing industry, the Siam Royal View Marina was opened. It provides a much-needed harbor and marina for yacht owners and sailors in Koh Chang and the rest of the Gulf of Thailand.

GOLF

Although there are more than 260 golf courses in Thailand, many in Phuket, Pattaya, Bangkok, Chiang Mai and Isan, the best courses are in Hua Hin ('The Queen of Tranquility'), the closest beach resort to Bangkok. Hua Hin has challenging courses set against a mountainous backdrop with stunning coastal and hillside views. The diverse setting combined with excellent club houses, facilities and golf tour programs have turned King Bhumibol's once-favorite holiday destination into an attractive spot for golfing holidays. Two of the finest courses are the Royal Hua Hin and the Black Mountain Golf Club.

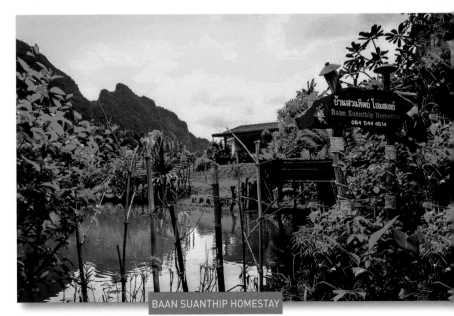

BAAN SUANTHIP HOMESTAY

Pattaya is also home to many great golf courses, around 30 in all. Because of the seaboard city's proximity to Bangkok, it attracts many weekend golfers as well as national and international golfers who visit for the sun, sea and golf. Courses of note include the Laem Chabang International Country Club and the Siam Country Club.

It goes without saying that Phuket, a playground for retirees, also has a number of great golf courses, eight at last count. The Blue Canyon Country Club has even hosted a Tiger Woods championship win in the past. Honorable mentions must also go to the Mission Hills and Loch Palm golf clubs.

HOMESTAYS AND VOLUNTEERISM

There are many tourists who choose homestays or enroll in volunteer programs when visiting Thailand. A truly authentic and genuine experience can be very rewarding and show you a side of Thailand well off the beaten tourist path. Some teach English at state schools, while others learn about rice farming, silk weaving or even how to make traditional Thai handicrafts.

There are also homestays where visitors can learn the age-old traditions of a Muslim fishing community or discover how families survive off the land in forests high in the Chiang Mai hills. The Tourism Authority of Thailand (TAT) has sanctioned a number of Official

Teach at a school, work on a farm, feed elephants at a conservation center, visitors to Thailand are spoilt for choice on how to spend their time and money.

Home Stay options throughout every region. They bear the TAT seal and guarantee a level of cultural authenticity.

Unfortunately, there are also a number of disreputable and exploitative companies throughout the country offering picturesque poverty and opportunities to see hill tribes and impoverished villages and to 'help endangered wildlife' that probably do more harm than good. It

is often these unethical companies that can afford to pay for the great websites and the necessary marketing tools to appeal to the tourist. Research into the industry of volunteering at Thai orphanages has found that demand by tourists to help and visit orphans has turned many orphanages into little more than tourist attractions and actually fueled the trade in child trafficking.

NOT WILD **ABOUT THE WILDLIFE**

Because of Thailand's animist roots, the country has always had a special relationship with the environment and its animals, as seen by the frequency with which they appear in the nation's folklores, its mysticism-fused religion and its reliance on rural living. Despite this, Thailand's wide variety of wildlife is often used as an unethical prop for tourism or is poached to meet overseas demand for meat or pelts.

Up until the banning of the practice in 1989, many elephants in Thailand worked in the logging industry. Now the majority work in elephant camps and take tourists for rides. Baby elephants are typically taken away from their mothers when they are very young. A similar fate has also befallen the Thai (Indochinese) tiger, with a worrying increase in tiger centers springing up and down the country. Whether 'sanctuary' or 'kingdom', baby tigers are hand-reared so that they are more comfortable around humans to enable tourists to have their photographs taken with them without getting mauled. There is no guarantee though, and in 2014 an Australian man was lucky to leave a cage in the Tiger Kingdom in Phuket alive. Once tigers reach maturity at such centers, they are destined to live their lives confined to cages.

Although it may be tempting to have your photograph taken with a snake, monkey, slow loris or tiger, know that there are repercussions that continue long after the camera has been put away.

A gibbon-holding hawker, complete with Polaroid camera, used to be quite a common sight on the streets of Phuket. Again, in order to train such animals to be comfortable in the company of humans, they are taken from their mothers in the jungle at an early age, have their teeth filed and are often drugged. Gibbons have since been replaced by the slow loris as the prop of choice.

In the lowlands of Thailand and in coastal regions like Koh Samui, macaque monkeys and gibbons work hand in hand with humans, helping to harvest coconuts. The monkeys climb the trees and twist coconuts until they fall to the ground and are then collected by the owner. Monkeys can harvest up to 400 coconuts a day, and a well-trained and efficient coconut-collecting monkey is a highly prized asset.

As tempting, quick and convenient as it is to have your photo taken with a gibbon on a tourist street, or sitting on the head of an elephant in Chiang Mai, or beside a sleeping tiger in a tiger center, the repercussions are far greater than the minute or two of contact. Animal trafficking, breaking of elephants, drugging of animals, slaughtering of mothers to steal babies and abuse on an almost record level has led to dwindling numbers of tigers, elephants and bears. Indeed, there are now more elephants and tigers in captivity than in the wild in Thailand.

Nearly 10 percent of the country's surface area is reserved for more than 50 wildlife sanctuaries in Thailand. However, traders and poachers are often better equipped and outnumber park rangers. This, combined with inconsistent punishment and outdated low fines mean that tigers, elephants, monkeys and many other Thai wildlife are being pushed or captured from their natural habitat.

It is the responsibility of not only those working within the industry but also every single tourist to stop the harrowing trade and abuse of Thailand's wildlife by refusing to be a part of it. It is easier said than done though, especially in Phuket, which remains a favorite holiday destination with celebrities. Rihanna visited in 2013 and had her photo taken with a slow loris. Beyonce visited in 2015 and was snapped on the back of a baby elephant.

A customer was mauled, but survived, at the Tiger Kingdom in Phuket in 2014.

ADVICE, TIPS AND WARNINGS

At first glance, Thailand, the Land of Smiles and the *mai phen rai* attitude, may seem to have a somewhat lackadaisical approach to rules and regulations. Laws relating to drink driving, prostitution and social disorder do exist, though, but the penalties and enforcement of these laws are not as stringent as in other countries. Living in Thailand is much like the common Thai phrase *laew tae khun* (up to you).

This gives many foreigners a false sense of freedom, of liberation. For those who are used to living in a nanny state, it can be quite a shock to the system, especially as the result of this freedom, this abandoning of responsibility and, in some cases, common sense, does not come with an equal or guaranteed measure of protection. In Thailand, how you live is up to you.

There are, however, certain things you should definitely not do while in Thailand if you want to continue seeing the smiles and enjoying the laid-back atmosphere. Restrictions do exist in the country even if they are rarely followed, such as the absence of speed limit signs on the roads. One is only likely to find out about such laws and their enforcement when they are infringed.

An absence of speed limit signs and a relaxed approach to road rules means driving in Thailand can be a maddening experience. Expect the unexpected.

THAI DRIVING HABITS

Thailand has the world's second-most dangerous roads, with an annual average of 44 deaths per 100,000 people.

Perhaps it's the ticking-down counter on traffic lights, or the motorcyclists driving the wrong way down roads, or the fact that obtaining a driving license is sometimes as easy as just turning up at the Department of Land Transport that makes traveling on Thai roads so dangerous. Many Thai drivers have never had a driving lesson in their life and thus take to the roads, minus motorcycle helmets, in the same cavalier manner they play video games.

When driving in Thailand, do so slowly, cautiously and defensively. Do not get angry or beep your horn—*mai phen rai*. So he almost killed you with his pick-up truck? Exhibit *kreng jai*.

Here are some tips when driving in Thailand:

- If you rent a motorcycle, make sure you wear a helmet, even if the majority of other riders don't.
- Wing mirrors on bikes are usually slightly inverted so the rider can check his/her hair at traffic lights. This obviously hampers their field of vision, so be mindful of this.
- In Thailand, people drive on the left. Motorbikes also tend to keep to the left side of the road, so undertaking on the left as opposed to overtaking on the right is quite common.
- Motorbike riders don't usually bother indicating, and instead just repeatedly glance to the left or right, depending on the direction in which they want to turn.

- A pillion passenger flapping his/her arms is not attempting to take off from the motorbike, but is instead indicating the direction the driver wishes to turn.
- Headlight flashes from oncoming cars don't mean they are giving you right of way, rather the opposite. It means that they are coming through and you should make way!
- Pedestrian crossings in Thailand are seen more as a form of decoration than a place where pedestrians can safely cross the road. Be aware that cars and motorbikes will not necessarily stop for passengers here.
- Thai drivers tend to drive almost bumper to bumper and certainly do not observe the two-car length rule. Keep to the left, drive at the speed limit and let them overtake you.
- When walking on sidewalks, be wary, especially in heavy traffic, of motorbike riders who may decide to take to the sidewalk to save time.
- Because of the numbers of cars and the limited parking spaces, you are required to leave your handbrake off in many lots, in case a car attendant needs to push your car out of the way to make room for others.
- Be wary of the *puang malai* street vendors who walk in and out of traffic when cars stop at traffic lights. They sell garlands of flowers that are supposed to bring good luck.

One explanation given for Thai driving habits and the frequency of accidents is the sheer number of objects that often obstruct a driver's view. For many Thais, their cars act as a sort of mobile shrine, with miniature monk statues on

Left When not totally congested or when closed for markets or festivals, Thai roads are notoriously dangerous.

Above It's common to see private ambulance crews stationed at busy intersections where many accidents occur.

Below A motorcycle built for four, or even five!

dashboards, garlands of flowers and other trinkets hanging from rear-view mirrors and Buddhist symbols etched upon roofs.

PRIVATE AMBULANCES

Because of the lack of state-run emergency services, responsibility for the roadside injured or dead falls on various charitable foundations.

Often crews are divided up between police-registered paid employees who work on behalf of the police in the care, transportation, fingerprinting and photographing of the dead, and volunteers who assist in driving and carrying the dead. It is the latter group that often has to participate in the unsettling 'trophy photos'. Although it may seem an incredibly insensitive and morbid practice, this posing and pointing at corpses for photos is for the benefit of the police should an investigation later take place.

Most of the staff are volunteers who do it to either to make merit or compete with one another to collect a small fee in exchange for deliveries of the injured or deceased to particular hospitals.

Commissions vary, but it is around 200–300 baht (US$6–9) depending on the injury or the particular hospital taken to. It is quite common, therefore, especially in the evenings, to see different ambulance crews waiting at intersections for the next accident to

happen. It will then be a race, quite literally, to the death.

The night shift is the most profitable time to work for ambulance crews. They typically start at 10 pm and spend the night listening in to police radios, scanners and traffic reports. Certain ambulance crews will also receive tip-offs from taxi drivers and *tuk tuk* drivers.

DON'T FORGET

Thai time Although often bandied around as a derogatory notion that Thais are not the most punctual of people, the country does use a different time-keeping system. Unlike the 24-hour clock, Thais favor the six-hour clock, where each day is divided into four quarters. In fact, the Thai solar calendar Suriyakati, 543 years ahead of the Western calendar, is also more commonly used. In 2020, for example, it will be 2563 in Thailand.

Although it seems forever hot and humid, Thailand does have seasonal differences in temperature throughout the year. Apart from the coastal regions, which experience just two seasons, the rainy season (April-October) and hot season (the rest of the year), generally speaking Thailand has three seasons: cool season (November–February), which is not really cool per se, just cooler; hot season (March–June), where temperatures reach a boiling 35° C; and rainy season (July–October), the most sporadic and unpredictable season, where it literally never rains but pours.

The majority of visitors need a visa to travel in Thailand. Either apply for a Tourist Visa at a Thai Embassy, which is valid for 60 days' travel, or get a visa-on-arrival at a Thai border checkpoint or Thai airport, which, depending on nationality, entitles the visitor to either 15 or 30 days in the kingdom. These can also be extended for a maximum of 30 days at an immigration center. After that, visitors must go on visa runs to neighboring countries to repeat the process all over again. This can be an

exhausting, and thanks to breakneck speeds at which the drivers scoot along, extremely dangerous exercise.

To prevent tourists abusing the system and effectively living in Thailand illegally, immigration officers reserve the right to refuse visitors entry. Visitors may be asked to show a departure flight ticket or proof of funds.

There are also different visas depending on your official purpose for being in Thailand, such as Education Visa, Business Visa, Media Visa, Retirement Visa and many more. Rules regarding visas are constantly changing, so take a moment, or most likely an afternoon, to familiarize yourself with the country's particular rules.

Should you overstay, you will be liable for a fine of 500 baht (US$15) per day.

As a foreigner, you will need a work permit, which is applied for independently of your visa.

Even if you have a year-long visa, or Retirement Visa, you will need to visit an immigration center every 90 days to notify them you still have a valid visa and are staying at the same address.

Foreigners cannot legally own 100 percent of a business in Thailand and so you will need to have Thai shareholders.

Foreigners cannot own land in Thailand. The only option for those who want to buy is to purchase a condominium unit freehold.

DO'S AND DON'TS

Show respect and reverence for the Thai royal family. It is customary to stand when the national anthem is played, for example, before movie screenings and at public parks. Thailand is one of the few countries where the monarchy is protected by the lèse majesté law, and it is still quite common for both Thais and foreigners to receive jail sentences for any offence against the king or royal family.

Dress decently in palaces and temple grounds. Vests, shorts and skimpy attire are not acceptable. Men going shirtless anywhere other than the beach or a pool is considered quite disrespectful. Outside of tourist areas, Thais are quite conservative and such exhibitionism is considered very rude.

Show respect to Buddhist images and Buddhism in general. If in doubt, don't touch an image. Women are not permitted to touch monks. Smoking and drinking are also prohibited on temple grounds.

Behave appropriately. Thais consider the head the highest point of the body and therefore it should not be touched by strangers.

Conversely, the feet are considered the lowest point of the body, so do not show the soles of your feet in public or point or attempt to maneuver anything with them.

Give a *wai*. Although handshaking is slowly becoming more popular, especially among the younger generation and with foreigners, the *wai* is still the most common form of greeting, giving thanks and saying farewell. Giving a *wai* is also a more practical gesture in a tropical climate where hands can become sweaty. *Wai* back, especially to show appreciation.

Don't show affection in public. Although attitudes are slowly changing, public displays of affection are still frowned upon. Don't kiss or be too touchy-feely in public. Remember that even on TV couples will perform what is known as a cheek sniff rather than a kiss on the lips.

Remove your shoes before entering a Thai house, apartment or even a studio room. It is quite common to see a dozen or more pairs haphazardly placed or neatly stacked outside a home. Thais also take off their shoes in pharmacies and in smaller family-owned stores, hence the Thais' fondness for slip-on shoes.

Show respect to your elders. Thailand is a patriarchal society, where most of its citizens show deep reverence for the social structure. The elderly are typically placed at the top and are treated as such.

Don't raise your voice in public. This will get you nowhere and is likely to inflame the situation, not dissipate or rectify it.

Exercise caution with *soi* dogs (street dogs/stray dogs) but don't be overly fearful. They don't generally show as much aggression or fear as the stray dogs in many other countries because of the unique way in which they are treated and tolerated in Thailand. It's quite common to see stray dogs cooling down in an air-conditioned 7-Eleven or being fed by local security guards. Often whole streets will take communal ownership of a dog, feed and take care of

In general, Thai *soi* dogs are often friendlier than their domesticated, pampered canine kin.

it until it becomes part and parcel of the fabric of that neighborhood.

Show respect to the police. Thai police officers wield a lot of power and are not particularly willing to let a cross or angry word go. Be wary of how you communicate with them or you may find yourself fined or even imprisoned. Corruption among the Thai police force remains a problem.

Don't buy drugs. A common scam is for somebody to set up a drug deal with the sole purpose of informing the police. Police will then swoop in to catch the patsy.

Be wary of scams. Use common sense. Taxi drivers who claim to be able to drive you around town for 20 baht (US 60 cents) will probably have a prescribed route, involving several of their colleagues' souvenir shops.

Be wary of renting jet skis on Thailand's beaces. A standard scam is to extort the user for 'damage' to the machine.

Check to see if the Grand Palace or any other Bangkok tourist attraction is, indeed, closed. Don't believe the taxi driver who tells you it is. He is likely to also suggest taking you to another attraction.

Don't buy gems no matter how much the vendor says you can sell them for in your home country. If it sounds too good to be true, it probably is.

Exercise caution when in tourist zones. Don't automatically trust someone because they are from the same country or ethnicity as you. Many time-share companies hire a smorgasbord of nationalities armed with scratch cards and smiles in order to attract potential customers. Be warned that if you do stop and take a scratch card and win a prize from a time-share tout, you will have to attend an all-day high-pressured sales pitch in order to claim it.

Be careful when using ATM machines and someone offers to help you. ATM skimming gangs are rife in Thailand.

Keep your luggage with you when you travel. Many people have had their luggage stolen from the undercarriage compartment on overnight or long-haul journeys.

Don't play cards with strangers. First and foremost, this is because gambling in Thailand is illegal. Secondly, the game has more than likely been constructed around you with the sole purpose of extracting all your money.

Pay attention to the flags on beaches in Thailand. If there is a red flag on the beach, don't swim.

Many beaches in Thailand are without lifeguards, meaning that if you do want to swim, then you are quite often taking your life into your own hands. Every year, especially during the monsoon season (June–October), hundreds of tourists and Thais drown on the country's seemingly perfect, picturesque beaches.

Don't drink water from taps. It is untreated and will make you ill.

Drive carefully on the roads. Road safety, rules and regulations are probably not what you are used to back home.

Have safe sex. This is extremely important in a country like Thailand, which has almost 10,000 new cases of HIV infection every year.

Get the necessary vaccinations. Those recommended by the World Health Organization (WHO) for travelers to Thailand include Adult Diphtheria, Tetanus and Pertussis, Hepatitis A, Hepatitis B, Measles, Mumps and Rubella, Polio, Typhoid, Varicella and Rabies.

Buy health insurance. If you have an accident, the hospital costs could well cost more than your entire holiday expenses.

Contact your embassy or the Tourist Police on 1155 if you encounter any problems.

Published by Tuttle Publishing, an imprint of
Periplus Editions (HK) Ltd

www.tuttlepublishing.com

Library of Congress Control Number:
2015949992

ISBN: 978-0-8048-4448-2

Distributed by
North America, Latin America & Europe
Tuttle Publishing
364 Innovation Drive
North Clarendon, VT 05759-9436 U.S.A.
Tel: 1 (802) 773-8930; Fax: 1 (802) 773-6993
info@tuttlepublishing.com
www.tuttlepublishing.com

Japan
Tuttle Publishing
Yaekari Building, 3rd Floor
5-4-12 Osaki
Shinagawa-ku
Tokyo 141-0032
Tel: (81) 3 5437-0171; Fax: (81) 3 5437-0755
sales@tuttle.co.jp
www.tuttle.co.jp

Asia Pacific
Berkeley Books Pte. Ltd.
61 Tai Seng Avenue, #02-12
Singapore 534167
Tel: (65) 6280-1330; Fax: (65) 6280-6290
inquiries@periplus.com.sg
www.periplus.com

18 17 16 15
10 9 8 7 6 5 4 3 2 1

Printed in Singapore   1510CP

ABOUT TUTTLE
BOOKS TO SPAN THE EAST AND WEST

Our core mission at Tuttle Publishing is to create books
which bring people together one page at a time. Tuttle
was founded in 1832 in the small New England town of
Rutland, Vermont (USA). Our fundamental values
remain as strong today as they were then—to publish
best-in-class books informing the English-speaking world
about the countries and peoples of Asia. The world has
become a smaller place today and Asia's economic,
cultural and political influence has expanded, yet the
need for meaningful dialogue and information about this
diverse region has never been greater. Since 1948, Tuttle
has been a leader in publishing books on the cultures,
arts, cuisines, languages and literatures of Asia. Our
authors and photographers have won numerous awards
and Tuttle has published thousands of books on subjects
ranging from martial arts to paper crafts. We welcome
you to explore the wealth of information available on
Asia at **www.tuttlepublishing.com**